Lecture Notes in Computer Science   10221

Commenced Publication in 1973
Founding and Former Series Editors:
Gerhard Goos, Juris Hartmanis, and Jan van Leeuwen

More information about this series at http://www.springer.com/series/7408

Goetz Botterweck · Claudia Werner (Eds.)

Mastering Scale and Complexity in Software Reuse

16th International Conference on Software Reuse, ICSR 2017
Salvador, Brazil, May 29–31, 2017
Proceedings

 Springer

Editors
Goetz Botterweck 🆔
Lero - University of Limerick
Limerick
Ireland

Claudia Werner
Federal University of Rio de Janeiro
Rio de Janeiro
Brazil

ISSN 0302-9743   ISSN 1611-3349 (electronic)
Lecture Notes in Computer Science
ISBN 978-3-319-56855-3   ISBN 978-3-319-56856-0 (eBook)
DOI 10.1007/978-3-319-56856-0

Library of Congress Control Number: 2017936356

LNCS Sublibrary: SL2 – Programming and Software Engineering

Printed on acid-free paper

This Springer imprint is published by Springer Nature
The registered company is Springer International Publishing AG
The registered company address is: Gewerbestrasse 11, 6330 Cham, Switzerland

Foreword

This volume contains the proceedings of the International Conference on Software Reuse (ICSR 16) held during May 29–31, 2017, in Salvador, Brazil.

The International Conference on Software Reuse is the premier international event in the software reuse community. The main goal of ICSR is to present the most recent advances and breakthroughs in the area of software reuse and to promote an intensive and continuous exchange among researchers and practitioners.

The conference featured two keynotes by Mark Harman, University College London, and Thomas Zimmermann, Microsoft Research. We received 34 submissions (excluding withdrawn submissions). Each submission was reviewed by three Program Committee members. The committee decided to accept 11 papers, out of which eight full papers and three short ones, resulting in an acceptance rate of 32.3%. The program also included invited talks, a workshop, a doctoral symposium, and two tutorials. Abstracts of all these are also included in this volume. The program was complemented by tool demos and doctoral symposium.

This conference was a collaborative work that could only be realized through many dedicated efforts. First of all, we would like to thank Eduardo Almeida and Ivan Machado for their work as general chair and local chair, respectively. Rafael Capilla organized the workshop and tutorial program. Deepak Dhungana organized the demonstrations and tools track. Rohit Gheyi was Doctoral Symposium Chair. Tassio Vale and Alcemir Santos both served as Web chairs, while Crescencio Lima and Iuri Souza served as financial chairs. We would also like to thank Paulo Silveira for his work as proceedings chair.

We would also like to thank Fapesb, Secretaria de Ciência, Tecnologia e Inovação, Governo do Estado da Bahia, and CAPES for their financial support of the conference, which was paramount to holding the conference in Salvador, Brazil.

Last but not least, as program co-chairs of ICSR 2017, we would like to sincerely thank all authors who submitted papers to the conference for their contributions. We also thank the members of the Program Committee and the additional reviewers for their detailed and timely reviews as well as their participation in the discussions of the submissions.

February 2017

Goetz Botterweck
Claudia Werner

Organization

General Chair

Eduardo Santana
de Almeida   Federal University of Bahia and RiSE Labs, Brazil

Program Co-chairs

Goetz Botterweck   Lero - University of Limerick, Ireland
Claudia Werner   Federal University of Rio de Janeiro, Brazil

Doctoral Symposium Chair

Rohit Gheyi   Federal University of Campina Grande, Brazil

Workshops and Tutorials Chair

Rafael Capilla   King Juan Carlos University, Spain

Tool Demonstrations Chair

Deepak Dhungana   Siemens, Austria

Program Committee

Mathieu Acher   Inria, France
Colin Atkinson   University of Mannheim, Germany
Paris Avgeriou   University of Groningen, The Netherlands
Ebrahim Bagheri   Ryerson University, Canada
Maurice H. Ter Beek   ISTI-CNR, Italy
David Benavides   Universidad de Sevilla, Spain
Jan Bosch   Chalmers, Sweden
Regina Braga   Federal University of Juiz de Fora, Brazil
Jim Buckley   University of Limerick, Ireland
Rafael Capilla   Universidad Rey Juan Carlos, Madrid, Spain
Andrea Capiluppi   Brunel University, UK
Sholom Cohen   SEI, USA
Florian Daniel   Politecnico di Milano, Italy
Davide Falessi   Cal Poly, USA
John Favaro   Intecs SpA, Italy
William B. Frakes   Virginia Tech, USA
Harald Gall   University of Zurich, Switzerland

Keynote Abstracts

Alice in Dataland: Reuse for Data Science in Software Teams

Thomas Zimmermann

Microsoft Research, Redmond, USA
tz@acm.org

Abstract. Data is changing the world and how we build software. Running software produces large amounts of raw data about development processes and customer usage of software. In this talk, I will motivate the need for data analytics and show how data scientists work in a large software companies such as Microsoft helping software teams to infer actionable insights. I will highlight opportunities related to software reuse for researchers, practitioners, and educators.

Bio. Thomas Zimmermann is a Senior Researcher in the Research in Software Engineering (RiSE) group at Microsoft Research, Redmond, USA. His research interests include software productivity, software analytics, recommender systems, and games research. He is best known for his research on systematic mining of software repositories to conduct empirical studies and to build tools to support developers and managers. His work received several awards, including Ten Year Most Influential Paper awards at ICSE'14 and MSR'14, five ACM SIGSOFT Distinguished Paper Awards, and a CHI Honorable Mention. He currently serves as General Chair for SIGSOFT FSE'16 and as Program Co-Chair for ICSME 2017. He is Co-Editor in Chief of the Empirical Software Engineering journal and serves on the editorial boards of several journals, including the IEEE Transactions on Software Engineering. He received his PhD in 2008 from Saarland University in Germany. His homepage is http://thomas-zimmermann.com.

Software Transplantation for Reuse

Mark Harman

University College London, London, UK
mark.harman@ucl.ac.uk

Abstract. This talk describe recent advances in automated software transplantation and genetic improvement, focusing on their potential for reuse. Transplantation automatically transfers code from one system, a donor, into another unrelated system, the host, transforming it in order to transfer functionality from donor to host. Genetic improvement automatically improves operational characteristics of existing systems, such as execution time, memory requirements, and energy consumption.

This keynote is based on joint work with Earl Barr, Bobby Bruce, Yue Jia, Bill Langdon, Alexandru Marginean, Justyna Petke, Federica Sarro, Fan Wu and Yuanyuan Zhang in the CREST centre at UCL. CREST's work on automated transplantation won an ACM distinguished paper award (at ISSTA 2015) and the gold medal for human competitive results at the GECCO 2016 Humie awards.

Bio. Mark Harman is professor of Software Engineering in the Department of Computer Science at University College London, where he directs the CREST centre and is Head of Software Systems Engineering. He is widely known for work on source code analysis and testing and co-founded the field of Search Based Software Engineering (SBSE). SBSE research has rapidly grown over the past five years and now includes over 1600 authors, from nearly 300 institutions spread over more than 40 countries.

Contents

Documentation Reuse and Repositories

DevRec: A Developer Recommendation System
for Open Source Repositories 3
    Xunhui Zhang, Tao Wang, Gang Yin, Cheng Yang, Yue Yu,
    and Huaimin Wang

Documentation Reuse: Hot or Not? An Empirical Study 12
    Mohamed A. Oumaziz, Alan Charpentier, Jean-Rémy Falleri,
    and Xavier Blanc

Software Product Lines

A Preliminary Assessment of Variability Implementation Mechanisms
in Service-Oriented Computing 31
    Loreno Freitas Matos Alvim, Ivan do Carmo Machado,
    and Eduardo Santana de Almeida

No Code Anomaly is an Island: Anomaly Agglomeration as Sign
of Product Line Instabilities 48
    Eduardo Fernandes, Gustavo Vale, Leonardo Sousa,
    Eduardo Figueiredo, Alessandro Garcia, and Jaejoon Lee

ReMINDER: An Approach to Modeling Non-Functional Properties
in Dynamic Software Product Lines 65
    Anderson G. Uchôa, Carla I.M. Bezerra, Ivan C. Machado,
    José Maria Monteiro, and Rossana M.C. Andrade

Variability Management and Model Variants

Clustering Variation Points in MATLAB/Simulink Models
Using Reverse Signal Propagation Analysis 77
    Alexander Schlie, David Wille, Loek Cleophas, and Ina Schaefer

Discovering Software Architectures with Search-Based Merge
of UML Model Variants 95
    Wesley K.G. Assunção, Silvia R. Vergilio,
    and Roberto E. Lopez-Herrejon

Tracing Imperfectly Modular Variability in Software Product
Line Implementation 112
    Xhevahire Tërnava and Philippe Collet

Verification and Refactoring for Reuse

Composition of Verification Assets for Software Product Lines
of Cyber Physical Systems.................................... 123
  Ethan T. McGee, Roselane S. Silva, and John D. McGregor

Engineering and Employing Reusable Software Components
for Modular Verification 139
  Daniel Welch and Murali Sitaraman

Refactoring Legacy JavaScript Code to Use Classes: The Good,
The Bad and The Ugly 155
  Leonardo Humberto Silva, Marco Tulio Valente, and Alexandre Bergel

Tools Demonstrations

DyMMer-NFP: Modeling Non-functional Properties and Multiple Context
Adaptation Scenarios in Software Product Lines 175
  *Anderson G. Uchôa, Luan P. Lima, Carla I.M. Bezerra,
  José Maria Monteiro, and Rossana M.C. Andrade*

Identification and Prioritization of Reuse Opportunities with JReuse 184
  *Johnatan Oliveira, Eduardo Fernandes, Gustavo Vale,
  and Eduardo Figueiredo*

Doctoral Symposium

EcoData: Architecting Cross-Platform Software Ecosystem Applications 195
  Marcelo França

Investigating the Recovery of Product Line Architectures:
An Approach Proposal....................................... 201
  Crescencio Lima, Christina Chavez, and Eduardo Santana de Almeida

Towards a Guideline-Based Approach to Govern Developers in Mobile
Software Ecosystems.. 208
  Awdren de Lima Fontão, Arilo Dias-Neto, and Rodrigo Santos

Erratum to: Towards a Guideline-Based Approach to Govern Developers
in Mobile Software Ecosystems E1
  Awdren de Lima Fontão, Arilo Dias-Neto, and Rodrigo Santos

Tutorials

Building Safety-Critical Systems Through Architecture-Based
Systematic Reuse 217
  John D. McGregor and Roselane S. Silva

Reusable Use Case and Test Case Specification Modeling 219
   Tao Yue and Shaukat Ali

Workshop

2nd Workshop on Social, Human, and Economic Aspects of Software
(WASHES): Special Edition for Software Reuse 223
   Rodrigo Santos, Eldanae Teixeira, Emilia Mendes, and John McGregor

Author Index 225

Documentation Reuse and Repositories

DevRec: A Developer Recommendation System for Open Source Repositories

Xunhui Zhang$^{(\boxtimes)}$, Tao Wang, Gang Yin, Cheng Yang, Yue Yu, and Huaimin Wang

National University of Defense Technology, Changsha, Hunan, China
{zhangxunhui,taowang2005,yingang,yuyue,hmwang}@nudt.edu.cn,
delpiero710@126.com

Abstract. The crowds' active contribution is one of the key factors for the continuous growth and final success of open source software. With the massive amounts of competitions, how to find and attract the right developers to engage in is quite a crucial yet challenging problem for open source projects. Most of the current works mainly focus on recommending experts to specific fine-grained software engineering tasks and the candidates are often confined to the internal developers of the project. In this paper, we propose a recommendation system *DevRec* which combines users' activities in both social coding and questioning and answering (Q&A) communities to recommend developer candidates to open source projects from all over the community. The experiment results show that *DevRec* is good at solving cold start problem, and performs well at recommending proper developers for open source projects.

Keywords: Developer recommendation · Collaborative Filtering · StackOverflow · GitHub

1 Introduction

Nowadays, open source software (OSS) has formed a brand-new development paradigm and achieved its unprecedented success. Compared to the traditional software development in industry, open source software is driven by a massive number of stackholders including developers, users, managers and so on. These stakeholders involve in OSS projects by interests, and most of them have their own full-time job and only spend spare time on OSS. Although crowds may join in an OSS project occasionally, and then withdraw from it at any time, OSS has achieved great success at creating high-quality software like Linux, MySQL, Spark and so on. Nowadays, OSS is viewed as "eating the software world" by the Future of Open Source Survey [1].

On GitHub alone, one of the largest open source communities, there are more than 48 million open source projects hosted. However, according to our statistics, 95.2% of them do not received any attention by public (i.e. no watcher and forked repository) and 15.1% of them were not updated for more than one year. Even for

© Springer International Publishing AG 2017
G. Botterweck and C. Werner (Eds.): ICSR 2017, LNCS 10221, pp. 3–11, 2017.
DOI: 10.1007/978-3-319-56856-0_1

those projects which used to experience their success will languish without the crowds' continuous contributions. Therefore, to find and attract the right developers to participate in is quite crucial for OSS.

However, due to the massive amounts of competitive OSS, the crowds are often limited by their time and energy to choose from all the related projects. An automatic approach to bridge the gap between developers and projects is useful for both the developers and projects. In this paper, we propose a hybrid recommendation system called *DevRec*, which combines the development activity (DA)[1] based approach and knowledge sharing activity (KA)[2] based approach respectively to recommend proper developers for open source projects. The main contributions of this paper include:

- We propose a DA-based recommendation approach, by mining the crowds' development activities to discover and recommend proper collaborators for a given project from all over the community.
- We combine the developers' knowledge sharing and development activities, which helps to solve the cold-start problem for newly released projects.
- We conducted experiments on a large-scale dataset containing 165,741 projects and 72,877 developers, to show the effectiveness of our approach.

2   Related Work

In the age of global and distributed software development, finding the right person to collaborate and complete the right task is of great importance. Bhattacharya et al. [2] employed the incremental learning approach and multi-feature tossing graphs to improve the bug triaging. Xuan et al. [3] combined network analyzing and text classification approaches to recommend proper developers for a specific bug. Yu et al. [4–6] analyzed the pull-request mechanism, and embedded the social factors into typical recommendation approaches of bug triaging, to recommend pull-request reviewers. Besides, there are some works related to software recommendation. Lingxiao Zhang et al. [7] recommended relevant projects according to the relationship between developers and projects. Naoki Orii combined the probabilistic matrix factorization and topic model method to recommend repositories to programmers [8]. Different from these works, our work aims to recommend developers at the granularity of repository and the range of the whole software community.

There are also many researches focusing on the interplay between Q&A and social coding communities. Bogdan Vasilescu et al. [9] did some researches about the relationship of users' activities between StackOverflow and GitHub. Wang et al. [10] proposed an approach to link Android issues and corresponding discussions. Giuseppe Silvestri et al. [11] studied whether the relative importance of users vary across social networks, including StackOverflow, GitHub and Twitter.

---

[1] development activity: users' activities in social coding communities.

[2] knowledge sharing activity: users' activities in Q&A communities.

Venkataramani et al. [12] recommended suitable experts from GitHub to Stack-Overflow questions, taking developers' reputation into account. However, there are few studies about recommending users in Q&A communities to OSS, which gives full play to users' expertise and helps to speed up the rate of development.

3 Recommendation Approach

3.1 Overview of Recommendation System

DevRec explores the activities in social coding and Q&A communities to measure the technical distance between a given project and the developers, and combines the two results together to rank and recommend developer candidates for OSS. The architecture of *DevRec* is shown in Fig. 1.

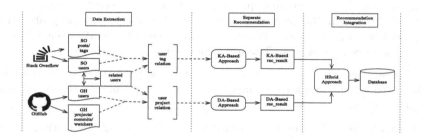

Fig. 1. Architecture of *DevRec*

Data Extraction: This step aims to gather datasets from StackOverflow and GitHub, and generate the user tag and user project association matrix.

Separate Recommendation: When a project comes, we calculate the relevance of each candidate according to the user association matrix, which is obtained from the user project and user tag association matrix.

Recommendation Integration: We combine the separate results by weight, and finally get the recommendation results for the hybrid approach.

3.2 Developer Recommendation Based on Social Coding Activities

There are kinds of activities in GitHub, including commit, fork and watch, which represent developers' interests to specific repositories. The basic intuition of this approach is that developers with similar technical interests tend to have similar development activities [7]. There are three parts in this approach.

UP Connector: This part is to create the association matrix of users and projects based on the activities in GitHub. Here we get a two-value matrix R_{u-p}, where 1 stands for participation and 0 stands for the opposite.

User Connector: This part is to calculate the association between users based on the user project association matrix using Jaccard algorithm.

Match Engine: In this part, we calculate the association between users and projects according to the user association matrix R_{u-u}. If we use $UA_p\langle u_1, u_2, ..., u_n \rangle$ to represent users that have already participated in the target project p, we can obtain the match score of each user towards project p using Eq. 1.

$$result = \sum_{i=1}^{|UA_p|} R_{u-u}[UA_p[i]] \tag{1}$$

3.3 Developer Recommendation Based on Knowledge Sharing Activities

Asking and answering technical questions are common activities among developers. Those with similar technical interests tend to focus on same posts, which are marked by same tags, and We suppose that they also tend to participate in the same kind of repositories. There are four parts in this approach.

Tag Extractor: This part is used to extract the fields that users proficient in. We consider that tags that mark users' related posts can represent user's interests or research fields.

Relation Creator: In this part, we calculate the user tag association matrix. Here we use *TF-IDF* method. If we use $U\{u_1, u_2, ..., u_n\}$ to represent users in StackOverflow, $T_u = \{t_1, t_2, ..., t_n\}$ to represent the tags that related to user u, and $C(t, u)$ to represent the number of times tag t relates to user u. Then we can calculate user tag association matrix using Eq. 2.

$$R_{u-t}(u, t) = \frac{C(t, u)}{\sum_{i=1}^{|T_u|} C(T_u[i], u)} * \log(\frac{\sum_{k=1}^{|U|} \sum_{q=1}^{|T_{U[k]}|} C(T_{U[k]}[q], U[k])}{\sum_{j=1}^{|U|} C(t, U[j])}) \tag{2}$$

User Connector: After obtaining the user tag association matrix R_{u-t}, we calculate the association of users using Vector Space Similarity algorithm.

Match Engine: The same as the match engine part in DA-based approach.

3.4 Hybrid Approach for Developer Recommendation

According to the above two approaches, we can get two recommendation results of the same repository. The combination of the two approaches takes users' activities into consideration comprehensively, and will probably improve the recommendation results. The specific steps are as follows:

Overlapped candidates' selection: Applying the aforementioned approaches and getting the top 10000 recommendation results of each project. Finding the same candidates in both sets by calculating the intersection.

Overlapped candidates' ranking: Setting a balance proportional coefficient which assign different weights for different approaches. The rank of the candidates is calculated with Eq. 3.

$$rank = W_{DA} * rank_{DA} + W_{KA} * rank_{KA} \qquad (3)$$

In which $\frac{W_{DA}}{W_{KA}}$ is the proportional coefficient of DA-based and KA-based approaches, and $rank_{DA}$ and $rank_{KA}$ represent the ranks of the candidates of the two approaches. Initially, we set the coefficient to $\frac{0.75}{0.25}$.

4   Experiment

4.1   Research Questions

In order to verify the effectiveness of our recommendation approaches and explore the influence when considering about different repositories. We focus on the following two research questions.

- Q1: What is the performance difference among three approaches over repositories with different popularities?
- Q2: How will the balance coefficient between the two kinds of activities affect the recommendation performance?

4.2   Experiment Datasets

To address the above research questions and validate our approach, we use the data in GitHub and StackOverflow. Here we choose the GHTorrent[3] MySQL dump released on March 2016, and the 2015 snapshot of StackExchange[4].

We find users both active in StackOverflow and GitHub by matching email MD5. After removing fake or deleted users, 72,877 left. For projects, we get 1,355,043 that at least one of the related users participated in before point-in-time (2014-09-14) and 165,741 projects that have new users after point-in-time.

We use h.d. (history developers) to represent the number of related users who focused on projects before point-in-time, and l.d. (latent developers) means the number of users who participate in the projects after point-in-time for the first time. Here we just consider about the projects that are popular after point-in-time because these projects can be used to validate the effectiveness of the approaches. After filtering, we get 136 popular projects whose h.d. bigger than 300 and l.d. bigger than 300. Also, we get 99 unpopular projects whose h.d. less than 2 and l.d. bigger than 100.

---

[3] http://ghtorrent.org/downloads.html.
[4] https://archive.org/details/stackexchange.

4.3   Evaluation Metrics

Accuracy: We use the accuracy to represent the availability of approaches, which is calculated by the division of the number of matched projects and the total number of test projects.

MRR: Mean Reciprocal Rank is widely used to evaluate the performance of recommendation systems. If the correct results rank in the front, the MRR value is high. Here, we use $rank_i$ to represent the rank of result i, $P\{p_1, p_2, ..., p_n\}$ to represent the set of test repositories, and $R_p\{r_1, r_2, ..., r_m\}$ to represent correctly matched results for project p. Then the MRR value is shown in Eq. 4.

$$MRR = \frac{1}{|P|} \sum_{i=1}^{|P|} (\frac{1}{|R_{P[i]}|} \sum_{j=1}^{|R_{P[i]}|} \frac{1}{rank_{R_{P[i]}[j]}}) \tag{4}$$

5   Experiment Results

5.1   Influence of Different Activities Towards Different Projects

Figures 2 and 3 present the accuracy of three different recommendation approaches for unpopular and popular projects. From the two figures, we can see that the accuracy of DA-based approach is better than that of KA-based approach. That is to say, the development activity is more important when recommending, which is consistent with reality. Developers may focus on many techniques, but will just apply one or two when developing projects. Asking or answering a question is much easier than following a repository.

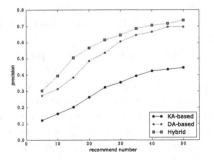   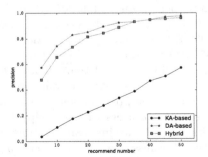

Fig. 2. Accuracy for unpopular projects   **Fig. 3.** Accuracy for popular projects

In Fig. 2, the hybrid approach performs the best, which means that for unpopular projects, knowledge sharing activity can help to improve the result. The reason is that the user association matrix generated from StackOverflow is more dense than that from GitHub. In Fig. 3, for popular projects, hybrid approach doesn't perform the best. This is because there are many developers focusing on

Table 1. MRR for unpopular and popular projects ($coefficient = \frac{0.75}{0.25}$)

Unpopular repositories										
	5	10	15	20	25	30	35	40	45	50
KA-based	.445	.295	.246	.229	.198	.172	.164	.155	.145	.136
DA-based	**.472**	**.323**	.267	**.206**	**.176**	159	**.142**	**.134**	.126	.120
Hybrid	**.503**	**.355**	.241	**.208**	**.182**	**.166**	**.148**	**.138**	.126	.112
Increase rate (%)	**6.57**	**9.91**	−9.74	**0.97**	**3.41**	**4.40**	**4.23**	**2.99**	0	−6.67
Popular repositories										
KA-based	.380	.187	.135	.113	.100	.085	.071	.063	.059	.052
DA-based	**.491**	**.321**	**.263**	**.225**	**.193**	**.167**	.149	.135	.125	.117
Hybrid	**.568**	**.362**	**.281**	**.244**	**.208**	**.170**	.148	.134	.123	.115
Increase rate (%)	**15.7**	**12.8**	**6.84**	**8.44**	**7.77**	**1.80**	−0.67	−0.74	−1.6	−1.7

the target project before point-in-time, which increases the prepared information for Collaborative Filtering algorithm.

From Table 1, we can see that hybrid approach tends to hit correct results in the front very often.

5.2   Influence of Different Coefficient Values in Hybrid Approach

Figures 4 and 5 show that coefficient value will influence the hybrid approach. In Fig. 4, the accuracy of hybrid approach increases with the decrease of coefficient value when recommending 5 to 10 developers to unpopular projects. However, for popular projects in Fig. 5, the result is opposite.

Meanwhile, Table 2 shows that for unpopular projects, the MRR of hybrid approach increases a lot when setting the coefficient to $\frac{0.25}{0.75}$, however decreases a lot for popular projects. Compare Table 2 to Table 1, when considering about MRR, small coefficient is more stable for unpopular projects because all the

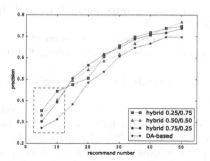

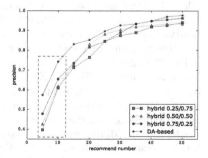

Fig. 4. Accuracy for unpopular projects with different coefficients

Fig. 5. Accuracy for popular projects with different coefficients

Table 2. MRR for unpopular and popular projects ($coefficient = \frac{0.25}{0.75}$)

Unpopular repositories										
	5	10	15	20	25	30	35	40	45	50
KA-based	.445	.295	.246	.229	.198	.172	.164	.155	.145	.136
DA-based	**.472**	**.323**	.267	**.206**	**.176**	159	.142	**.134**	**.126**	**.120**
Hybrid	**.483**	**.357**	**.297**	**.250**	**.213**	**.178**	**.161**	**.148**	**.142**	**.131**
Increase rate (%)	**2.33**	**10.5**	**11.2**	**21.4**	**21.0**	**11.9**	**13.4**	**10.4**	**12.7**	**9.17**
Popular repositories										
KA-based	.380	.187	.135	.113	.100	.085	.071	.063	.059	.052
DA-based	.491	.321	.263	.225	.193	.167	.149	.135	.125	.117
Hybrid	.394	.286	.228	.188	.159	.143	.131	.120	.109	.102
Increase rate (-%)	19.8	10.9	13.3	16.4	17.6	14.4	12.1	11.1	12.8	12.8

increasing rate are positive, however big coefficient is more suitable for popular projects with hybrid approach because the increasing rate tends to be positive.

In conclusion, using hybrid approach with small coefficient value to recommend for unpopular projects will get better accuracy and MRR value at the same time compared with DA-based approach. However, for popular projects, if the target repository considers more about the accuracy (wants to get suitable developers more probably), then choose DA-based approach. If it considers more about the MRR (wants to get suitable developers with fewer results), then use hybrid approach with big coefficient.

Acknowledgements. The research is supported by the National Natural Science Foundation of China (Grant No.61432020,61472430,61502512,61303064) and National Grand R&D Plan (Grant No. 2016-YFB1000805).

References

1. Silic, M.: Dual-use open source security software in organizations-Dilemma: help or hinder? Comput. Secur. **39**, 386–395 (2013)
2. Bhattacharya, P., Neamtiu, I., Shelton, C.R.: Automated, highly-accurate, bug assignment using machine learning and tossing graphs. J. Syst. Softw. **85**(10), 2275–2292 (2012)
3. Xuan, J., Jiang, H., Ren, Z., Zou, W.: Developer prioritization in bug repositories. In: ICSE, vol. 8543, no: 1, pp. 25–35 (2012)
4. Yu, Y., Wang, H., Filkov, V., Devanbu, P., Vasilescu, B.: Wait for it: determinants of pull request evaluation latency on GitHub. In: 2015 IEEE/ACM 12th Working Conference on Mining Software Repositories (MSR), pp. 367–371. IEEE (2015)
5. Yu, Y., Wang, H., Yin, G., Wang, T.: Reviewer recommendation for pull-requests in GitHub: what can we learn from code review and bug assignment? Inf. Softw. Technol. **74**, 204–218 (2016)

6. Yu, Y., Wang, H., Yin, G., Ling, C.X.: Reviewer recommender of pull requests in GitHub. In: ICSME, pp. 609–612. IEEE (2014)
7. Zhang, L., Zou, Y., Xie, B., Zhu, Z.: Recommending relevant projects via user behaviour: an exploratory study on GitHub (2014)
8. Orii, N.: Collaborative topic modeling for recommending GitHub repositories (2012)
9. Vasilescu, B., Filkov, V., Serebrenik, A.: Stackoverflow and github: associations between software development and crowdsourced knowledge. In: ASE/IEEE International Conference on Social Computing, pp. 188–195 (2013)
10. Wang, H., Wang, T., Yin, G., Yang, C.: Linking issue tracker with q and a sites for knowledge sharing across communities. IEEE Trans. Serv. Comput. **PP**, 1–14 (2015)
11. Silvestri, G., Yang, J., Bozzon, A., Tagarelli, A.: Linking accounts across social networks: the case of stackoverflow, github and twitter. In: International Workshop on Knowledge Discovery on the WEB, pp. 41–52 (2015)
12. Venkataramani, R., Gupta, A., Asadullah, A., Muddu, B., Bhat, V.: Discovery of technical expertise from open source code repositories. In: International Conference on World Wide Web Companion, pp. 97–98 (2013)

Documentation Reuse: Hot or Not?
An Empirical Study

Mohamed A. Oumaziz[(✉)], Alan Charpentier, Jean-Rémy Falleri,
and Xavier Blanc

CNRS, Bordeaux INP, Univ. Bordeaux LaBRI, UMR 5800, 33400 Talence, France
{moumaziz,acharpen,falleri,xblanc}@labri.fr

Abstract. Having available a high quality documentation is critical for
software projects. This is why documentation tools such as Javadoc are
so popular. As for code, documentation should be reused when possible to
increase developer productivity and simplify maintenance. In this paper,
we perform an empirical study of duplications in JavaDoc documentation
on a corpus of seven famous Java APIs. Our results show that copy-
pastes of JavaDoc documentation tags are abundant in our corpus. We
also show that these copy-pastes are caused by four different kinds of
relations in the underlying source code. In addition, we show that popular
documentation tools do not provide any reuse mechanism to cope with
these relations. Finally, we make a proposal for a simple but efficient
automatic reuse mechanism.

Keywords: Documentation · Reuse · Empirical study

1 Introduction

Code documentation is a crucial part of software development as it helps developers understand someone else's code without reading it [13,25]. It is even more
critical in the context of APIs, where the code is developed with the main intent
to be used by other developers (the users of the API) that do not want to read
it [12,16,17]. In this context, having a high quality reference documentation is
critical [5].

Further, it has been shown that the documentation has to be close to its corresponding code [8,9,14]. Developers prefer to write the documentation directly
in comments within the code files rather than in external artifacts [22]. Popular
documentation tools, such as JavaDoc or Doxygen, all share the same principle
which is to parse source code files to extract tags from documentation comments
and to generate readable web pages [20,24].

Writing documentation and code are highly coupled tasks. Ideally, developers should write and update the documentation together with the code. However, it has been shown that the documentation is rarely up-to-date with the
code [8,9,14] and is perceived as very expensive to maintain [4,5].

G. Botterweck and C. Werner (Eds.): ICSR 2017, LNCS 10221, pp. 12–27, 2017.
DOI: 10.1007/978-3-319-56856-0_2

We think that one possible reason for this maintenance burden is that documentation tools lack reuse mechanisms whereas there are plenty of such mechanisms in programming languages. Developers that write documentation therefore copy-paste many documentation tags, which is suspected to increase the maintenance effort [11].

As an example, let us consider a case of delegation as shown in the Fig. 1. In this example, the right method is just returning directly a value computed from the left method. As expected, some documentation tags from the left method are copy-pasted in the right method: the common parameters and the return value. As a consequence, if the documentation of the callee method is updated, an update of the caller documentation will have to be carried out manually, which is well known to be error-prone [11].

```
/**
 * @param a the first collection, must
     not be null
 * @param b the second collection, must
     not be null
 * @return true iff the collections
     contain the same elements with the
     same cardinalities.
 */
public static boolean
    isEqualCollection(final
    Collection a, final
    Collection b) {
...
return true;
}
```

```
/**
 * @param a the first collection, must
     not be null
 * @param b the second collection, must
     not be null
 * @param equator the Equator
     used for testing equality
 * @return true iff the collections
     contain the same elements with the
     same cardinalities.
 */
public static  boolean
    isEqualCollection(final
    Collection a, final
    Collection b, final Equator
    equator) {
...
return
    isEqualCollection(collect(a,
    transformer), collect(b,
    transformer));
}
```

Fig. 1. Extract of a documentation duplication due to method delegation (in the Apache Commons Collections project). Duplicated tags are displayed in bold.

In this paper, we investigate this hypothesis and more formally answer the two following research questions:

- RQ1: Do developers often resort to copy-paste documentation tags?
- RQ2: What are the causes of documentation tags copy-paste and could they be avoided by a proper usage of documentation tools?

We answer our research questions by providing an empirical study performed on a corpus of seven popular Java APIs where the need of documentation is critical (see Sect. 2.1). We answer the first research question by showing how big is the phenomenon of documentation tags copy-pasting (see Sect. 3). To that extent, we automatically identify what we call documentation tags duplications (Sect. 2.2), count them, and manually check if they are intended copy-pastes or just created by coincidence. We answer the second research question by investigating the intended copy-pastes we observed with the objective to find out their causes. Then we analyze whether existing documentation tools can cope with them (see Sect. 4). We further extend our second research question by providing a proposal for a simple but useful documentation reuse mechanism.

Our results show that copy-pastes of documentation tags are abundant in our corpus. We also show that these copy-pastes are caused by four kinds of relations that take place in the underlying source code. In addition, we show that popular documentation tools do not provide any reuse mechanism to cope with these relations.

The structure of this paper is as follows. First, Sect. 2 presents our corpus and the tool we create to automatically identify documentation duplications. Then, Sect. 3 and Sect. 4 respectively investigate our two research questions. Finally, Sect. 5 describes the related works about software documentation and Sect. 6 concludes and describes future work.

2   Experimental Setup

In this section, we first explain how we create our corpus (Sect. 2.1), and give general statistics about it. Then, we describe how we extract documentation duplications contained in our corpus (Sect. 2.2).

2.1   Corpus

The corpus of our study is composed of seven Java APIs that use JavaDoc, arbitrary selected from the top 30 most used Java libraries on GitHub as computed in a previous work of Teyton *et al.* [23]. We just considered the source code used to generate the documentation displayed on their websites. We also choose to focus only on methods' documentation, as this is where there is most of the documentation. In the remainder of this paper, we therefore only discuss about the documentation of Java methods written in JavaDoc.

Table 1 presents these seven APIs. All the data gathered for this study is available on our website[1]. As we can see in the *General* section of this table, the projects are medium to large sized (from 33 to 1,203 classes). As expected, they contain a fair amount of documentation: from about 28% to 97% of the methods are documented. The *Tags* section of this table gives some descriptive statistics of the JavaDoc tags used. As we can see, the most frequent tags are usually, in order: @description, @param, @return and @throw. Finally, the *inheritDoc* section of this table shows that there are few @inheritDoc tags. Such tags are used to express a documentation reuse between two methods but the method that reuses the documentation must override or implement the method that contains the reused documentation.

---

[1] http://se.labri.fr/a/ICSR17-oumaziz.

Table 1. Statistics computed from our corpus and the documentation it contains.

	acc[a]	acio[b]	ggson[c]	Guava	JUnit	Mockito	SLF4J
General							
# of classes	466	119	72	1,203	205	375	33
# of methods	4,078	1,173	569	9,928	1,319	1,716	433
% of documented methods	61.53	97.27	52.55	36.37	43.44	28.15	36.49
Tags							
# of @description	1,939	922	265	3,073	448	436	128
# of @param	1,199	734	106	749	178	237	51
# of @throw	438	209	65	462	12	11	5
# of @return	892	322	92	414	90	131	42
inheritDoc							
# of usage	85	18	0	112	2	0	0

[a] Apache Commons Collections
[b] Apache Commons IO
[c] google-gson

2.2 Documentation Duplication Detector

A documentation duplication is a set of JavaDoc tags that are duplicated among a set of Java methods. If it is intended then it was created by a copy-paste, if not then it was created by coincidence. We propose a documentation duplication detector that inputs a set of Java source code files and outputs the so-called documentation duplications[2].

The detector first parses the Java files and identifies all the documentation tags they contain by using the GumTree tool [7]. To detect only meaningful duplications, it extracts the most important tags of JavaDoc: `@param`, `@return`, `@throws` (or its alias `@exception`). It also extracts the main description of Java methods as if it is tagged too (with an imaginary `@description` tag). Finally, to avoid missing duplications because of meaningless differences in the white-space layout, it cleans the text contained in the documentation tags by normalizing the white-spaces (replacing tabs by spaces, removing carriage returns and keeping only one space between two words). For the same reasons, it also transforms all text contained in documentation tags to lowercase.

As a next step, the detector makes a comparison between tags, and checks if they are shared between different Java methods. Table 2 shows the result of this step w.r.t. to the Java code of Fig. 1.

The third and last step of the process consists in grouping the Java methods and the tags they share with the objective to identify maximal documentation duplications. This step is complex as it can lead to a combinatorial explosion, but fortunately, it can be solved efficiently using Formal Concept Analysis [10]

---

[2] https://github.com/docreuse/docreuse.

Table 2. The methods and their respective tags computed from Fig. 1 source code (duplicated tags are depicted in bold).

	@param a	@param b	@return	@param equator
I1: isEqualCollection(final Collection a, final Collection b)	✕	✕	✕	
I2: isEqualCollection(final Collection a, final Collection b, ...)	✕	✕	✕	✕

(FCA). FCA is a branch of lattice theory that aims at automatically finding maximal groups of *objects* that share common *attributes*. In our context, the objects simply correspond to Java methods, and the attributes correspond to documentation tags.

FCA returns a hierarchy of so-called *formal concepts*. A formal concept is composed of two sets: the extent (a set of Java methods in our context) and the intent (a set of documentation tags in our context). The extent is composed of objects that all share the attributes of the intent. In other words in our context, a formal concept is a collection of Java methods that share several documentation tags.

The hierarchy returned by FCA then expresses inclusion relationships between the formal concepts. The Fig. 2 shows such a hierarchy from the formal context of Table 2. To identify duplicated documentation tags, we search within the hierarchy the concepts that have at least two objects in their extent, and discard all other concepts as they do not correspond to duplications. The formal concepts corresponding to maximal duplications are shown in plain line in Fig. 2, the others are not relevant in our context. In our example, one maximal documentation duplication has been identified.

3   Research Question 1

In this section, we answer our first research question: *Do developers often resort to copy-paste documentation tags?*. To investigate if documentation duplications are frequent, we simply apply our documentation duplication detector to our corpus and report statistics about the extracted duplications. To ensure that these duplications are intentional, we draw at random a subset of the extracted duplications and ask three developers to manually decide for each duplication if it is intentional or coincidental.

3.1   Frequency of Duplications

As shown in the *Documentation* part of Table 3, our detector has identified about 2, 800 documentation duplications in the seven APIs of our corpus. As we can

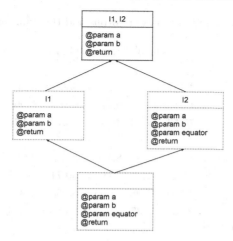

Fig. 2. Hierarchy computed by FCA from the formal context of Table 2. Retained concepts are depicted with plain lines, while discarded concepts are depicted with dotted lines.

see, at most 4% of the documented methods have their documentation completely duplicated (line `% of complete dupl.`). This indicates that completely duplicating a method's documentation is rare. On the contrary, about 40% to 75% of the documented methods have their documentation partially duplicated (line `% of partial dupl.`). This indicates that duplicating some method's documentation tags is very frequent, at least much more frequent than using the `@inheritDoc` tags as seen in the Table 1, which raises questions about the limitations of this mechanism as we will see in Sect. 4.

Fig. 3. Diagrams presenting the number of Java methods and tags of the identified duplications in Guava (left) and Mockito (right). The rows correspond to the number of Java methods, and the columns correspond to the number of documentation tags. The color in a cell correspond to the number of duplications (the darker the cell is, the more duplications).

In addition, we can see in the *Documentation tags* part of Table 3 a fine-grained analysis of the duplicated tags. Even though the frequency of duplications for each tag depends on the project, `param` and `throws` are often the most duplicated tags (from 20% to 40% of these tags are duplicated). The `return` tags are also largely duplicated (from 14% to 31%). Finally, the `description` tag is rarely duplicated (from 4% to 15%).

Table 3. Statistics computed from our corpus and the duplications it contains.

	acc[a]	acio[b]	ggson[c]	Guava	JUnit	Mockito	SLF4J
Documentation							
# of dupl	1,137	684	59	630	134	86	36
% of complete dupl	1.51	4.03	0.67	0.80	0.00	0.00	0.00
% of partial dupl	75.53	77.83	48.49	38.72	42.76	58.59	73.42
Documentation tags							
% of dupl. @description	11.24	14.53	8.30	6.57	14.96	4.13	3.91
% of dupl. @param	41.78	42.78	22.64	30.71	37.08	17.72	39.22
% of dupl. @throw	49.09	55.98	21.54	33.33	8.33	27.27	40.00
% of dupl. @return	27.35	31.37	15.22	25.85	14.44	19.85	26.19

[a] Apache Commons Collections
[b] Apache Commons IO
[c] google-gson

Figure 3 presents the number of documentation tags and Java methods of the identified duplications for Mockito and Guava projects. Due to the lack of space, we only show these two projects, but the figures are very similar for all the projects in our corpus, and can be found on our website. The figure shows that most of the identified duplications have few documentation tags and few Java methods: many duplications involve only two Java methods that share a single documentation tag. On these figures, we notice that the maximum number of duplications' documentation tags ranges from 3 (in SLF4J) to 8 (in Apache Commons Collections). The maximum number of Java methods ranges from 22 (in google-gson) to 183 (in Apache Commons IO). Thus, there exist duplications involving a lot of method and only a few tags or a lot of tags and a few methods. Finally, there is no duplication with both a large number of methods and a large number of tags.

3.2 Copy-Pastes Vs. Coincidental Duplications

To answer the second part of our research question we perform a qualitative experiment that relies on the manual judgement of several developers. We choose to involve three experienced Java developers for the experiment, as advised in [2], because judging if a duplication is an intended copy-paste or not is subjective. Involving three developers allows us to have a trust level on the status of a duplication. In our experiment, the developers are three of the paper's authors.

We then decided to create a sample composed of 100 duplications randomly drawn from our dataset of identified duplications, representing about 5% of the population of that dataset. Due to limitations in time we had to limit our manual analysis to 100 duplications, we randomly selected them to have a representative ratio of the corpus. Each of the 100 duplications was then presented to each developer through a web interface that also presented the associated code.

The developers then had as much time as they needed to judge whether the duplication was an intended copy-paste or not. Of course, the developers were not authorized to talk about the experiment until its completion.

A duplication labeled as "intended" is called from now on a *copy-paste* while a duplication labeled as "not intended" is called an coincidental duplication. When a developer is not able to decide whether the answer should be "intended" or "not intended", he must label the duplication as "not intended", to ensure that the number of copy-pastes that are found is a solid lower bound. We therefore define the two following trust levels. First, a copy-paste has a "majority" trust level when it has been labeled as "intended" by at least two participants. Last, a copy-paste has a "unanimity" trust level when it has been labeled as "intended" by the three participants.

Finally, we apply the bootstrapping statistical method [6] on our sample to compute a 95% confidence interval for the ratio of copy-pastes in our corpus. The bootstrapping method is particularly well-suited in our context since it makes no assumption about the underlying distribution of the values.

Before presenting our experiment results, it should be noted that the developers replied an identical answer on 69 out of 100 duplications. This indicates that the task of rating a duplication is not too subjective. Moreover, on these 69 cases, the developers agreed on a copy-paste 68 times, and on a coincidental duplication only one time[3]. It means that agreeing on a copy-paste is easy while agreeing on an coincidental duplication is difficult.

The main results of the experiment are presented in the Fig. 4. About 85% to 96% of the duplications are copy-pastes when using the majority trust level. When using the stricter unanimity trust level, about 57% to 76% of the duplications are copy-pastes. In both cases, more than half of the duplications are copy-pastes.

3.3   Threats to Validity

Our experiment bears two main threats to validity. First, the developers are authors of the paper, therefore, it could bias their answer when judging the duplications. Even if they took extra care to be as impartial as possible, replicating the study would enforce its validity and that it is why all the experiment's data is available.[4] Second, the results obtained from this experiment cannot be generalizable to all APIs, because we used the duplications of only seven Java open-source APIs. Even if we only considered well known and mature open-source projects for the experiment, it would be better to replicate the study with other APIs wether open-source or not and in various programming languages.

4   Research Question 2

In this section we answer our second research question: *What are the causes of documentation copy-pastes and could they be avoided by a proper usage of*

---

[3] http://se.labri.fr/a/ICSR17-oumaziz/RandomExperiment.
[4] http://se.labri.fr/a/ICSR17-oumaziz.

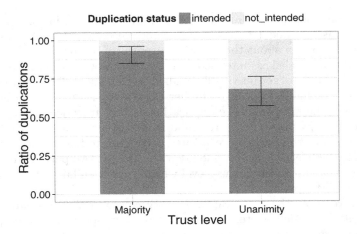

Fig. 4. Ratio of intended or coincidental duplications for the majority and unanimity trust levels, shown with their 95% confidence interval.

documentation tools? We start by an analysis of the causes that lead to documentation copy-paste, and their root in the source code (see Sect. 4.1). Then we check whether the existing documentation reuse mechanisms can cope with these causes (see Sect. 4.2). Finally, we propose a new documentation reuse mechanism that can be used to cope with the unsupported causes (see Sect. 4.3).

4.1   Causes of Documentation Copy-Pasting

To identify the causes that lead to copy-paste, we manually analyzed the source code corresponding to the 61 copy-pastes (68 initially with 7 containing only main tags which we did not keep) identified to answer RQ1 (see Sect. 3). After performing our manual analysis we identified four different causes: delegation, sub-typing, code clone and similar intent.

A *delegation*, as shown in Fig. 1, appears when a method calls another one, and thus has a part of its documentation coming from the called one.

A *sub-typing* appears when a method overrides another one that is defined in a same hierarchy. In this case, it is common that the overriding method's documentation comes from the one of the overridden method.

A *code clone* appears when a method shares similar lines of code with another one, hence duplicating a part of its body. Figure 5 shows an example of code clone as the two methods share common lines of code.

Finally, a *similar intent* appears when a method performs a computation that is similar to another method, which is why they share some documentation tags.

Figure 6 shows such an example. Here the two methods only differ because of the return type (float or int). It is not a clone because there is no common line between them. Further, the funny thing is that the developer made a mistake as

```
/**                                 /**
 * Writes a String to the {@link     * Writes a portion of a character
    StringBuilder}.                      array to the {@link
 *                                        StringBuilder}.
 * @param value The value to write   *
 */                                  * @param value The value to write
@Override                           * @param offset The index of the
public void write(final String         first character
   value) {                         * @param length The number of
 if (value != null) {                    characters to write
  builder.append(value);           */
 }                                  @Override
}                                   public void write(final char[]
                                       value, final int offset, final
                                       int length) {
                                     if (value != null) {
                                      builder.append(value, offset,
                                         length);
                                     }
                                    }
```

Fig. 5. Example of copy-paste due to code clone in the Apache Commons IO project. Duplicated tags are displayed in bold.

```
/**                                 /**
 * Delegates to {@link               * Delegates to {@link
    EndianUtils#                         EndianUtils#
readSwappedInteger(InputStream)}    readSwappedFloat(InputStream)}
 * @return the read long             * @return the read long
 * @throws IOException if an I/O error * @throws IOException if an I/O error
    occurs                               occurs
 * @throws EOFException if an end of  * @throws EOFException if an end of
    file is reached unexpectedly         file is reached unexpectedly
 */                                  */
public int readInt() throws         public float readFloat()
   IOException, EOFException {          throws IOException,
 return                                 EOFException {
 EndianUtils.readSwappedInteger(in); return
}                                    EndianUtils.readSwappedFloat(in);
                                    }
```

Fig. 6. Extract of copy-paste due to two methods with a similar intent in the Guava project. Duplicated tags are displayed in bold.

he clearly copied the documentation of the long method but didn't change the documentation of the int and float ones. In Java, most of similar intent cases we observed are due to developers implementing several times a same feature for each primitive type.

Table 4 shows the occurrences of each relation in our corpus based on our analysis. We can see that the main cause of documentation copy-pastes is delegation (60%) and then code clone (28%). There are very few sub-typing (8%) and similar intent (3%) cases. Further, looking at the tag level we notice that this distribution is quite consistent whatever the tag.

Table 4. Percentage of copy/paste for each cause in our corpus.

	Cause			
	Delegation	Sub-typing	Code clone	Similar intent
copy-pastes	37/61 (60%)	5/61 (8%)	17/61 (28%)	2/61 (3%)
@description	8/15 (53%)	1/15 (7%)	6/15 (40%)	0/15 (0%)
@param	27/41 (66%)	4/41 (10%)	9/41 (22%)	1/41 (2%)
@return	18/30 (60%)	3/30 (10%)	8/30 (27%)	1/30 (3%)
@throw	18/30 (60%)	1/30 (3%)	9/30 (30%)	2/30 (7%)

4.2 Existing Documentation Tools

As a second step, we first look at the different documentation tools to obtain the
mechanisms they provide for reusing documentation. As there are too many documentation tools (about fifty) [5], and due to time constraints, we choose to focus
on the most popular ones. As a proxy to compute the popularity, we compute
for each tool the number of questions asked by developers on StackOverflow, for
the tools where a dedicated StackOverflow tag is available.

Table 5. The five documentation tools with the most questions in StackOverflow

Tool	Language	#Questions
JavaDoc	Java	2, 022
Doxygen	C, C++, Java, C#, VBScript, IDL Fortran, PHP, TCL	1, 894
phpDocumentor	PHP	636
JSDoc	JavaScript	574
Doc++	C, C++, IDL, Java	570

We then analyze in detail the five tools having the most related questions on
StackOverflow, whether they are compatible with Java or not, in order to be sure
that there is no mechanism available for other languages that could avoid copy-
pastes and therefore should be implemented for Java. These tools are shown in
Table 5.

As a second step for our experiment, for each tool, we go through the whole
user-guide to find out the list of reuse mechanisms. We find out that these reuse
mechanisms have two main aspects. The first aspect is about the reuse granularity: some allow only to reuse a whole method documentation, some allow to
reuse documentation tags separately. The second aspect is about the location of
the reused documentation. Some mechanisms only allow to reuse documentation

---

[5] https://en.wikipedia.org/wiki/Comparison_of_documentation_generators.

Table 6. Aspects of the reuse mechanisms. Reuse granularity indicates if the documentation has to be completely reused (Whole) or if it is possible to select some tags (Choice). Source location indicates where can be the source of the reused documentation: in an overridden method (Override) or in a method anywhere in the code (Anywhere).

Source location	Reuse granularity	
	Whole	Choice
Override	JavaDoc, JSDoc	JavaDoc
Anywhere	Doxygen, JSDoc	

located in an overridden method, some allow to reuse documentation located in any method. Table 6 summarizes the aspects of the mechanisms offered by the documentation tools.

First, it is important to notice that only three tools out of five provide reuse mechanisms: DOC++ and phpDocumentor have no support at all to reuse documentation. More surprisingly, no tool supports the reuse of documentation tags anywhere in the code. Indeed, JavaDoc allows to reuse documentation tags, but only in an overridden method, while JSDOC and Doxygen allow to reuse complete method documentations in the code, but not specific documentation tags.

As a result for our classification, *delegation*, *code clone* and *similar intent* relations are not yet handled by any existing mechanism. On the contrary, duplications due to *sub-typing* relations are already properly handled by JavaDoc.

4.3   Documentation Reuse Revisited

Based on our findings, we suggest a novel mechanism to allow developers to automatically reuse documentation tags from a method to another one. Our proposal is an inline tag for JavaDoc. An inline tag can be used inside another tag, giving therefore the possibility to reuse the content of a specific tag but also to add more content before and after the reused one. We define it as: {@reuseClass:Method(type[, type])[:TagName]}.

For instance, by using this new mechanism, the documentation of the right method in Fig. 1 becomes as in Fig. 7.

As you can see in Fig. 7, while using the @reuse tag inside @param, there is no need to specify which tag name to reuse, by default it will automatically reuse the tag with the same name as the tag it belongs to, therefore the @param named a.

```
/**
 * @param a {@reuse Class:isEqualCollection(Collection, Collection)}
 * @param b {@reuse Class:isEqualCollection(Collection, Collection)}
 * @param equator the Equator used for testing equality
 * @return {@reuse Class:isEqualCollection(Collection, Collection)}
 */
```

Fig. 7. Example of a documentation reuse with our @reuse inline tag.

We implemented our proposal as a doclet for JavaDoc, the source code can be accessed in our website[6]. By using this mechanism, it is possible to avoid at least all the copy-pastes due to *delegation*, the most frequent ones in our corpus (60% of the copy-pastes). While this mechanism could also be used for copy-pastes due to *code clone* and *similar intent*, one main problem would be to decide which method should be the documentation origin which is a still open research question. Finally, our proposal is not able to cope with @description tags, as they are not materialized in JavaDoc. We also plan to conduct a more thorough study of our proposal as a future work.

5   Related Work

This section describes the work done on the subject of software documentation: studies and tools. We start by describing the existing studies on this subject, which all agree on the fact that developers need more assistance for maintaining the documentation.

Forward et al. [9] perform a qualitative study on 48 developers and managers about how they feel about software documentation as well as the tools that support it. They discover that their favourite tools are word processors and Javadoc-like tools. They also discover that the participants think that the documentation is usually outdated. Finally, they discover that the participants would greatly appreciate tools that help in maintaining the documentation.

Dagenais and Robillard [5] perform a qualitative study involving 12 core open-source contributors writing documentation and 10 documentation readers. They analyze the evolution of 19 documentation documents across 1500 revisions. They identify three documentation production modes: initial effort, incremental changes and bursts (big amount of change in a small period). They also discover that Javadoc-like documentation is perceived as a competitive advantage for libraries, and is easy to create but costly to maintain.

Finally, Correia et al. [4] show that maintaining a documentation is highly challenging. They identify four so-called patterns to help tackling this challenge: information proximity, co-evolution, domain structured information and integrated environment.

In order to help creating and maintaining the documentation, several tools have been developed. We describe these tools in the remainder of this section, even if none of them supports documentation reuse as presented in our study.

DocRef [26] helps detecting errors in software documentation by combining code analysis and natural language processing techniques. This tool has then been validated on 1000 detected documentation errors from open-source projects, and has proven usefulness as many errors have been fixed after having been reported.

Childs and Sametinger [3] suggest the use of object-oriented programming techniques such as inheritance and information hiding in documentation to avoid

---

[6] http://se.labri.fr/a/ICSR17-oumaziz.

redundancy. They also describe documentation reuse concepts and how to apply them using literate programming on documentation that is either or not related to source code.

Parnas [18] explains the lack of interest of researchers about the documentation topic. He further explains that his team and him developed a new mathematical notation that is more adapted for documentation but didn't convince academics and practitioners.

Buse and Weimer [1] present a tool that can statically infer and characterize exception-causing conditions in Java and then output a human-readable documentation of the exceptions. The tool is evaluated on over 900 instances of exception documentation within 2 million lines of code. They find out that the output is as good as or better than the existing one in the majority of the cases.

Pierce and Tilley [19] suggest using reverse engineering techniques to automate the documentation process. They propose an approach based on this principle in their Rational Rose tool. This approach offers the possibility to automatically generate up-to-date documentation. However their approach is not subjected to a serious evaluation.

McBurney and McMilla [15] describe a new method that uses natural processing language with method invocation analysis to generate a documentation not only explaining what the method does but also what is its purpose in the whole software project.

Robillard and Chhetri [21] describe a tool, Krec, that is able to extract relevant fragments of documentation that correspond to a given API element. The tool has been evaluated on a corpus of 1000 documentation units drawn from 10 open source projects and has shown to have a 90% precision and 69% recall.

6   Conclusion

Code documentation is a crucial part of software development. Like it is the case with source code, developers should reuse documentation as much as possible to simplify its maintenance.

By performing an empirical study on a corpus of seven popular Java APIs, we show that copy-pastes of documentation tags are unfortunately too abundant. By analyzing these copy-pastes, we identified that they are caused by four different kinds of relationships in the underlying source code.

Our study pinpoints the fact that popular documentation tools do not provide any reuse mechanism to cope with these causes. For instance, there is definitely no mechanism supporting documentation reuse in the case of delegation, which is the major cause of copy-paste.

We looked towards a proposal providing a simple tag that makes the documentation reuse simple but efficient. As a further work, we obviously plan to extend our study. We plan to analyze other programming languages and documentation tools, and to detect not only identical documentations but also similar ones, aiming to find duplications with tiny differences. We finally plan to extend and validate our proposal from a developer point of view.

References

1. Buse, R.P., Weimer, W.R.: Automatic documentation inference for exceptions. In: Proceedings of the 2008 International Symposium on Software Testing and Analysis, pp. 273–282. ACM (2008)
2. Charpentier, A., Falleri, J.R., Lo, D., Réveillère, L.: An empirical assessment of Bellon's clone benchmark. In: Proceedings of the 19th International Conference on Evaluation and Assessment in Software Engineering, EASE 2015, pp. 20:1–20:10. ACM, Nanjing (2015)
3. Childs, B., Sametinger, J.: Literate programming and documentation reuse. In: Proceedings of Fourth International Conference on Software Reuse, pp. 205–214. IEEE (1996)
4. Correia, F.F., Aguiar, A., Ferreira, H.S., Flores, N.: Patterns for consistent software documentation. In: Proceedings of the 16th Conference on Pattern Languages of Programs, p. 12. ACM (2009)
5. Dagenais, B., Robillard, M.P.: Creating and evolving developer documentation: understanding the decisions of open source contributors. In: Proceedings of the Eighteenth ACM SIGSOFT International Symposium on Foundations of Software Engineering, pp. 127–136. ACM (2010)
6. Efron, B., Tibshirani, R.J.: An Introduction to the Bootstrap. Chapman & Hall, New York (1993)
7. Falleri, J.R., Morandat, F., Blanc, X., Martinez, M., Monperrus, M.: Fine-grained and accurate source code differencing. In: Proceedings of the 29th ACM/IEEE International Conference on Automated Software Engineering, ASE 2014, pp. 313–324. ACM, New York (2014)
8. Fluri, B., Würsch, M., Gall, H.C.: Do code and comments co-evolve? on the relation between source code and comment changes. In: 14th Working Conference on Reverse Engineering, WCRE 2007, pp. 70–79. IEEE (2007)
9. Forward, A., Lethbridge, T.C.: The relevance of software documentation, tools and technologies: a survey. In: Proceedings of the 2002 ACM Symposium on Document Engineering, DocEng 2002, NY, USA, pp. 26–33. ACM, New York (2002)
10. Ganter, B., Wille, R.: Formal Concept Analysis: Mathematical Foundations, 1st edn. Springer-Verlag, Secaucus (1997)
11. Juergens, E., Deissenboeck, F., Hummel, B., Wagner, S.: Do code clones matter? In: IEEE 31st International Conference on Software Engineering, ICSE 2009, pp. 485–495, May 2009
12. Kramer, D.: API documentation from source code comments: a case study of Javadoc. In: Proceedings of the 17th Annual International Conference on Computer Documentation, pp. 147–153. ACM (1999)
13. Lakhotia, A.: Understanding someone else's code: analysis of experiences. J. Syst. Softw. **23**(3), 269–275 (1993)
14. Lethbridge, T.C., Singer, J., Forward, A.: How software engineers use documentation: the state of the practice. IEEE Softw. **20**(6), 35–39 (2003)
15. McBurney, P.W., McMillan, C.: Automatic documentation generation via source code summarization of method context. In: Proceedings of the 22nd International Conference on Program Comprehension, pp. 279–290. ACM (2014)
16. Monperrus, M., Eichberg, M., Tekes, E., Mezini, M.: What should developers be aware of? an empirical study on the directives of API documentation. Empirical Softw. Eng. **17**(6), 703–737 (2012)

17. Parnas, D.L.: A technique for software module specification with examples. Commun. ACM **15**(5), 330–336 (1972)
18. Parnas, D.L.: Software aging. In: Proceedings of the 16th International Conference on Software Engineering, pp. 279–287. IEEE Computer Society Press (1994)
19. Pierce, R., Tilley, S.: Automatically connecting documentation to code with rose. In: Proceedings of the 20th Annual International Conference on Computer Documentation, pp. 157–163. ACM (2002)
20. Pollack, M.: Code generation using Javadoc. JavaWorld (2000). http://www.javaworld.com/javaworld/jw-08-2000/jw-0818-javadoc.html
21. Robillard, M.P., Chhetri, Y.B.: Recommending reference API documentation. Empirical Softw. Eng. **20**(6), 1558–1586 (2015)
22. de Souza, S.C.B., Anquetil, N., de Oliveira, K.M.: A study of the documentation essential to software maintenance. In: Proceedings of the 23rd Annual International Conference on Design of Communication: Documenting & Designing for Pervasive Information, SIGDOC 2005, pp. 68–75. ACM, New York (2005)
23. Teyton, C., Falleri, J.R., Palyart, M., Blanc, X.: A study of library migrations in Java. J. Softw. Evol. Process **26**(11), 1030–1052 (2014)
24. Van Heesch, D.: Doxygen (2004)
25. Van De Vanter, M.L.: The documentary structure of source code. Inf. Softw. Technol. **44**(13), 767–782 (2002). Special Issue on Source Code Analysis and Manipulation (SCAM)
26. Zhong, H., Su, Z.: Detecting API documentation errors. In: ACM SIGPLAN Notices, vol. 48, pp. 803–816. ACM (2013)

Software Product Lines

A Preliminary Assessment of Variability Implementation Mechanisms in Service-Oriented Computing

Loreno Freitas Matos Alvim[(✉)], Ivan do Carmo Machado,
and Eduardo Santana de Almeida

Computer Science Department, Federal University of Bahia - Salvador,
Salvador, Brazil
lorenoalvim@gmail.com, {ivanmachado,esa}@dcc.ufba.br

Abstract. Service-Oriented Computing and Software Product Lines are software development strategies capable to provide a systematic means to reuse existing software assets, rather than repeatedly developing them from scratch, for every new software system. The inherent characteristics of both strategies has led the research community to combine them, in what is commonly referred to as Service-Oriented Product Lines (SOPL) strategies. Despite the perceived potential of such a combination, there are many challenges to confront in order to provide a practical generalizable solution. In particular, there is a lack of empirical evidence on the actual support of variability implementation mechanisms, typical in SPL engineering, and their suitability for SOPL. In line with such a challenge, this paper presents a preliminary assessment aimed to identify variability implementation mechanisms which may improve measures of complexity, instability and modularity, quality attributes particularly important for modular and reusable software systems, as is the case of SOPL. Based on the results of these evaluations, an initial decision model is developed to provide software engineers with an adequate support for the selection of variability mechanisms.

Keywords: Software Product Lines · Service-Oriented Product Lines · Decision model

1 Introduction

Software Product Lines (SPL) engineering is a software development paradigm aimed at fostering systematic software reuse. SPL engineering involves creating a set of product variants from a reusable collection of software artifacts [7]. These product variants share a set of functions (commonalities), but also deliver customer-specific ones (variabilities), key element of SPL engineering. Several software companies, from small to large-sized ones, have developed their software systems, in a range of application domains, based on such a development paradigm. SPL engineering promises improvements in the quality of delivered products, reductions in time-to-market, and gains in productivity [6].

G. Botterweck and C. Werner (Eds.): ICSR 2017, LNCS 10221, pp. 31–47, 2017.
DOI: 10.1007/978-3-319-56856-0_3

Service-Oriented Computing (SOC) is a well-established paradigm of Software Engineering [16]. It allows decomposing software into services, then provide a well-defined functionality while hiding systems implementation [3]. Services are autonomous, platform-independent computational units that can be described, published, discovered, and dynamically composed and assembled [15]. Thus, programmers may integrate distributed services, even if they are written in different programming languages [3]. It makes SOC an alternative to solve integration and interoperability-related issues, and increase business flexibility.

In order to achieve the benefits from both SPL and SOC, the research community has investigated their combination, in what has been called Service-Oriented Product Lines (SOPL) [5]. A number of studies [4,8,10,18] have analyzed how the commonly variability implementation mechanisms from SPL could also be suitable to SOPL. Such studies analyzed the mechanisms used by the software industry to implement variability in SOPL. However, understanding the actual use of the techniques is still challenging to assess and report its value.

In this paper, we present a preliminary assessment to investigate the variability implementation mechanisms suitable for SOPL. More specifically, we analyze the choice of a particular mechanism, according to three quality attributes: *complexity, modularity* and *stability*. We implemented two SPLs and released three product instances for each SPL. Next, we carried out an adaptation, by transforming the SPL features into services. Based on gathered evidence, we defined a measurement framework and a decision model to support the analysis of SPL.

2   Variability Implementation Mechanisms

This section provides a brief introduction about the variability implementation mechanisms used in this work: **Conditional Compilation (CComp), Aspect-oriented Programming (AOP),** and the **Open Services Gateway Initiative (OSGi).**

2.1   Conditional Compilation

CComp is one of the most elementary, yet most powerful approaches to enable variability implementation [9]. Preprocessors provide an intuitive means to implement variability. Its simplicity and flexibility attracts many practitioners [13]. Also, projects with strict requirements on the overhead resulting from the composition process of their variants rely on the overhead-free mechanisms offered by the preprocessor.

One advantage of conditional compilation is to allow that code be marked at different granularities from a single line of code to a whole file. As a consequence, it is possible to encapsulate multiple implementations in a single module.

2.2   Aspect-Oriented Programming

AOP is a widely-known technique for improving Separation of Concerns (SoC) [11]. An aspect (or *concern*) is a concept, goal or area of interest. A system can be considered as a collection of several concerns. There are core-level and system-level concerns. The former includes the business logic, and the latter includes aspects that affect the entire system [12]. Many such system-level concerns may influence multiple implementation modules. They are also called crosscutting concerns. As these concerns affect many implementation modules, even with programming approaches such as object-orientation, they make the resulting system harder to understand, design and implement.

AOP focuses on identifying such crosscutting concerns in the system and implement them as a collection of loosely coupled aspects. As a result, implementation modules become more independent and reusable. AOP is an affordable strategy to analyze the commonalities and variabilities of an SPL [12].

2.3   Open Services Gateway Initiative

The OSGi[1] technology is a set of specifications that defines an open, common architecture to develop, deploy and manage services in a coordinated way for the Java language. These specifications aim to facilitate the development, reduce the complexity and increase the reuse of developed services. OSGi is based on a service-oriented architecture where functional units are decoupled and components can be managed independently of each other [17]. An important characteristic is that the OSGi enables applications to discover and use services provided by other applications running inside the same OSGi platform [18].

OSGi is also suitable for implementing variation points because it offers an easy way to include new components and services without being required to recompile the whole system. In other words, it is possible to perform changes between different implementations in a dynamic fashion [1].

3   The Measurement Framework

The measurement of internal attributes such as size and instability may not mean anything when observed in isolation [19]. However, the metrics are more effective when combined to produce a measurement framework, which enables software engineers to understand and interpret the meanings of the measured data. By establishing a relationship among metrics, as introduced in [18], we herein propose a measurement framework, aimed to assess the code quality in the context of SOPL. The metrics reused in this framework for data collection were defined in previous studies [1,10,14,19].

Figure 1 shows the proposed framework. It encompasses three levels, as follows: (i) **code quality** - the response variable studied in this work; (ii) **reusability and maintainability** - the quality attributes observed in the system; and (iii) the **factors** (complexity, instability and modularity) - which influence the quality attributes, and could be categorized and quantified using the metrics, which provide the necessary conditions to analyze the source code quality. These metrics are further discussed in details.

---

[1] https://www.osgi.org/.

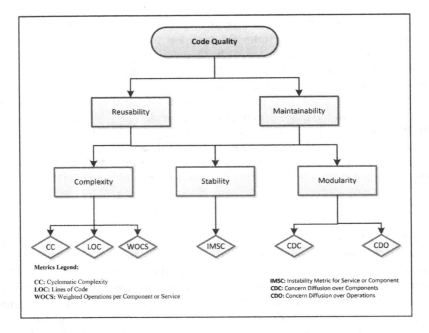

Fig. 1. The Measurement Framework.

3.1   Complexity Metrics

A critical issue in SPL engineering is how to efficiently implement SoC and modularize the system in order to have modules and components well defined, testable and reusable [19]. In this scenario, structural dependencies between services and components have a significant influence on the system complexity [18]. The following metrics could be used to assess source code complexity:

1. **Cyclomatic Complexity (CC).** It is a measure of the logical complexity of a program. CC calculations are useful to keep the size of components or services manageable and allow the testing of all independent paths. In this sense, CC can be used to analyze the complexity of each component [1].
2. **Lines of Code (LOC).** It counts all lines for each implementation, excluding comments and blank lines. This measure provides a baseline for comparing any two distinct systems, in terms of size. In this sense, it is necessary to ensure the same programming style in every project [19], given that different programming styles can bias the results of this metric. However, this might be difficult to ensure in SOC, where applications can be built by different companies, and the source code cannot always be accessed.
3. **Weighted Operations per Component or Service (WOCS).** It determines the complexity of service or component based on its operations (methods) that will be required by other services or components [18]. Let us

consider a component or service C with operations $O_1, \ldots, O_n$. Let $c_1, \ldots, c_n$ be the complexity of the operations, then:

$$WOCSC = c_1 + \ldots + c_n \qquad (1)$$

For this metric, the number of parameters of an operation is the key of complexity. Thus, operations with many parameters are more likely to be complex than other which requires few parameters. In this way, the complexity of operation O_k is defined as: $ck = \alpha k + 1$, where αk denotes the number of formal parameters of O_k.

3.2 Stability Metrics

A single change can begin a chain of changes of independent modules or services when there is a fragile design and difficulties are faced during reuse. Thus, the designer might face difficulties to predict both the extent of change and its impact [19]. Instability is the probability of a system to change, due to changes occurring in different parts of the system [2]. In this context, the metric to measure instability of source code artifacts used was:

1. Instability Metric for Service or Component (IMSC). It is supported by `fan.in` and `fan.out`, where `fan.in` (for function `A`) is calculated by the number of functions that call function `A`. On the other hand, `fan.out` is the opposite procedure, i.e., it represents the number of external functions called by `A`. The value measured by IMSC reflects the interaction between services or components [18]. Thus, this metric can be defined as follows:

$$IMCS = \frac{fan.out}{fan.in + fan.out} \qquad (2)$$

3.3 Modularity Metrics

Decomposition mechanisms used both in design and implementation are closely related to SoC. Concerns are an alternative for decomposing software in smaller parts and at the same time they are deemed to be more manageable and comprehensible. Besides, concerns are commonly regarded as equivalent to *features* [10]. Thus, the following metrics were chosen to support the modularity analysis of source code artifacts:

1. **Concerns Diffusion over Components (CDC).** It quantifies the degree of feature scattering considering the granularity level of components. *CDC* counts the number of components whose purpose is to contribute to the implementation of a concern. A high *CDC* indicates that a feature implementation can be scattered [10].
2. **Concerns Diffusion over Operations (CDO).** It is similar to *CDC*, as it also quantifies the degree of feature scattering, however it is focused on the level of granularity of the methods. It counts the number of methods and constructors performing a feature [10].

4   First Case Study - Warehouse

This section presents the case study aimed at analyzing the variability implementation mechanisms. We applied the GQM (Goal/Question/Metric) structure to define our goal, as follows:

G. *Analyze the* variability implementation mechanisms (conditional compilation, OSGi, and aspects) *for the purpose of* evaluation *with respect to* complexity, instability and modularity *from the point of view of* software engineers and researchers *in the context of* an SOPL project.

Q1. How complex are the services and components developed using CComp, AOP or OSGi? This research question investigates structural dependencies between components or services. This kind of dependency may influence the system complexity, thus, the goal is to identify which mechanism produces better results. In order to answer this question we used the framework complexity metrics (CC, LOC, and WOCS).

Q2. How stable are the services and components developed using CComp, AOP or OSGi? This research question identifies which mechanism produces better results for instability. With a fragile design and development, whenever a single component changes, an independent chain of changes may be triggered. Thus, this aspect is worth investigating. The framework instability metric (IMSC) was employed in an attempt to answer this question.

Q3. How modular are the services and components developed using CComp, AOP or OSGi? Developers often seek to implement modular software and, at the same time, they want to deliver more manageable and more comprehensible software artifacts. In this context, this research question aims at supporting our analysis about the modularity level of services and components. The modularity metrics CDC and CDO were employed to answer this question.

4.1   Hypotheses

For this study, it means that there is no difference among the techniques to implement variability:

$$H_{0_a} : CComp_{CC} = AOP_{CC} = OSGi_{CC}$$
$$H_{0_b} : CComp_{LOC} = AOP_{LOC} = OSGi_{LOC}$$
$$H_{0_c} : CComp_{WOCS} = AOP_{WOCS} = OSGi_{WOCS}$$
$$H_{0_d} : CComp_{IMSC} = AOP_{IMSC} = OSGi_{IMSC}$$
$$H_{0_e} : CComp_{CDC} = AOP_{CDC} = OSGi_{CDC}$$
$$H_{0_f} : CComp_{CDO} = AOP_{CDO} = OSGi_{CDO} \tag{3}$$

Conversely, whether there are differences among the variability implementation mechanisms, the null hypotheses are rejected.

4.2   Case Study Execution

The SPL under evaluation is a simulator of a warehouse. The project was developed by two graduate students. The project was inspired by the scenario proposed in [3], which provides conditions to investigate the source code related to modularity and software variability. The *Warehouse SPL* is composed of 23 features that allow the simulation of basic functions such as to get customer requests, to check the availability of ordered goods, to order the goods from an inventory, and billing.

In the first phase, the SPL was built from scratch, by using CComp as its variability implementation mechanism. Three releases were developed. The first release contains the core asset of the SPL and the latter ones incorporate changes to implement other features. Next, the remaining implementations proceeded. The developers refactored the SPL by using AOP and OSGi, based on the features from the first release. For the OSGi version, the services were used to resolve features, i.e., the services are the main core assets, where for each feature, a corresponding service was developed in the implemented SPL.

4.3   Results

This section presents and analyzes the data gathered from the first case study. We carried out a quantitative analysis regarding the quality attributes complexity, instability and modularity.

Complexity Analysis. Table 1 shows the mean values for each release of the Warehouse SPL. OSGi yielded the lowest CComp values. Among the OSGi releases, there was a minor variation, remaining at roughly 1.2. CComp presents the higher mean. However, in release 2, the AOP mechanism had similar mean values, around 1.5.

Unlike the CComp analysis, OSGi demanded a higher LOC, when compared to the other techniques. When CComp is used in the implementation, the range was 2487 to 3309 LOC among the releases. The variation between products for AOP was lower, between 2649 to 2933. Finally, the range for OSGi was from 2992 to 3309. The observed LOC differences could be partially explained by the fact that CComp inserts its preconditions in pieces of code commented only in the base product. Thus, when the remaining releases were derived, the preconditions were removed. In fact, some mechanisms are more verbose than others.

WOCS was the last metric used to measure code complexity. In this metric, OSGi achieved the lowest values. The difference among the values measured was considerable, as the OSGi average was half the AOP version. The highest WOCS values were observed in the CComp version. It can be explained by the fact that it had the implementation with the lowest number of methods and classes among the techniques. Thus, the number of parameters (key to calculate this metric) is distributed in fewer methods, which led to an increased CComp value.

Stability Analysis. By observing the measured values it is possible to identify that OSGi is the mechanism with more unstable components or services in all

Table 1. Results for the quantitative analysis for the Warehouse SPL project.

Variability mechanism	Metric	Release 1	Release 2	Release 3
CComp	CC	1.609	1.586	1.609
	LOC	2487	2697	2934
	WOCS	8.756	8.744	8.848
	IMSC	0.272	0.2651	0.2585
	CDC	0.088	0.091	0.082
	CDO	0.048	0.045	0.036
AOP	CC	1.482	1.528	1.511
	LOC	2649	2813	2933
	WOCS	7.620	7.904	7.661
	IMSC	0.270	0.269	0.268
	CDC	0.083	0.086	0.077
	CDO	0.047	0.044	0.036
OSGi	CC	1.275	1.268	1.229
	LOC	2992	3160	3309
	WOCS	3.892	3.814	3.541
	IMSC	0.342	0.327	0.337
	CDC	0.074	0.076	0.065
	CDO	0.048	0.046	0.039

the analyzed releases. In turn, AOP and CComp had very similar results. The OSGi values could be explained for its dynamic characteristic, in which it is not possible to separate the persistence from the Bundle, which resulted in a high coupling among services that produces increased instability values.

Modularity Analysis. Regarding CDC, Table 1 shows that OSGi implementation is the most modular when the observed criterion refers to the degree of feature scattering at component level. AOP had an intermediate mean value, and CComp yielded the worst result for this metric, with the highest means. This result was expected due to the intrinsic features of the mechanisms. During the development of the OSGi version, each feature was isolated in a service. It could provide a given modularity level. In an analogous way, features were inserted in aspects when the development used AOP. Nevertheless, CComp implementation does not have a native way to isolate features.

CDO was the last metric applied in this case study. In contrast with the CDC results, the achieved values do not clarify which mechanism yielded the best results. They are very similar and sometimes a technique has slightly superior values. It is inconclusive at this point.

4.4   Descriptive and Exploratory Analysis

We used the nonparametric Kruskal-Wallis test (KW) to compare the different variability mechanisms as in most samples the normality hypothesis was rejected by the Shapiro-Wilk test (SW), which prevents using the variance analysis. The underlying hypothesis test is:

H_0: All populations have identical distributions.
H_1: At least two populations have different distributions.

Table 2 shows the results. The comparison of variability mechanisms indicates that LOC and CDO did not present statistically significant differences at a confidence level of 5%. The instability variable had a borderline significance. It means that there is a difference only in one of the mechanisms, when compared to the others, where only OSGi version had higher values. Thus, these results rejected the null hypotheses defined for the case study except for LOC and CDO metric that did not present significant results in this study.

Table 2. Results of the quantitative analyses for the Warehouse SPL project.

Variable	Kruskal-Wallis Chi-squared	H-value	df
CC	7.2000	5.6	2
WOCS	7.2000	5.6	2
LOC	5.4222	5.6	2
IMSC	5.6000	5.6	2
CDC	5.9556	5.6	2
CDO	0.5650	5.6	2

4.5   Threats to Validity

Internal Validity. This case study addressed different areas, such as, SOC, variability implementation mechanisms, and the combination of SOC and SPL, known as SOPL. Understanding all of these areas would take a long time and effort. Thus, it is possible that some concepts may have been poorly understood. Trying to solve these possible issues, we investigated related work that could provide useful metrics to this investigation, as well as a formalized strategy on how to proceed during the evaluation process.

External Validity. This study aims at identifying the most suitable variability mechanism, it may be used as baseline for comparison in further studies developed in similar contexts. However, the small domain analyzed is a threat because the Warehouse is an academic small-sized project that may hinder any generalization of findings. In the future, we plan to carry out replications, by considering systems from distinct application domains and size.

5   Second Case Study - RiSEEvents

This section presents a replicated case study. It was carried out with the aim to analyze the variability mechanisms used to implement SPL and SOPL, and to compare the results with the previous case study. For this reason, the protocol used in this replicated study was identical to the applied in the former, to ensure their similarity, and foster comparisons.

5.1   Case Study Execution

The SPL under evaluation consists of a desktop application that assists users in the management of scientific events. The development team for the base version of the SPL used in this study was composed of three graduate students. They were not aware of the first case study.

The RiSEEvents SPL is composed of 28 features which provide the required functions to manage the life-cycle of a scientific event, encompassing submission, registration and evaluation phases, attendee registration procedures, semi-automated generation of the event proceedings, and an automated generation of documents such as reports, and certificate of attendance. Based on the initial version implemented with CComp, the developers were asked to deliver two additional releases aiming to complete the number of products required to assess this variability mechanism. As in the first case study, the Release 1 only comprised the core assets of the application. Next, changes were incorporated to implement all features designed for this SPL. At the end of this process, three scenarios for each variability mechanism through inclusion, changing, or removing classes were implemented.

5.2   Results and Findings

This section discusses the findings of the replicated case study.

Complexity Analysis. In Table 3, it is possible to observe the CComp collected from the implemented scenarios. The releases implemented through CComp had the highest CC among the studied mechanisms. Another observation is the difference of values measured by each technique. The mean values for the CComp and AOP versions were rather closer to each other, and distinct from that observed in the OSGi version. The first two had mean values measured at around 2.1 while in the OSGi version the values of the releases 1 and 2 were about 1.8 and in the release 3 the value was 1.745.

An opposite situation was observed for the LOC metric. In this context, AOP becomes the mechanism with the highest measured values, and CComp required the smallest LOC. The exception was observed in release 3, in which the OSGi version yielded the highest LOC.

Regarding WOCS measurement, it was observed a particular wide variation in the results for the OSGi version. In the first release, OSGi had (with a large difference from other mechanisms) the smallest measured value. However, in release 2, the situation changed and it made the technique more complex. In release 3, this situation was repeated, but with the mean closer to other mechanisms. Except in the first release, AOP was the technique with the best results.

Stability Analysis. From Table 3, we could also observe that the components built with OSGi are the most unstable. The other mechanisms had similar instability levels, with a slight trend for the implementations that use CComp to be more stable.

Modularity Analysis. The last group of metrics used in these studies is related to the modularity of programs. According to the CDC measures, we could state that features implemented with OSGi are a little less diffuse among the components than the others developed with AOP and CComp. They had very similar results, which were not expected, since it did not occur in the first case study.

Alike in the first study, CDO calculations were also inconclusive. OSGi presented a large variation and the others had identical results in both releases. It is possible that during migration from CComp to AOP some external factor had influenced this process.

Table 3. Results of the quantitative analysis for the RiSEEvents SPL project.

Variability mechanism	Metric	Release 1	Release 2	Release 3
CComp	CC	2.165	2.137	2.15
	LOC	9623	20420	26349
	WOCS	7.098	7.533	7.285
	IMSC	0.435	0.441	0.448
	CDC	0.09	0.06	0.05
	CDO	0.056	0.049	0.039
AOP	CC	2.101	2.112	2.125
	LOC	9922	20684	26719
	WOCS	7.032	7.409	7.149
	IMSC	0.484	0.498	0.503
	CDC	0.097	0.06	0.049
	CDO	0.054	0.049	0.039
OSGi	CC	1.849	1.878	1.745
	LOC	9911	20516	26741
	WOCS	6.105	8.33	7.448
	IMSC	0.624	0.666	0.664
	CDC	0.088	0.058	0.043
	CDO	0.069	0.051	0.038

Descriptive and Exploratory Analysis. As in the first study, we used the nonparametric Kruskal-Wallis test to compare the different mechanisms of variability and the results are presented in Table 4. They indicate that (for RiSEEvents) only the results from CC and Instability which presented statistically significant differences at a confidence level of 5%. As a result, most mechanisms presented similar behavior.

With these results, only the two null hypotheses related to cyclomatic complexity and instability defined for this case study could be rejected. Consequently, the other metrics did not produce significant results in this study.

Table 4. Results for the quantitative analysis for RiSEEvents.

Variable	Kruskal-Wallis Chi-squared	H-value	df
CC	7.2000	5.6	2
WOCS	0.6222	5.6	2
LOC	0.6222	5.6	2
IMSC	72.000	5.6	2
CDC	0.6050	5.6	2
CDO	0.0904	5.6	2

5.3   Threats to Validity

Internal Validity. The wide knowledge areas addressed in this study together with the context of RiSEEvents SPL are also threats for the study alike in the preceding one. In order to mitigate these issues, a compilation of the results through a comparison with data from both studies was performed.

External Validity. The same observation from the first case study still holds for this second one. It is hard to generalize the findings, given the size of the projects involved in both studies. However, we believe such results could serve as baseline values for further replications.

6   Comparative Analysis

In this section, we synthesize gathered evidence, by providing a comparison of the achieved results.

Complexity Comparison. The individual analysis allows to observe that both case studies had similar data related to the first complexity criterion - CC. OSGi was the mechanism with the best results in all products followed by AOP with intermediary results. However, in the RiSEEvents the values for releases implemented with CComp were very similar to the AOP releases.

For the second criterion - LOC, the results from both studies converged again, but in RiSEEvents the measured values were similar. They presented CComp as the mechanism demanding fewer LOC. OSGi had a higher LOC in its implementation for the Warehouse SPL. However, AOP had a higher LOC in its implementation for two products of the RiSEEvents SPL (releases 1 and 2).

Finally, considering WOCS measurement, there was an unusual fluctuation of results obtained. OSGi had WOCS values in Warehouse and in the first release of RiSEEvents smaller than other mechanisms. However, for the second release of RiSEEvents, the measured results had a considerable increase, which led OSGi to achieve the worst results in both releases 2 and 3 of RiSEEvents. These values indicate that the services responsible for the implementation of features are composed of possible god-classes, i.e., classes that control too many other objects in the system and as such they might become classes with several responsibilities. The same variation did not occur in Warehouse results, where OSGi had best results followed by AOP and CComp.

Stability Comparison. Both case studies had the components developed with CComp more stable that the other ones. This result can be observed more clearly in the replicated case that had the largest difference between data from CComp and AOP.

Modularity Comparison. The results indicate that OSGi had the best components regarding the CDC metric. It could be observed only in the first case study where the mean of OSGi had, in general, 0.01 of difference from another mechanism. In the second study, the results did not allow any inferences. Concerning to CDO, we could not identify any significant differences among the three approaches in both systems. Therefore, we could not discard the null hypotheses with the use of CDO metric.

7 Decision Model

The descriptive and exploratory analysis indicate that we should consider some factors when using the techniques to implement variability. In order to support the choice of the most suitable technique we defined a decision model. In the development process, we considered only the data that rejected the null hypotheses. Thus, there is no indication for the most suitable techniques when software modularity is assessed, for example, by CDO metric in the decision model. Moreover, as a result of the lack of significant differences among the techniques, two mechanisms could be indicated as first options for a particular observed metric.

The decision model is centered on variability mechanisms and has three inputs that produce the most suitable indication for the observed criteria. The first input concerns the variability mechanisms target of the study (CC, AOP, and OSGi); the second one consists of the criteria to compare the techniques (complexity, instability, and modularity); and the last one are the metrics used to quantify the criteria observed in the case studies.

Based on the results from the first case study, the decision model showed in Fig. 2 was designed. In this model, there are priorities (for each metric) that indicate the most suitable variability mechanism in the analyzed context. For example, OSGi is the technique that produces the best components considering CC.

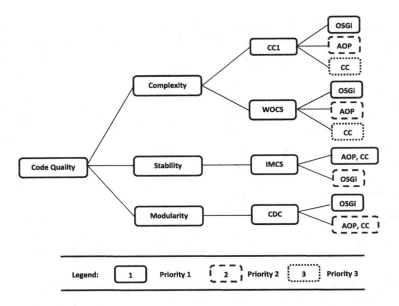

Fig. 2. Warehouse Decision model.

Similarly, we developed another decision model based on the replicated case study results. In this case, only the results from CC and instability which presented statistically significant differences at a confidence level of 5% were considered. Figure 3 shows the decision model based on the RiSEEvents SPL.

Furthermore, by comparing the results we could assume this one as the model produced with the results of both studies. Since the CC and instability results were evaluated in the original case study and reinforced with new assessments in the replicated case study. Thus, this second assessment allowed understanding what results were influenced by the context, and provided support for making these generalizations regarding the CC and instability.

8   Related Work

In this section, we provide an overview of previous research efforts related to the scope of this paper.

In [4], authors performed an exploratory study to analyze solutions used in dynamic variability implementation. The evaluation was performed with respect to size, cohesion, coupling, and instability of the source code with the aid of a measurement framework. Although similar, our work focuses in context of SOPL and their work are mostly focused on dynamic SPL engineering.

Quantitative and qualitative analysis were carried out aimed to identify how feature modularity and change propagation behave in the context of two evolving SPLs [8]. In order to gather quantitative data, the authors developed each SPL

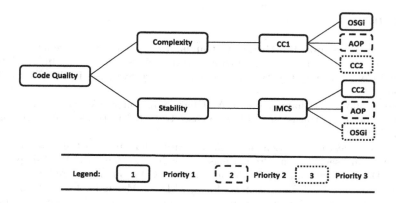

Fig. 3. RiSEEvents Decision model.

using three different variability mechanisms. Moreover, the compositional mechanism available in Feature-oriented Programming (FOP) was evaluated by using other two variability techniques as baseline (CComp and Design Patterns). Such a study was further expanded [10], aimed at investigating whether the simultaneous use of aspects and features through the Aspectual Feature Modules approach (AFM) facilitates the evolution of SPLs. All these works compare some variability techniques through quantitative and qualitative analysis, however, neither of them in the context of SOPL.

In [18], authors proposed an approach for implementing core assets in SOPL providing guidelines and steps that enable the implementation in the SOPL context (components, services providers and consumers). This study contributed with our work to indicate how features could be resolved by services. Moreover, it provided inputs for the development of our measurement framework that aims to collect data to evaluate the different implementations.

9 Concluding Remarks

This paper presented a preliminary assessment of variability mechanisms to support SOPL implementation. The assessment comprised the planning, execution and reporting of two case studies, aimed at evaluating the techniques with respect to complexity, instability and modularity. The results of the studies indicated that, in general, there are small differences among the techniques, and some hypotheses could not be rejected. This paper also describes the proposal of a framework to design decision models to aid the selection of a particular mechanism based on a set of parameters.

As future work, we plan to improve the empirical assessment, by considering another set of measurements, in order to increase the coverage of the framework. Moreover, we will consider to use combination of mechanisms aiming to provide variability to the services in our study context.

References

1. Almeida, E., Santos, E., Alvaro, A., Garcia, V.C., Meira, S., Lucredio, D., Fortes, R.: Domain implementation in software product lines using OSGi. In: 7th International Conference on Composition-Based Software Systems (ICCBSS), pp. 72–81 (2008)
2. Ampatzoglou, A., Chatzigeorgiou, A., Charalampidou, S., Avgeriou, P.: The effect of GoF design patterns on stability: a case study. IEEE Trans. Softw. Eng. 41(8), 781–802 (2015)
3. Apel, S., Kaestner, C., Lengauer, C.: Research challenges in the tension between features and services. In: Proceedings of the 2nd International Workshop on Systems Development in SOA Environments (SDSOA), pp. 53–58. ACM (2008)
4. Carvalho, M.L.L., Gomes, G.S.S., Silva, M.L.G., Machado, I.C., Almeida, E.S.: On the implementation of dynamic software product lines: a preliminary study. In: 10th Brazilian Symposium on Components, Architecture, and Reuse (SBCARS) (2016)
5. Castelluccia, D., Boffoli, N.: Service-oriented product lines: a systematic mapping study. SIGSOFT Softw. Eng. Notes 39(2), 1–6 (2014)
6. Clements, P., McGregor, J.: Better, faster, cheaper: pick any three. Bus. Horiz. 55(2), 201–208 (2012)
7. Clements, P., Northrop, L.: Software Product Lines: Practices and Patterns. Addison-Wesley, Boston (2001)
8. Ferreira, G.C.S., Gaia, F.N., Figueiredo, E., de Almeida Maia, M.: On the use of feature-oriented programming for evolving software product lines - a comparative study. Sci. Comput. Program. 93(PA), 65–85 (2014)
9. Gacek, C., Anastasopoules, M.: Implementing product line variabilities. In: Proceedings of the 2001 Symposium on Software Reusability: Putting Software Reuse in Context SSR 2001, pp. 109–117. ACM, New York (2001)
10. Gaia, F.N., Ferreira, G.C.S., Figueiredo, E., de Almeida Maia, M.: A quantitative and qualitative assessment of aspectual feature modules for evolving software product lines. Sci. Comput. Program. 96(P2), 230–253 (2014)
11. Kiczales, G., Lamping, J., Mendhekar, A., Maeda, C., Lopes, C., Loingtier, J.-M., Irwin, J.: Aspect-oriented programming. In: Akşit, M., Matsuoka, S. (eds.) ECOOP 1997. LNCS, vol. 1241, pp. 220–242. Springer, Heidelberg (1997). doi:10.1007/BFb0053381
12. Kuloor, C., Eberlein, A.: Aspect-oriented requirements engineering for software product lines. In: 10th IEEE International Conference and Workshop on the Engineering of Computer-Based Systems, pp. 98–107, April 2003
13. Liebig, J., Apel, S., Lengauer, C., Kästner, C., Schulze, M.: An analysis of the variability in forty preprocessor-based software product lines. In: 32nd International Conference on Software Engineering (ICSE), pp. 105–114. ACM (2010)
14. McCabe, T.: A complexity measure. IEEE Trans. Softw. Eng. 2, 308–320 (1976)
15. Mohabbati, B., Asadi, M., Gašević, D., Lee, J.: Software product line engineering to develop variant-rich web services. In: Bouguettaya, A., Sheng, Q.Z., Daniel, F. (eds.) Web Services Foundations, pp. 535–562. Springer, New York (2014)
16. Papazoglou, M.P., Traverso, P., Dustdar, S., Leymann, F.: Service-oriented computing: state of the art and research challenges. Computer 40(11), 38–45 (2007)
17. Rellermeyer, J.S., Alonso, G.: Concierge: a service platform for resource-constrained devices. SIGOPS Oper. Syst. Rev. 41(3), 245–258 (2007)

18. Ribeiro, H.B.G., Almeida, E.S., de Lemos Meira, S.R.: An approach for implementing core assets in service-oriented product lines. In: 1st Workshop on Services, Clouds, and Alternative Design Strategies for Variant-Rich Software Systems (SCArVeS). ACM (2011)
19. Santanna, C., Garcia, A., Chavez, C., Lucena, C., von Staa, A.: On the reuse and maintenance of aspect-oriented software: an assessment framework. In: Proceedings of the XVII Brazilian Symposium on Software Engineering (2003)

No Code Anomaly is an Island

Anomaly Agglomeration as Sign of Product Line Instabilities

Eduardo Fernandes[1,2(✉)], Gustavo Vale[3], Leonardo Sousa[2], Eduardo Figueiredo[1],
Alessandro Garcia[2], and Jaejoon Lee[4]

[1] Department of Computer Science, Federal University of Minas Gerais, Belo Horizonte, Brazil
{eduardofernandes,figueiredo}@dcc.ufmg.br
[2] Informatics Department, Pontifical Catholic University of Rio de Janeiro, Rio de Janeiro, Brazil
{lsousa,afgarcia}@inf.puc-rio.br
[3] Department of Informatics and Mathematics, University of Passau, Passau, Germany
vale@fim.uni-passau.de
[4] School of Computing and Communications, Lancaster University, Lancaster, UK
j.lee3@lancaster.ac.uk

Abstract. A software product line (SPL) is a set of systems that share common and varying features. To provide large-scale reuse, the components of a SPL should be easy to maintain. Therefore, developers have to identify anomalous code structures – i.e., code anomalies – that are detrimental to the SPL maintainability. Otherwise, SPL changes can eventually propagate to seemly-unrelated features and affect various SPL products. Previous work often assume that each code anomaly alone suffices to characterize SPL maintenance problems, though each single anomaly may represent only a partial, insignificant, or even inexistent view of the problem. As a result, previous studies have difficulties in characterizing anomalous structures that indicate SPL maintenance problems. In this paper, we study the surrounding context of each anomaly and observe that certain anomalies may be interconnected, thereby forming so-called anomaly agglomerations. We characterize three types of agglomerations in SPL: feature, feature hierarchy, and component agglomeration. Two or more anomalies form an agglomeration when they affect the same SPL structural element, i.e. a feature, a feature hierarchy, or a component. We then investigate to what extent non-agglomerated and agglomerated anomalies represent sources of a specific SPL maintenance problem: instability. We analyze various releases of four feature-oriented SPLs. Our findings suggest that a specific type of agglomeration indicates up to 89% of sources of instability, unlike non-agglomerated anomalies.

Keywords: Code anomaly agglomeration · Software product line · Instability

1 Introduction

A software product line (SPL) is a set of systems that share common and varying features [22]. Each feature is an increment in functionality of the product-line systems [2]. The combination of features generates different products [4]. Thus, the main goal of SPL is

© Springer International Publishing AG 2017
G. Botterweck and C. Werner (Eds.): ICSR 2017, LNCS 10221, pp. 48–64, 2017.
DOI: 10.1007/978-3-319-56856-0_4

to provide large-scale reuse with a decrease in the maintenance effort [22]. The implementation of a feature can be distributed into one or more source files, called components. To support large-scale reuse, the components and features of a SPL should be easy to maintain. Therefore, developers should identify anomalous code structures that are detrimental to the SPL maintainability. Otherwise, changes can eventually be propagated to seemly-unrelated features and affect various SPL products.

Code anomalies are anomalous code structures that represent symptoms of problems in a system [12]. They can harm the maintainability of systems in several levels by affecting classes and methods, for instance [12, 16]. Code anomalies affect any system, including SPL [7]. Previous work states that SPL-specific anomalies can be easier to introduce, harder to fix, and more critical than others, due to the inherent SPL complexity [18]. An example of code anomaly is *Long Refinement Chain* [7], related to the feature hierarchy (see Sect. 3.1). This anomalous code structure may hinder developers in understanding and performing proper changes. Eventually, these changes might affect several SPL products in the whole product-line. Thus, understanding the negative impact of anomalies in the SPL maintainability is even more important than in stand-alone systems, as their side effects may affect multiple products. Still, there is little understanding about the impact of such anomalies on the SPL maintainability.

Some studies assume that each anomaly alone suffices to characterize SPL maintenance problems [7, 23]. However, each single anomaly may represent only a partial view of the problem. This limited view is because, in several occasions, a maintenance problem is scattered into different parts of the code [20]. For instance, *Long Method* is a method with too many responsibilities that, if isolated, represents a punctual, simple problem [12]. In turn, *Long Refinement Chain* is a method with too many refinements in different features [7] that, in isolation, does not indicate a critical problem depending on the refined method. However, if we observe both anomalies in the same method, we may assume an increasing potential of the anomalies in hindering the SPL maintainability, since an anomalous method is excessively refined and causes a wider problem. As a result, previous studies have limitations to characterize anomalous structures that indicate SPL maintenance problems. On the other hand, previous work has observed that certain anomalies may be interconnected, forming so-called anomaly agglomerations. They investigate to what extent these anomaly agglomerations support the characterization of maintenance problems of a single system [21]. The authors define a *code anomaly agglomeration* as a group of two or more anomalous code elements directly or indirectly related through the program structure of a system [21]. However, they do not characterize and study specific types of anomaly agglomerations in SPLs.

In this paper, we first characterize common types of anomaly agglomerations in SPLs. Then, we investigate how often non-agglomerated versus agglomerated anomalies occur in SPLs and if they indicate sources of instability, a specific SPL maintenance problem. In fact, our findings suggest that "no code anomaly is an island", i.e., code anomalies often interconnect to other anomalies in critical elements of a SPL, such as a feature, a feature hierarchy, or a component. We also confirm that non-agglomerated anomalies do not support the identification of structures that often harm the SPL maintainability. We then investigate to what extent certain types of agglomerations represent sources of instabilities. We propose three types of agglomeration based on the key SPL decomposition characteristics, i.e. features, refinement chains, and components. Two or more anomalies form an agglomeration when they affect together a feature, a feature hierarchy, or a component. We then analyze the relationship between agglomerations and instabilities. Our analysis relies on different releases of four feature-oriented SPLs.

For each proposed type of agglomeration, we compute the strength of the relationship between agglomerations and instability in SPLs. We also compute the accuracy of agglomerations in indicating sources of instability. Our data suggest that feature hierarchy agglomerations and instability are strongly related and, therefore, this type of agglomeration is a good indicator of instabilities. The high precision of 89% suggests feature hierarchy can support developers in anticipating SPL maintenance problems. These findings are quite interesting because SPLs implemented with feature-oriented programming (FOP) are rooted strongly on the notion of feature hierarchies. It indicates that developers of FOP-based SPLs should design carefully the feature hierarchies, since they might generate hierarchical structures that hamper the SPL maintainability.

The remainder of this paper is organized as follows. Section 2 provides background information. Section 3 proposes and characterizes three types of anomaly agglomerations in SPL. Section 4 describes the study settings. Section 5 presents the study results. Section 6 discusses related work. Section 7 presents threats to the study validity with respective treatments. Section 8 concludes the paper and suggests future work.

2   Background

This section provides background information to support the paper comprehension. Section 2.1 presents feature-oriented SPLs. Section 2.2 discusses instability in SPL.

2.1   Feature-Oriented Software Product Lines

In this paper, we analyze SPLs developed with feature-oriented programming (FOP) [4]. FOP is a compositional technique in which physically separated code units are composed to generate different product-line systems. We analyze SPLs implemented using the AHEAD [4] specific-language technique and the FeatureHouse [3] multi-language technique. We chose these technologies because they compose features in separated code units and are well-known in FOP community. Both technologies implement SPLs through successive refinements, in which complex systems are developed from an original set of mandatory features by incrementally adding optional features, called SPL variability [4]. A feature is composed by one or more component (*constants* or *refinements*) that represents a code unit. A constant is the basic implementation of functionality and a refinement adds or changes the functionality of a constant [4].

To illustrate the FOP main concepts, Fig. 1 presents the partial design view of MobileMedia [10], a SPL for management of media resources. In Fig. 1, there are 3 features and 13 components. Lines connecting components indicate a *refinement chain* with a constant in the topmost feature and refinements in the features below. When generating a SPL product, only the bottom-most refinement of the chain is instantiated, because it implements all the capabilities assigned to the respective chain [4]. In this study, we also refer to refinement chains as feature hierarchies, due to the order of components stablished by a refinement. As an example, the feature *SMSTransfer* has four constants and one refinement (`MediaController`). This refinement is part of a feature hierarchy that cuts across the three features presented in Fig. 1.

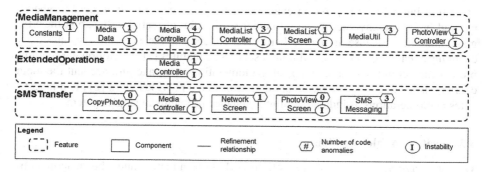

Fig. 1. Partial design view of the MobileMedia SPL

2.2 Sources of Instability in SPL

Instability is the probability of a system to change, due to changes performed in different parts of the source code [1]. A previous work states that instability relates mostly to the maintenance of a system and, therefore, instability harms the SPL maintainability [25]. Moreover, a previous work has found evidence that code anomalies can induce to instability in systems [14]. Stability is even more important for SPLs than single systems, since changes in one feature can propagate to other features and affect seemly-unrelated configurations of a SPL [10]. In this study, we assess to what extent anomaly agglomerations support the identification of sources of instability in SPLs. We are concerned about the relationship between agglomerated anomalies in indicating parts of the code that change frequently and represent an instability.

In this study, we consider a component as instable if it has changed in at least two SPL releases. We made this decision because there are few available releases per analyzed SPL, seven at most. As a SPL evolves, components may change and be improved. However, after a manual inspection of the target SPLs, we observed that most of the changes reflected poor SPL design decisions. Thus, we considered instability as harmful to the SPL maintainability. Figure 1 presents instable components in MobileMedia by assigning "I" to each instable component of the SPL. For instance, all presented components of feature *MediaManagement* are instable, except `Constants` and `MediaUtil`. We do not consider comment-related changes in the count of instability.

3 Code Anomalies and Agglomerations in SPL

Section 3.1 discusses code anomalies and agglomerations. Sections 3.2, 3.3, and 3.4 characterize feature, feature hierarchy, and component agglomerations, respectively.

3.1 Agglomerating Code Anomalies

Code anomalies are symptoms of deeper problems in a software system [12]. They make a specific source code element difficult to understand and maintain. Any software system is prone to have anomalies and the SPL variability can introduce anomalies, e.g., because of feature interactions [7]. As an example, a *Long Refinement Chain* occurs when a method has too many successive refinements in different features. It harms the SPL maintainability because it makes harder to understand the side effects caused by changing a feature or selecting a different set of SPL features [7]. The following sections present the definition of three types of agglomerations that take into account the main characteristics of SPLs. We based our definitions on a previous work [21] that investigates agglomerations as indicators of maintenance problems in single systems.

3.2 Feature Agglomeration

We define *feature agglomerations* as follows. Let f be a feature and c be an anomalous component. Let $c \rightarrow f$ when an anomalous component c contributes to implement the feature f. A *feature agglomeration* of a feature f is a set of anomalous components C in which there exists a relation $c \rightarrow f$ for all $c \in C$ and $|C| \geq 2$. There is a simple reason for considering a feature as a natural grouping of code anomalies, i.e., FOP expects that developers implement all components related to a specific functionality of the SPL into the same feature [2, 4]. Although there might be no explicit, syntactic relationship among components of the same feature, they are typically located in the same folder at the SPL source code. Thus, grouping components by feature reflects the semantical relationship among components. With this type of agglomeration, we hypothesize that the occurrence of different anomalies in components of the same feature are indicators of instabilities in SPL. In other words, we analyze anomalies from different components as a single anomalous structure at the feature-level. We expect that this wider view of anomalies may better indicate instabilities in the SPL.

Figure 1 presents the feature *MediaManagement* with seven constants. For each component, we have the respective number of code anomalies represented by "#" on the upon-right side of the component. All these components are anomalous and, therefore, this set of components corresponds to a feature agglomeration. By analyzing in details each anomalous component separately, we observe that most of them have only one anomaly. For instance, `Constants` and `PhotoViewController` contain only *Long Parameter List*. Although this anomaly is a symptom of maintenance problems, it provides a limited view of the maintenance problem that affects the SPL.

In turn, by analyzing the entire anomaly agglomeration, we may observe wider issues. As an example, the components `MediaController` and `MediaUtil` have both, *God Class*, *Long Method*, and *Long Parameter List*. In general, these anomalies relate to high difficulty to maintain the affected code elements (classes or methods, in this case). Since components of the same feature implement the same functionality, we expect that they access and use to one another. Thus, these anomaly occurrences in the same feature may lead to major maintenance problems in the feature as a whole. Moreover, attempts to treat these problems can lead to the overall feature instability. Therefore, feature agglomeration may help us to understand problems that affect multiple source files in the same feature that implement together the same SPL functionality.

3.3 Feature Hierarchy Agglomeration

We define a *feature hierarchy agglomeration* as follows. Let r be a refinement chain and c be an anomalous component. Let $c \rightarrow r$ when an anomalous component c belongs to the refinement chain r. A *feature hierarchy agglomeration* of a refinement chain r is a set of anomalous components C in which there exists a relation $c \rightarrow r$ for all $c \in C$ and $|C| \geq 2$. A refinement is an inter-component relation explicitly declared in the refinement's code that indicates the refined constant. For instance, the components MediaController of the three features in Fig. 1 compose a refinement chain. Since all these components are anomalous, they form a feature hierarchy agglomeration. We observe that two of the components individually have only one anomaly; MediaController of both *MediaManagement* and *SMSTransfer* have only *Long Parameter List*. This anomaly provides a limited view of maintenance problems (Sect. 3.2).

However, by analyzing in detail the feature hierarchy of MediaController, we can reason about major maintenance problems that encompass the entire refinement chain. The component MediaController of feature *MediaManagement* is a constant and, therefore, the components below it in the feature hierarchy are refinements. This constant has four code anomalies: *God Class*, *Long Method*, *Long Parameter List*, and *Long Refinement Chain*. The high number of anomalies that affect locally MediaController suggests this component has one or more problems. Besides that, there are two other components refining the constant. Because of the *Long Parameter List*, that may indicate an overload of responsibilities in the method, it is even more critical the fact that we have too many refinements of the constant, i.e. the *Long Refinement Chain* is potentially critical. Therefore, the impact of these anomalies is wider than an analysis of individual components may cover. Feature hierarchy agglomeration aims to indicate problems that affect a scattered concern associated with multiple features.

3.4 Component Agglomeration

We define a *component agglomeration* as follows. Let c be a component and e be a code element. Let $e \rightarrow c$ when a code element e belongs to the component c. A *component agglomeration* of a component c is a set of anomalous code elements E when there exists a relation $e \rightarrow c$ for all $e \in E$ and $|E| \geq 2$. In Fig. 1, the component that contains the highest amount of anomalies is MediaController of feature *MediaManagement*. Four anomalies with potential to harm the SPL maintainability occur in this component: *God Class*, *Long Method*, *Long Parameter List*, and *Long Refinement Chain*. By analyzing each anomaly separately, we limit our observations to the possible problems that the respective anomaly may cause. In turn, by agglomerating anomalies that affect the same component may lead to observations that are more conclusive. For instance, if we consider *God Class* and *Long Method* separately, we may overlook two important issues regarding MediaController. First, this component is a constant and many other components refine its implementation. Second, this component has a *Long*

Refinement Chain that makes code harder to understand and evolve. This anomaly, summed to the occurrences of *Large Class* and *Long Method*, tend to harm the SPL maintainability even more. Thus, component agglomeration may support the identification of major SPL maintenance problems in a component caused by inter-related anomalies.

4   Study Settings

Section 4.1 describes the study goal and research questions. Section 4.2 presents the target SPLs used in our analysis. Section 4.3 describes the study protocols.

4.1   Goal and Research Questions

We aim to investigate whether non-agglomerated and agglomerated anomalies indicate sources of instability in SPL. Our research questions (RQs) as discussed below.

RQ1.   *Can non-agglomerated code anomalies indicate instability in SPL?*
RQ2.   *Can agglomerated code anomalies indicate instability in SPL?*
RQ2.1.   *How strong is the relationship between agglomerations and instability?*
RQ2.2.   *How accurate is the relationship between agglomerations and instability?*

To the best of our knowledge, we did not find studies that investigate non-agglomerated anomalies as indicators of instability in SPL. Therefore, we assess if non-agglomerated anomalies can provide instability hints in SPL (RQ1). RQ2 focuses on the investigation of whether agglomerations can be indicators of instability. We address this question according to two perspectives. First, we compute the strength of the relationship between each type of agglomeration and instability (RQ2.1). That is, we assess the potential of agglomerated anomalies in indicating instabilities. We say a relationship is strong if agglomerated anomalies are able to identify at least 100% more instabilities than non-agglomerated anomalies. We chose this rounded threshold based on the guidelines of Lanza and Marinescu [16]. Second, we then compute the accuracy of agglomerations in identifying instability (RQ2.2), in terms of precision and recall. In other words, we assess if agglomerated anomalies can identify instabilities correctly.

4.2   Target SPLs

We selected four SPLs implemented in AHEAD or FeatureHouse: MobileMedia [10], Notepad [15], TankWar [23], and WebStore [13]. We selected these SPLs for some reasons. First, these SPLs are part of a SPL repository proposed in a previous work [24]. Second, they have been published and investigated in the literature [9, 23]. Third, there are different releases per SPL and, therefore, we could compute instability for the SPLs throughout consecutive releases. MobileMedia provides products for media management in mobile devices, and it has seven releases [9, 24]. Notepad aims to generate text editors and it has two releases [24]. TankWar is a war game for personal computers and mobile devices and it has seven releases [23]. Finally, WebStore derives Web applications with product management, and it has six releases [9, 24]. Fourth, developers of these SPLs were available for consultation, except in the case of Notepad.

According to the developers of the four SPLs, each of them evolved to address different issues. MobileMedia initially supported photo management only, but evolved to manage other media types, such as video and music. This evolution required a revision of the SPL assets [9]. Notepad was completely redesigned in the two available releases [15]. Developers added new functions and created new ones to ease the introduction of functions and to improve the feature modularization. TankWar evolved only to refactor the SPL without changing any functions but to improve its maintainability. Finally, WebStore initially supported a few payment types and data management options. As WebStore evolved, it has changed to cover these and other new functionalities. Although this is a similar scenario to MobileMedia, the initial development of WebStore took into account future planned evolutions, making this SPL more stable [9].

4.3 Data Collection and Analysis Protocols

Our data collection and analysis comprised three activities presented as follows. The artifacts produced during this process are available in the research website [8].

Identifying Sources of Instabilities. We first computed instability per SPL. We manually computed the number of changes per component between releases. Then, we identified the main sources of instability per SPL, based on the changed components. We used the instability computation for MobileMedia and WebStore provided by a previous work [9]. To increase the data reliability and to compute instability for TankWar and Notepad, we a tool for source code file comparison called WinMerge[1]. We count an instability index if the file changes between consecutive releases. As stated in Sect. 2.2, we considered as instable a component with two or more changes, due to the few available releases per SPL. Regarding the sources of instabilities, we analyzed the reasons that lead to instability per component to identify groups of components with similar instability sources, e.g. because a new feature was added, and represent a major source of instability. Whenever was possible, we validated the detected instability with developers of the target SPL by showing them the numbers obtained per component.

Table 1 presents the sources of instabilities identified in the four analyzed SPLs. The first column indicates the category and the sum of affected components per source. The second column presents the description of each source of instability. The last line (i.e., Others) represents the sources of instability that we were not able to categorize. As an example, we named "Add crosscutting feature" when a new feature is added to the SPL and it affects the implementation of existing features. This particular instability is interesting in the SPL context because, according to the open/closed principle, software entities should be open for extension, but closed for modification [19].

Identifying Code Anomalies and Agglomerations. Our process of identifying code anomalies consists in three steps: (i) to define the anomalies for study, (ii) to define the

---

[1] http://winmerge.org/.

metric-based detection strategies to identify each anomaly, and (iii) to apply the defined detection strategies to each SPL. We investigate eight anomalies defined in our website [8], namely: *Data Class, Divergent Change, God Class, Lazy Class, Long Method, Long Parameter List, Shotgun Surgery* [12, 16], and *Long Refinement Chain* [7]. Our analysis relies mostly on such general-purpose anomalies, except for *Long Refinement Chain* [7], but all of them relate somehow to the SPL composition. These anomalies affect the source code of SPLs in different levels, including feature hierarchies.

Table 1. Sources of instabilities in SPL

Source	Description
Add crosscutting feature (122)	When we add a new feature to the SPL and, consequently, the new functionalities are of interest of components from several existing features. Many components from different features change
Distribute code among features (39)	When we extract code parts of a component from an existing feature and, then, distributed these code parts to components from existing features
Change from mandatory to optional (19)	When we distribute the implementation of an existing feature to: (i) a new, basic mandatory feature, and (ii) a new optional features, with specific functionalities
Pull up common feature code (63)	When we extract code parts that are common into child features to a parent feature above in the feature hierarchy
Others (195)	General sources unrelated explicitly to SPL maintenance, e.g. attribute renaming

As an example, *Divergent Change* is a class that changes due to divergent reasons [16]. If these reasons relate to different features, this anomaly may harm the SPL modularization. *Long Method* is a method with too many responsibilities [12]. This anomaly is harmful in SPLs if the responsibilities of the method relate to different features, for instance. Finally, *Long Refinement Chain* [7] is a method with excessive number of successive refinements. This SPL-specific anomaly is harmful since it hampers the understanding of side effects of changes in the generation of SPL products. To detect each anomaly, we adapted detection strategies from the literature [16] whenever possible. We extracted the metric values per SPL via the VSD tool [24]. Once detected the anomalies, we computed manually the three types of agglomerations per SPL (see Sect. 3). Two authors contributed to double-check the results in order to prevent errors.

Correlating Agglomerations and Instabilities. To answer our research questions, we defined a criterion for correlating agglomerations and instabilities. Consider a general agglomeration that can be either a feature, a feature hierarchy, or even a component agglomeration. We say that such agglomeration indicates an instability when there exists an instable code element in the feature, feature hierarchy, or component that have the agglomeration. Even though agglomerations and instabilities may be located in more than two anomalous elements, our criterion considers sufficient if the agglomeration is affected by at least one problem. Thus, an agglomeration fails to indicate instability when none of its components relates to an instability. With respect to the number of agglomerations that indicate instability in the analyzed SPLs, we observed that an average of 94%, 78%, and 32% of the agglomerations indicate 2 or more instable components for feature, feature hierarchy, and component agglomeration respectively.

5   Results and Analysis

Section 5.1 presents the results for non-agglomerated anomalies. Section 5.2 discusses the results for the three proposed types of anomaly agglomeration in SPLs.

5.1   Non-agglomerated Code Anomalies

First, we investigate whether non-agglomerated code anomalies are sufficient indicators of instabilities in SPL. Therefore, we aim to answer RQ1.

RQ1.   Can non-agglomerated code anomalies indicate instabilities in SPL?

We computed the strength of the relation between non-agglomerated anomalies and instabilities via Fisher's test [11]. We also used the Odds Ratio [5] to compute the possibility of the presence or absence of a property (i.e., the non-agglomeration) to be associated with the presence or absence of other property (i.e. instability). We computed both statistics via the R tool[2]. Table 2 presents the results for non-agglomerated anomalies. The first column lists each SPL. The second column present the number of non-agglomerated anomalies that indicate instabilities. The third column presents the number of agglomerated anomalies that do not indicate instabilities, i.e. they indicate stability. The fourth column presents the total number of anomalies per SPL.

Table 2. Analysis results for non-agglomerated anomalies

SPL	Non-agglomerated and instability	Agglomerated and stability	Total number of anomalies
MobileMedia	1	11	87
Notepad	0	1	24
TankWar	0	2	106
WebStore	0	4	29

By comparing the second and third columns, we observe that for the 4 SPLs the number of non-agglomerated anomalies that indicate instability is very low. In general, this number is even lower than the number of agglomerated anomalies that indicate stability. Since each SPL has several anomalies (fourth column), we may assume that agglomerations are potentially useful to identify instabilities in SPL. In addition, considering all the four analyzed SPLs, we have a p-value of 0.1488 and Odds Ratio equals

---

[2] https://cran.r-project.org/.

0.0816. Thus, our results suggest that the possibility of a non-agglomerated anomaly to indicate instabilities is close to 0 when compared with an agglomerated anomaly.

Summary for RQ1. Our data suggest that non-agglomerated anomalies may not suffice to indicate instabilities in SPL. The low number of non-agglomerated anomalies that indicate instabilities supports this finding. On the other hand, there is a potential for agglomerations in indicating instabilities.

5.2 Agglomerated Code Anomalies

In this section, we analyze the relationship between agglomerations and instabilities. We aim to answer RQ2 decomposed into RQ2.1 and RQ2.2 discussed as follows.

RQ2.1.   How strong is the relationship between agglomerations and instability?

Table 3 presents the results per type of agglomeration. The first column lists each type of agglomeration. The second column presents the number of agglomerations that indicate correctly an instability for the four analyzed SPLs. The third column presents the number of non-agglomerations that does not indicate instability. The last two columns present the p-value computed via Fisher's test and the results for Odds Ratio.

Table 3. Analysis results for agglomerated anomalies

Type of agglomeration	Agglomeration and instability	Non-agglomeration and stability	p-value	Odds ratio
Feature	31	6	1	1.1598
Feature hierarchy	28	13	0.0478	3.8492
Component	28	124	0.8761	0.9290

Note that, for all types of agglomerations, we obtained similar numbers of agglomerations that indicate instability, but the values of non-agglomerations that indicate stability vary according to the type of agglomeration. Regarding p-value, we assume a confidence level higher than 95%. Only feature hierarchy agglomerations presented p-value lower than 0.05 and, therefore, it is the only type of agglomeration with statistical significance with respect to the correlation between agglomerations and instabilities. Regarding Odds Ratio, we have a value significantly greater than 1 only for feature hierarchy agglomerations, around 3.8. That means that the possibility of a feature hierarchy agglomeration to relate with instabilities is almost 4 times higher than a non-agglomerated code anomaly. For the other two types of agglomerations, we have values close to 1 and, therefore, we may not affirm that such types of agglomeration have more possibilities to "host" instabilities when compared to non-agglomerated anomalies.

Thus, regarding RQ2.1, we conclude that the relationship between agglomerations and instabilities is strong for *feature hierarchy agglomeration*. We then answer RQ2 partially. This observation is quite interesting, since in FOP the features encapsulate the implementation of SPL functionalities. Besides that, our data suggest the refinement relationship may hinder this encapsulation by causing instability into multiple features.

This problem is even more critical since the instabilities caused by a feature hierarchy agglomeration can eventually propagate to several seemly-unrelated SPL products.

We also investigate the accuracy of code anomaly agglomerations to indicate instabilities in SPLs, per type of agglomeration. We answer RQ2.2 as follows.

RQ2.2. *How accurate is the relationship between agglomerations and instability?*

To assess accuracy of each type of agglomeration, we compute precision and recall in terms of true positives (TP), false positives (FP), true negatives (TN), and false negatives (FN) [6]. TP is the number of agglomerations that indicate correctly instabilities. FP is the number of agglomerations that indicate incorrectly instabilities, i.e. indicate stability. TN is the number of non-agglomerations that does not indicate instability. Finally, FN is the number of non-agglomerations that indicate instability. The formula for precision and recall are $P = TP/(TP + FP)$ and $R = TP/(TP + FN)$ [6].

Since even small-sized systems have several anomalies [17], developers should focus their maintenance effort on anomalies that represent the most critical maintenance problems. Thus, agglomerating anomalies can reduce the search space for finding those problems. We focus our analysis on accuracy computed in terms of precision and recall. In this study, we compute precision and recall per type of agglomeration considering all the instable components, regardless the sources of instability of each component. We made this decision because some instable components have multiple sources that relate to different types of agglomeration. For instance, the component `MediaController` of feature *MediaManagement* has changed because of an "Add crosscutting feature" and a "Distribute code among features" in MobileMedia, Release 4.

Table 4 presents precision (P), recall (R), and the number of instable components indicated per type of agglomeration (#IC). This table also presents median, mean, and standard deviation for the results obtained for the four SPLs under analysis. We provide a discussion of our results per type of agglomeration as follows.

Table 4. Precision and recall per type of agglomeration

Agglomeration	Feature			Feature hierarchy			Component		
SPL	P	R	#IC	P	R	#IC	P	R	#IC
MobileMedia	76%	72%	65	100%	59%	30	50%	10%	8
Notepad	50%	20%	4	75%	50%	8	50%	25%	3
TankWar	92%	61%	37	82%	82%	66	65%	23%	17
WebStore	75%	60%	26	100%	24%	10	0%	0%	0
Median	**76%**	**61%**	**32**	**91%**	**54%**	**20**	**50%**	**16%**	**6**
Mean	**73%**	**53%**	**33**	**89%**	**54%**	**29**	**41%**	**14%**	**7**
Std. dev.	**15%**	**20%**	**22**	**11%**	**21%**	**23**	**25%**	**10%**	**6**

Feature Agglomeration. The first three columns in Table 4 correspond to the results for feature agglomeration. We observed a precision with median of 76% and mean of 73%. We then observe that each 3 out of 4 feature agglomerations indicate instabilities. These results are expressive if we consider that agglomerations aim to provide a precise indication of instability, based on high frequencies of code anomalies that may occur in any system. To illustrate the effectiveness of a feature agglomeration in indicating instability, let us consider again the example of MobileMedia from Sect. 3.2. In fact, the feature agglomeration formed by components from feature *MediaManagement* indicated relevant instabilities generated by a source of instability categorized as "Distribute code among features". In this case, the implementation of the component BaseController from feature Base, the most important controller of the SPL, was distributed to several features including *MediaManagement*. This distribution of source code to other features made the components of the feature agglomeration instable.

Regarding recall, we obtained a mean of 53%, with median of 61%, for the SPLs under analysis. We observed a percentage of recall equals or higher than 60% in 3 out of 4 SPLs. Indeed, low percentages of recall are expected in this study, since not all instabilities in SPL are related to anomalous code structures. Through a manual analysis of the four SPLs, we identified various sources of instability that do not relate with code anomalies. For instance, in MobileMedia some components have changed from one release to another because of the inclusion of new functionalities by means of features (e.g., in Releases 1 to 2). In TankWar, some components have changed due to the inclusion of FOP-specific mechanisms (e.g., in Releases 2 to 3).

Note that, for Notepad, the low rates of both precision and recall may be justified by the small percentage for both instable and anomalous components. As an example, Notepad has only 37.5% of instable components, against 58.9%, 79.3%, and 44.2% for MobileMedia, TankWar, and WebStore respectively. Despite of that, in general our results suggest that there is a high rate of feature agglomerations that, possibly, may indicate instabilities in the SPLs. However, since we did not observe statistical significance for this type of agglomeration (see Sect. 5.2), we may not affirm that feature agglomerations are indicators of instability in SPLs.

Feature Hierarchy Agglomeration. The three next columns in Table 4 present precision, recall, and #IC for the analysis of feature hierarchy agglomeration. We obtained values similar to the first analysis, with respect to the feature analysis. First, regarding precision, we have a mean value of 89%, the highest value among types of agglomeration. This data suggests the only a few feature hierarchy agglomerations – that is, related to a refinement chain formed by components and its refinements – are not related to instabilities. We additionally obtained a mean recall of 54% for the target SPLs, that is, the best value among agglomeration types. This result indicates that a significant number of feature hierarchy agglomerations are candidates to indicate instabilities. We conclude that the feature hierarchy agglomeration is an indicator of instabilities in SPL.

To illustrate a feature hierarchy agglomeration that indicated instability, let us consider the example of MobileMedia from Sect. 3.3. The feature hierarchy agglomeration formed by components of the refinement chain of MediaController indicated several relevant sources of instability. For instance, this agglomeration captured the instability caused by a source categorized as "Pull up common feature code". In this case, due to the addition of new types of media in MobileMedia, it was reorganized the implementation of feature *CopyPhoto* into two features: *CopyPhoto* and *CopyMedia*. This change affected all components from the agglomeration in terms of instability.

Component Agglomerations. The three last columns in Table 4 present precision, recall, and #IC for the analysis of component agglomeration. In this case, we obtained values significantly different when compared to the feature agglomeration analysis. With respect to the four SPLs, we obtained a mean precision of 41%. This result points that less than a half of the observed component agglomerations relate, in fact, to instabilities. Based on this data, we may not affirm that this type of agglomerations is effective in indicating instabilities. Moreover, we obtained a mean recall of 14% for the SPLs. This result is very low when considering that systems tend to present several instable components and code anomalies. Therefore, our data suggests that the component agglomeration is not an indicator of instabilities in SPL.

Although precision and recall are, in general, low, we observed interesting cases of component agglomerations that indicate instabilities. Consider the example presented in Sect. 3.4. Code elements from the component `MediaController`, of the feature *MediaManagement*, indicated correctly different sources of instability. These sources include (i) "Distribute code among features" regarding the implementation of component `BaseController` from feature *Base* and (ii) "Pull up common feature code" regarding the reorganization of feature *CopyPhoto*. We discuss both sources previously in this section, for feature agglomeration and feature hierarchy agglomeration.

Summary for RQ2. Our data suggest that feature hierarchy is the most effective type of agglomeration for identification of sources of instability in SPLs, due to the p-value lower than 0.05 (given a 95% confidence interval) and the highest Odds Ratio close to 3.8. When compared to non-agglomerated anomalies (RQ1), with Odds Ratio equals 0.08, we observe that feature hierarchy agglomeration is 3.8 times more effective in identifying instabilities. The high precision of 89% for this type reinforces our findings.

6 Related Work

Previous works propose or investigate anomalies that indicate potentially SPL maintenance problems [2, 7]. Apel et al. [2] introduce the term "variability smell", i.e. anomalies that capture the notion of SPL variability, and present a set of 14 anomalies that may occur in different phases of the SPL engineering. In turn, Fenske and Schulze [7] provide a complementary set of variability-aware anomalies, besides of an empirical study to assess the occurrence of these anomalies in real SPLs. However, none of these studies neither has used anomaly agglomeration nor has analyzed instability.

In particular, Oizumi et al. [21] investigate the use of inter-related anomalies, i.e. anomaly agglomerations, to identify design problems in general source code. They define strategies to group different anomaly occurrences in source code elements. The authors discuss that the defined agglomerations are better indicators of design problems than non-agglomerated anomalies. The results suggest that some types of agglomeration can indicate sufficiently problems with accuracy higher than 80%. However, the authors do not explore neither instability as a design problem nor the relationship between agglomerations and instability in SPL. In turn, this paper focus on the analysis agglomerations as indicators of instability in the context of feature-oriented SPL.

7   Threats to Validity

We discuss threats to the study validity, with respective treatments, as follows.

Construct and Internal Validity. We carefully designed our study for replication. However, a major threat to our study is the set of metrics used in the detection strategy composition. This set is restricted to the metrics provided by the SPL repository [24] adopted in our study. To minimize this issue, we selected some well-known and largely studied metrics, such as *McCabe's Cyclomatic Complexity (Cyclo)*. The list of detection strategies used in this study is available in the research website [8]. Regarding the small length of the analyzed SPLs, we highlight the limited number of SPLs available for research, as the limited number of releases for the available SPLs. The low number of available releases has lead us to consider a component as instable if it has changed in two or more releases. To minimize this issue, we analyzed the SPLs in all available releases. Finally, we conducted the data collection carefully. To minimize errors, two authors checked all the collected data and re-collected the data in case of divergence.

Conclusion and External Validity. We designed a data analysis protocol carefully. To compute the statistical significance and strength of the relationship between agglomerations and instabilities, we computed the Fisher's test [11] and Odds Ratio [5], two well-known and reliable techniques. We also computed precision and recall for the accuracy analysis of agglomerations, based on previous work [21]. These procedures aim to minimize issues regarding the conclusions we draw. Two authors checked the analysis to avoid missing data and re-conducted the analysis to prevent biases. Regarding the generalization of findings, we expect that our results are extensible to other SPL development contexts than FOP. However, further investigation is required.

8   Conclusion and Future Work

Some studies assume that each code anomaly alone suffices to characterize SPL maintenance problems [7, 23]. Nevertheless, each single anomaly may represent only a partial view of a problem. To address this issue, a previous work investigates to what extent agglomerating code anomalies may support the characterization of maintenance problems in single systems [21]. However, we lack studies to investigate and compare the use of anomalies and their agglomerations as indicators of problems that harm the SPL maintainability. In this paper, we focus on a specific maintenance problem in SPLs: instability. We first investigate if non-agglomerated anomalies may indicate instability in SPL. Our findings suggest that non-agglomerated anomalies do not support the identification of anomalous code structures that cause instability. We then investigate to what extent anomaly agglomerations represent sources of instability in SPL. Our study relies on the analysis of different releases of four feature-oriented SPLs.

Our data suggest that feature hierarchy agglomeration, one of the three types of agglomeration proposed in this study, is up to 3.8 times more effective than non-agglomerated anomalies in identifying sources of instability in SPL. The high precision of 89% for this type of agglomeration reinforces that it can support developers in anticipating critical instabilities that harm the SPL maintainability. These findings have clear implications in the FOP development. Since feature hierarchies are a basis for FOP, developers of feature-oriented SPLs should design carefully feature hierarchies to prevent the implementation of hierarchical structures that hamper the SPL maintainability. As future work, we intend to investigate alternative types of agglomeration for other SPL maintainability problems, as the impact of different anomalies on instability.

Acknowledgments. This work was partially supported by CAPES/Procad, CNPq (grants 424340/2016-0 and 290136/2015-6), and FAPEMIG (grant PPM-00382-14).

References

1. Ampatzoglou, A., Chatzigeorgiou, A., Charalampidou, S., Avgeriou, P.: The effect of GoF design patterns on stability. IEEE Trans. Softw. Eng. **41**(8), 781–802 (2015)
2. Apel, S., Batory, D., Kästner, C., Saake, G.: Feature-Oriented Software Product Lines. Springer, Heidelberg (2013)
3. Apel, S., Kätner, C., Lengauer, C.: FeatureHouse. In: 31st ICSE, pp. 221–231 (2009)
4. Batory, D., Sarvela, J., Rauschmayer, A.: scaling step-wise refinement. In: 25th International Conference on Software Engineering (ICSE), pp. 187–197 (2003)
5. Cornfield, J.: A method of estimating comparative rates from clinical data. J. Natl Cancer Inst. **11**(6), 1269–1275 (1951)
6. Fawcett, T.: An introduction to ROC analysis. Pattern Recogn. Lett. **27**(8), 861–874 (2006)
7. Fenske, W., Schulze, S.: Code smells revisited. In: 9th VaMoS, pp. 3–10 (2015)
8. Fernandes, E., Vale, G., Figueiredo, S., Figueiredo, E., Garcia, A., Lee, J.: No Code Anomaly is an Island: Anomaly Agglomeration as Sign of Product Line Instabilities – Data of the Study. http://labsoft.dcc.ufmg.br/doku.php?id=about:no_code_anomaly_is_an_island
9. Ferreira, G., Gaia, F., Figueiredo, E., Maia, M.: On the Use of Feature-Oriented Programming for Evolving Software Product Lines. Sci. Comput. Program. **93**, 65–85 (2014)
10. Figueiredo, E., Cacho, N., Sant'Anna, C., Monteiro, M., Kulesza, U., Garcia, A., Soares, S., Ferrari, F., Khan, S., Castor Filho, F., Dantas, F.: Evolving software product lines with aspects. In: 30th International Conference on Software Engineering (ICSE), pp. 261–270 (2008)
11. Fisher, R.: On the interpretation of x^2 from contingency tables, and the calculation of P. J. Roy. Stat. Soc. **85**(1), 87–94 (1922)
12. Fowler, M.: Refactoring. Object Technology Series. Addison-Wesley, Boston (1999)
13. Gaia, F., Ferreira, G., Figueiredo, E., Maia, M.: A quantitative and qualitative assessment of aspectual feature modules for evolving software product lines. Sci. Comput. Program. **96**(2), 230–253 (2014)
14. Khomh, F., Di Penta, M., Gueheneuc, Y.: An Exploratory Study of the Impact of Code Smells on Software Change-Proneness. In: 16th WCRE, pp. 75–84 (2009)
15. Kim, C.H.P., Bodden, E., Batory, D., Khurshid, S.: Reducing configurations to monitor in a software product line. In: Barringer, H., et al. (eds.) RV 2010. LNCS, vol. 6418, pp. 285–299. Springer, Heidelberg (2010). doi:10.1007/978-3-642-16612-9_22
16. Lanza, M., Marinescu, R.: Object-Oriented Metrics in Practice. Springer, Heidelberg (2006)
17. Macia, I., Garcia, J., Popescu, D., Garcia, A., Medvidovic, N., von Staa, A.: Are automatically-detected code anomalies relevant to architectural modularity? In: 11th International Conference on Aspect-Oriented Software Development (AOSD), pp. 167–178 (2012)

18. Medeiros, F., Kästner, C., Ribeiro, M., Nadi, S., Gheyi, R.: The love/hate relationship with the C prepocessor. In: 29th ECOOP, pp. 495–518 (2015)
19. Meyer, B.: Object-Oriented Software Construction. Prentice Hall, Upper Saddle River (1988)
20. Moha, N., Gueheneuc, Y., Duchien, L., Le Meur, A.: DECOR. IEEE Trans. Softw. Eng. **36**(1), 20–36 (2010)
21. Oizumi, W., Garcia, A., Sousa, L., Cafeo, B., Zhao, Y.: Code anomalies flock together. In: 38th International Conference on Software Engineering (ICSE), pp. 440–451 (2016)
22. Pohl, K., Böckle, G., van der Linden, F.: Software Product Line Engineering. Springer Science & Business Media, Heidelberg (2005)
23. Schulze, S., Apel, S., Kästner, C.: Code clones in feature-oriented software product lines. In: 4th GPCE, pp. 103–112 (2010)
24. Vale, G., Albuquerque, D., Figueiredo, E., Garcia, A.: Defining metric thresholds for software product lines. In: 19th SPLC, pp. 176–185 (2015)
25. Yau, S., Collofello, J.: Design stability measures for software maintenance. IEEE Trans. Softw. Eng. **11**(9), 849–856 (1985)

ReMINDER: An Approach to Modeling Non-Functional Properties in Dynamic Software Product Lines

Anderson G. Uchôa[1]([✉]), Carla I.M. Bezerra[1], Ivan C. Machado[3],
José Maria Monteiro[2], and Rossana M.C. Andrade[2]

[1] Federal University of Ceará, UFC Quixadá, Fortaleza, Brazil
andersonguchoa@gmail.com, carlailane@ufc.br
[2] Computer Science Department, Federal University of Ceará,
UFC Fortaleza, Fortaleza, Brazil
monteiro@lia.ufc.br, rossana@ufc.br
[3] Computer Science Department, Federal University of Bahia,
UFBA Salvador, Salvador, Brazil
ivanmachado@dcc.ufba.br

Abstract. This paper presents a systematic approach to modeling NFPs in DSPL feature models. In our proposed approach, feature models are annotated with the representation of NFPs, rules for the activation and deactivation of features, constraints between NFPs and features, and context adaptation scenarios. To evaluate the applicability of the proposed approach we carried out an empirical evaluation. The approach yielded good results at identifying NFPs in DSPLs.

Keywords: Dynamic Software Product Lines · Non-Functional Properties · Feature models

1 Introduction

DSPL engineering is an approach that extends the concept of conventional SPL to allow the generation of software variants at runtime [1]. DSPL aims to produce software capable to adapt according to the needs of users and resources constraints at runtime. In a DSPL, variation points are firstly bound when the software is released, matching initial environment settings. However, at runtime, whether the context changes, it is possible to rebind the variation points, in order to adapt the system to the new, changed, environment settings [2].

One of the most important assets of a DSPL is the feature model. This artifact captures the similarities and variabilities between the possible configurations of products of a DSPL in a given context. In a DSPL feature model the system characteristics can be added, removed and modified at runtime

---

R.M.C. Andrade—Research Scholarship - DT Level 2, sponsored by CNPq.

G. Botterweck and C. Werner (Eds.): ICSR 2017, LNCS 10221, pp. 65–73, 2017.
DOI: 10.1007/978-3-319-56856-0_5

in a managed way [1]. However, the feature model does not capture NFP explicitly neither influence these properties to achieve alternative configurations of a product variant.

Representing NFP in DSPL might be a rather complex activity. Given a particular context, configuration rules, features constraints and preferences of stakeholders, particularly the Functional Requirements (FR) and NFP [8], must all be considered. Although the NFP represent an important artifact associated to the quality of an SPL, modeling NFP techniques are not completely suitable for SPL engineering, as the approaches are commonly based on FR rather than NFP, as indicated in an extensive literature survey on the field [4].

In this paper, we present an approach to modeling NFPs in DSPL feature models. The approach is capable to identify, in a systematic fashion, the set of NFPs, constraints and context adaptation scenarios. To evaluate the approach we carried out an empirical evaluation, aimed to identify the relevant NFPs and context adaptation scenarios, with their respective constraints, to support the features modeling and the representation of NFPs in DSPL feature models. As results we obtained 70% accuracy in relation to the identification of NFPs, and 90% accuracy to identify context adaptations scenarios. Besides, we could observe that the approach could be useful to provide software engineers with an adequate support at identifying NFPs and their relation to the behavior of the feature models through interdependence constraints.

2   ReMINDER: An AppRoach to Modeling Non-FunctIoNal Properties in DSPL

The ReMINDER approach aims to provide a systematic way for identifying NFPs and context adaptation scenarios, with their respective constraints, as a means to support feature modeling and the representation of NFP in DSPL feature models. The proposed approach could be considered an endeavor to bridge an important gap, concerning to the lack of existing approaches to enable the representation of both NFP and context scenarios in feature models.

Figure 1 provides an overview of the ReMINDER approach. The ReMINDER approach encompasses two major phases: (1) identification and representation of NFPs in feature models; and (2) identification of constraints and context adaptations scenarios. The first phase aims to identify the NFPs that are critical for a DSPL and represent them in an quality feature model. The input of this phase are SPL or DSPL feature models without context, modeled with the FODA notation [3]. The output of this phase is a quality feature model. The second phase aims to identify the constraints between NFPs and context adaptations with the guidance of a Domain Engineer. The input of this phase is the SPL or DSPL feature models without context and the quality feature model built in the previous phase, while as output DSPL feature models with context, the quality feature model and context adaptation scenarios. The NFPs catalog, the quality feature model and the templates used by ReMINDER are available online[1]. Each step of the ReMINDER approach is discussed along the next sections.

---

[1] http://bit.ly/2lx3Ik2.

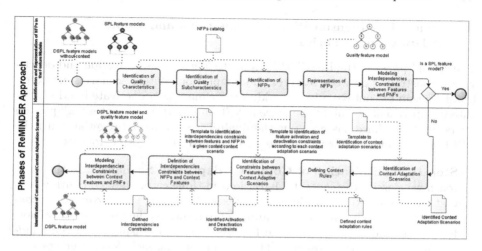

Fig. 1. Process of ReMINDER approach.

2.1 Phase I - Identification and Representation of NFPs in Feature Models

The first phase of the ReMINDER approach aims to identify the NFPs that are critical for a DSPL and represent them in a quality feature model. The quality feature model classifies these NFPs according to the quality characteristic and sub-characteristics presented in the product quality model of the ISO/IEC 25010 SQuaRE [6]. To assist in the identification of these NFPs, we created a NFPs catalog from [9]. This catalog also classifies the NFPs according to the SQuaRE quality characteristic and sub-characteristics. This phase encompasses four steps, as follows:

Step I - Identification of Quality Characteristics. It aims to identify the relevant quality characteristics based on the stakeholders needs.

Step II - Identification of Quality Sub-characteristics. Next, for each quality characteristic previously identified, it aims to identify the relevant quality sub-characteristics.

Step III - Identification of NFPs. This step consists of adding the NFPs established by the stakeholders, for each relevant sub-characteristic previously identified. The relevance of a NFP for a specific sub-characteristic is represented by qualifiers - high, medium or low. For example, for the quality sub-characteristics operability, the NFP effort can be measured as low.

Step IV - Representation of NFPs. The NFPs could be represented through a quality feature model, composed of quality characteristics, sub-characteristics, and NFPs. This artifact together with the DSPL feature model is given as input to the next phase.

2.2 Phase II - Identification of Constraint and Context Adaptation Scenarios

The second phase of the ReMINDER aims to identify the activation and deactivation constraints between features and adaptation context scenarios, based on the definition of context rules. In addition, define how an activated and deactivated context feature might influence a NFP in a particular context adaptation scenario. This phase has as input the quality feature model together with the DSPL feature model. For this phase we identified four steps, as follows:

Step I - Identification of Context Adaptation Scenarios. In this approach we classify the context adaptations in three categories: computing contexts, user contexts, and physical contexts. According to [5], *computing context* refers to the hardware configuration used, such as the processors available for a task, the devices accessible for user input and display, and the bandwidth. *User context* represents all the human factors, such as the user's profile, calendars, and profiles. *Physical context* refers to the non-computing-related information provided by a real-world environment, such as location, lighting, etc. The definitions of each context adaptation scenario describe situations relevant to the domain of an DSPL, based on a scenario ID and the following properties:

- **Contexts** - used to inform the type of context, computing context, user context, and physical context.
- **Context informations** - used to identify the information that varies according to each type of context, for example, battery level is a computational context information.
- **Qualifiers** - used to identify the qualifications of each context information. A qualification can be either boolean or classified in a qualitative scale (high, medium and low). For example, the context information "free memory level" can assume the values high or low. On the other hand, context information "internet connection" can assume the values true or false.
- **Quantifiers** - used to describe the values associated with each type of qualifier. These quantifiers are defined by relational operators: greater than ($>$), less than ($<$), greater than or equal to ($>=$), less than or equal to ($<=$), equal ($=$) and different ($<>$). Followed by a value of type: *string*, integer, *float* or boolean. If this quantifier is defined by a numeric range, a logical operator is added that can be of the type: (OR) or (AND), followed by another value of type *string*, integer, *float* or boolean. For example, high free memory level $>=$ 128 or low free memory level $<$ 128.
- **Status of quantifiers by scenario** - Used to indicate which of the values of each context information is valid in the scenario definition.

Step II - Defining Context Rules. After the identification of context adaptation scenarios, we can define the context rules that specify how a context information impacts on the configuration of the products of a DSPL. It indicates, for example, which features should be activated and deactivated.

These rules have as properties: an identifier and an expression. The expression is formed by an antecedent, the operator *implies*, and a consequent. The antecedent is an expression that can contain context information with its variation activated and deactivated. The operator *implies* determine that if the antecedent is true in the adaptation scenario, then the consequent should be or not included in the configuration of the feature models. The consequent is an expression that can contain features and logic operators. The expression determines which features need to be activated or deactivated according to each context adaptation scenario. For example, RC1 - LOW MEMORY LEVEL *implies* NOT (PERSISTENCE); RC2 - NOT (INTERNET CONNECTION) *implies* VIA SENSOR.

Step III - Identification of Constraints Between Features and Context Adaptive Scenarios. The next step is to identify the constraints of activation and deactivation features according to the context rules that will be executed based on the definitions of context adaptation scenarios and the features present in the initial configuration of the product. As exemplified previously, for a given context adaptation scenario, in which just the antecedent LOW MEMORY LEVEL is true, RC1 must be executed, i.e., PERSISTENCE must be deactivated.

Step IV - Definition of Interdependence Constraints Between NFPs and Context Features. After identifying the constraints between features and context adaptation scenarios, we need to identify the relations of interdependencies between the identified NFPs and the features, according to each context adaptation scenario. To specify and measure this interdependence constraints, we have added a concept of goal-oriented modeling, in particular the concept of contribution links [10]. In this way, we assign interdependence constraints between context features and NFPs, in a given context. These features can be represented visually (see footnote 1) and may have four types of interdependence constraints over an NFP:

- "++" - the feature completely satisfies an NFP if it is activated.
- "- -" - the feature does not completely satisfy an NFP if it is activated.
- "+" - the feature has a positive influence on an NFP if it is activated.
- "-" - the feature has a negative influence on an NFP if it is activated.

3   Empirical Evaluation

An observational study was executed to analyze the process defined in the ReMINDER approach. The DSPL used in this study is called DSPL Mobi-Line [7]. The MobiLine's feature model, used in the observational study is available online (see footnote 1). Two M.Sc. students and one PhD participated in this observation study.

3.1   Execution

For this empirical study, a questionnaire was applied to characterize each participant. Then, a training was held for participants on the steps used in the

ReMINDER approach. An observation activity occurred in a single session. Initially, participants had to assume the role of domain engineer in charge of specifying the relevant NFPs for the DSPL mobile visit guide. The effort expected to accomplish this task was medium. We consider a scale between high, medium and low. The participants identified an average, respectively, 50%, 100% and 62% of the expected NFPs. These results show that it is possible to identify and specify NFPs using ReMINDER.

Next, the engineers should identify which features should be activated and deactivated based on the context rules that are performed and the definitions of the context adaptation scenarios. The effort expected to accomplish this task was low. A set of 11 contextual rules and two contextual adaptation scenarios were defined. In the first scenario, 11 activated features and 2 deactivated were provided, whereas in the second scenario, 9 activated and 4 deactivated features were provided. Only one participant did not identify all features.

Finally, the participants had to identify the interdependence constraints between the NFP that were identified in the first part of the observation study and activated and deactivated features according to context adaptations scenarios identified in the second part. The effort expected to accomplish this task was medium or high. In this activity, we analyzed whether the constraints identified by each engineers were consistent. Only one of the engineers presented inconsistency in their constraints.

3.2   Results and Findings

After the observation activities, we performed a interview with the participants to contribute with the evaluation approach and answer the research questions.

Q1: What is the effort expended to identify the NFPs according to the quality characteristics and sub-characteristics of the SQuaRE standard, through the NFPs Catalog?
In general, the effort spent to identify the NFPs according to the quality characteristics and sub-characteristics was medium. However, prior knowledge about the quality characteristics and sub-characteristics of SQuaRE standard is required. Regard the number of correct answers in the NFP identification task, we verified 70% accuracy in relation to the expected result.

Q2: What is the effort expended to specify the interdependence constraints between identified NFP and features?
When it is necessary to specify the interdependence constraints between NFP and features, the overall effort spent was medium. The participants took on average about 29 min to specify the constraints, even with the support of the proposed template. Initially, the participants took about 20 min to specify the interdependence constraints in the first context adaptation scenario. In the second adaptation scenario, they took less time to accomplish the task, which indicates a reduced effort necessary.

Q3: What is the accuracy and effort expended to specify the adaptation scenarios and their constraints?

The use of the templates facilitated the specification of context scenarios adaptations and their constraints. According to the participants, with the templates it was possible to delimit the values of the context information, and manage their features and constraints. In addition, the ease of specifying context adaptation scenario is one of the greatest benefits of the approach. However, during the observation activity, the engineers made a high effort to identify which context rules should be executed. In relation to the number of correctness in specifying scenarios of context adaptations and their constraints, we verified 90% accuracy in relation to the expected result for the first scenario of context adaptation, while 89% accuracy regarding the expected result for the second context adaptation scenario.

Q4: What are the drawbacks and benefits of the approach?

The participants mentioned the approach was both intuitive and easy to understand, the phases are well divided and with specific objectives. The approach facilitated the identification of NFP and their relationship to the features of the product line. In addition, the templates and the NFP catalog were a useful support at identifying NFP in DSPL. However, they reported a greater effort to accomplish the task to specify the interdependence constraints between identified NFPs and context features.

3.3   Threats to Validity

We next discuss the threats to the validity of our empirical assesssment. **Construct Validity.** As the main researcher of this study is part of the same experimenter's research group, he had a strong influence on the conclusions. To mitigate this threat, other participants played the role of a domain engineer, during the process of using the approach. **Internal Validity.** The approach has a couple of phases and steps. It is possible that some concepts have been misinterpreted. To mitigate this threat, the researcher was, during an observation activity, all the time close to the participants. The Mobiline DSPL used in this study may not be the most appropriate. In order to mitigate this threat, we aim to continue to investigate the approach in other application scenarios. **External validity.** As the empirical study was executed in one small academic DSPL, it is difficult to generalize the findings. Hence, the discussions are limited for this DSPL context. Despite the limitations, researchers can extend the study by replicating it in different DSPL contexts following the design of this study.

4   Related Work

Zang et al. [11] presents an approach to modeling quality attribute and quality-aware product configuration in SPLs. Similar to the objective of this work, the authors proposed an approach for modeling quality attributes in the feature models leading to a quality-aware product configuration. However, in this work, we defined an approach for identification and representation of NFPs and identification of constraints and context adaptation scenarios to the DSPL feature models. Soares et al. [9] identified in a systematic review, a set of 52 NFP that may emerge at runtime. This set of 52 NFPs that emerge at runtime, by application domains that suffer adaptations at runtime, can also emerge in autonomic systems and context-aware systems. From this classification we have created a NFP catalog as one of the main artifacts of our approach. Sanchez et al. [8] presents an approach for self-adaptive systems, based on the process of specification, measurement and optimization of quality attribute properties in feature models. In addition, instead of extending the feature models in two submodules, we propose a quality feature model to support the NFP representation.

5 Conclusion and Future Work

This paper presented the ReMINDER approach that support the modeling of NFP in DSPL. We carried out an empirical evaluation to evaluate the applicability of the approach. The evaluation consisted of observation and interview activities with domain engineers. Among the observations, we examined the role of the approach as a guide to identification and specification of NFP. From an NFP catalog, stakeholders can find NFP related to the quality characteristics and sub-characteristics of a DSPL, according to the SQUaRE standard. As future work, we plan to extend the ReMINDER approach to formally verify whether the NFP in DSPL feature models match the expected results of the process of reconfiguration at runtime. In addition, we plan to add new NFPs to the NFPs catalog, which may emerge at runtime and develop a tool to assist in operationalizing the approach.

References

1. Bencomo, N., Hallsteinsen, S., De Almeida, E.S.: A view of the dynamic software product line landscape. Computer **45**(10), 36–41 (2012)
2. Capilla, R., Bosch, J., Kang, K.C.: Systems and Software Variability Management. Springer, Heidelberg (2013)
3. Czarnecki, K., Helsen, S., Eisenecker, U.: Formalizing cardinality-based feature models and their specialization. Softw. Process: Improv. Pract. **10**(1), 7–29 (2005)
4. Hammani, F.Z.: Survey of non-functional requirements modeling and verification of software product lines. In: 2014 IEEE Eighth International Conference on Research Challenges in Information Science (RCIS), pp. 1–6. IEEE (2014)
5. Hong, D., Chiu, D.K., Shen, V.Y.: Requirements elicitation for the design of context-aware applications in a ubiquitous environment. In: 7th International Conference on Electronic Commerce, pp. 590–596. ACM, Xi'an (2005)
6. ISO/IEC: 25010: Systems and software engineering - Systems and software Quality Requirements and Evaluation (SQuaRE) - System and software quality models. Technical report, ISO/IEC, Switzerland (2011)

7. Marinho, F.G., Andrade, R.M., Werner, C., Viana, W., Maia, M.E., Rocha, L.S., Teixeira, E., Ferreira Filho, J.B., Dantas, V.L., Lima, F., et al.: MobiLine: a nested software product line for the domain of mobile and context-aware applications. Sci. Comput. Program. **78**(12), 2381–2398 (2013)
8. Sanchez, L.E., Diaz-Pace, J.A., Zunino, A., Moisan, S., Rigault, J.P.: An approach based on feature models and quality criteria for adapting component-based systems. J. Softw. Eng. Res. Dev. **3**(1), 1–30 (2015)
9. Soares, L.R., Potena, P., Carmo Machado, I., Crnkovic, I., Almeida, E.S.: Analysis of non-functional properties in software product lines: a systematic review. In: 2014 40th EUROMICRO Conference on Software Engineering and Advanced Applications, pp. 328–335. IEEE (2014)
10. Van Lamsweerde, A.: Goal-oriented requirements engineering: a guided tour. In: Proceedings of the 2001 Fifth IEEE International Symposium on Requirements Engineering, pp. 249–262. IEEE (2001)
11. Zhang, G., Ye, H., Lin, Y.: Quality attribute modeling and quality aware product configuration in software product lines. Softw. Qual. J. **22**(3), 365–401 (2014)

Variability Management and Model Variants

Clustering Variation Points
in MATLAB/Simulink Models Using
Reverse Signal Propagation Analysis

Alexander Schlie[1(✉)], David Wille[1], Loek Cleophas[2,3], and Ina Schaefer[1]

[1] TU Braunschweig, Braunschweig, Germany
{a.schlie,d.wille,i.schaefer}@tu-braunschweig.de
[2] Stellenbosch University, Stellenbosch, South Africa
[3] TU Eindhoven, Eindhoven, The Netherlands
l.g.w.a.cleophas@tue.nl
https://www.tu-braunschweig.de/isf

Abstract. Model-based languages such as MATLAB/Simulink play an essential role in the model-driven development of software systems. During their development, these systems can be subject to modification numerous times. For large-scale systems, to manually identify performed modifications is infeasible. However, their precise identification and subsequent validation is essential for the evolution of model-based systems. If not fully identified, modifications may cause unaccountable behavior as the system evolves and their redress can significantly delay the entire development process. In this paper, we propose a fully automated technique called Reverse Signal Propagation Analysis, which identifies and clusters variations within evolving *MATLAB/Simulink* models. With each cluster representing a clearly delimitable variation point between models, we allow model engineers not only to specifically focus on single variations, but by using their domain knowledge, to also relate and verify them. By identifying variation points, we assist model engineers in validating the respective parts and reduce the risk of improper system behavior as the system evolves. To assess the applicability of our technique, we present a feasibility study with real-world models from the automotive domain and show our technique to be very fast and highly precise.

Keywords: MATLAB/Simulink · Variation point · Clustering

1 Introduction

For the *model-driven engineering* of complex systems, model-based languages such as *MATLAB/Simulink*[1] are of substantial importance in a variety of industrial domains. They allow for an abstraction of the overall complexity to a level more understandable for the various engineers involved in the process [1]. Certain domains favor the development of a *150% model* [2], that is a single system

---

[1] Mathworks®- https://mathworks.com/products/simulink/ - Nov. 2016.

© Springer International Publishing AG 2017
G. Botterweck and C. Werner (Eds.): ICSR 2017, LNCS 10221, pp. 77–94, 2017.
DOI: 10.1007/978-3-319-56856-0_6

comprising all functions, rather than multiple single-variant instances [3]. Consequently, nurturing the precise identification of performed modifications in an evolution scenario is essential to both system versions and system variants.

During their development, model-based systems can be subject to modification several times [4]. Due to their sheer size and complexity, the majority of such systems might remain unchanged between iterations. The parts subject to modification can, however, be substantial to the behavior of the entire system. Manually identifying variations induces a vast workload and is usually infeasible. With multiple engineers involved in the process, performed changes can unintentionally be overlooked. If not precisely detected in the first place, they can cause unaccountable system behavior in subsequent phases of development. The workload to redress unverified modifications can accumulate and cause severe problems. Consequently, the identification and validation of the respective parts is essential to the entire development process and subsequent maintenance.

In this paper, we address this problem by specifically utilizing domain-specific features of *MATLAB/Simulink* to analyze models. To this end, we propose *Reverse Signal Propagation Analysis (RSPA)* to identify and cluster variations in evolved model-based systems. We argue that by precisely identifying variations within models, our method is beneficial for the development process and supports engineers in evolving, maintaining and validating large-scale industrial models. We provide a feasibility study to assess our technique. Focusing on *MATLAB/Simulink* models, we make the following contributions:

- We introduce RSPA, a fully automated procedure to precisely identify and cluster syntactically connected variations within *MATLAB/Simulink* models, in order to allow for performed modifications to be validated.
- We evaluate our approach by means of a feasibility study with real-world models from the automotive domain and show our proposed technique to be very fast, highly precise and applicable to models of industrial size.

In the following sections, we briefly provide background information on *MATLAB/Simulink* models and domain-specific features we utilize (Sect. 2). We introduce and explain in detail our proposed technique (Sect. 3), present a feasibility study with models from the automotive domain and discuss the results produced by our technique (Sect. 4). We state related work (Sect. 5) and future work (Sect. 6).

2   Background

We provide the basic terminology to represent implementation-specific variability for evolved *MATLAB/Simulink* models. We further provide information on domain-specific properties for such models that we specifically exploit for RSPA.

2.1   MATLAB/Simulink Models

MATLAB/Simulink is a block-based behavioral modeling language that utilizes *functional blocks* and *signals* to specify functionality of a software system.

To capture the behavior of complex systems, *MATLAB/Simulink* models can comprise several thousand blocks [1,5]. To maintain an overview, logically connected blocks are often grouped within a *Subsystem* block, which hides the contained blocks from direct view until explicitly accessed. Subsystems can be nested and constitute a *model hierarchy*. Figure 1 shows two versions of a model, both encapsulated in the respective subsystem block shown in Fig. 2. We refer to the contained blocks as *sub blocks*. They are shifted within the model hierarchy by one *hierarchical layer* with respect to the subsystem block, which forms their *parent block*.

2.2   Variability in Models

During their evolution, software systems can undergo a multitude of iterations [4]. Modifications can affect various parts of the model and cause blocks and their associated signals to diverge. Hence, diverging elements can be scattered across the model. We refer to locations where two similar models differ as *Variation Points*. Depending on the extent of the performed modification, variation points can comprise multiple blocks and hierarchical layers. Figure 1 shows two versions of a model. Although mostly unchanged, the models diverge at the location circled in red. Here, the circled block represents a simple example of a variation point.

2.3   Signal Propagation in Models

Implementing new functionalities or performing modifications within a model results in additional or varying signals respectively. The change in the signals can propagate between hierarchical layers. This upward directed propagation is depicted in Figs. 1 and 2. For both figures, the lower portion reflects the model prior to the modification and the upper portion reflects the model after the modification. Circled in red in Fig. 1, there is an additional *Outport* block. This signal change propagates to the next higher layer and requires the corresponding parent block shown in Fig. 2 to provide an interface to further relay the signal.

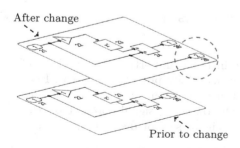

Fig. 1. Signal propagation on lower layer (Color figure online)

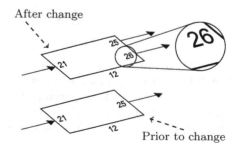

Fig. 2. Effect on higher layer

Our proposed RSPA specifically exploits this upward propagation to realize a lightweight but precise identification of all variation points.

2.4   The Simulink Identifier

The *Simulink Identifier (SID)* is a unique, non-volatile and unmodifiable identifier that persists for the lifetime of a block. It is automatically generated by the *MATLAB/Simulink* environment. For each block, its *SID* is comprised of the corresponding model name and a unique integer value greater than one, separated by a colon. Besides regular *MATLAB/Simulink* blocks, the *SID* also applies to *Stateflow*[2] elements, generally used to model decision logic based on state machines. Both element types are commonly used in combination when modeling complex functionality. For RSPA, we neglect the model name as part of a block's *SID* and only evaluate the unique integer value. We do so because the model name might change during evolution but *MATLAB/Simulink* guarantees the integer value itself to persist.

3   Reverse Signal Propagation Analysis

In this section, we propose our RSPA to identify and cluster variation points in *MATLAB/Simulink* models. Our approach is integrated into the *Family Mining Framework (FMF)* [6–8], which provides an environment for comparing models to identify and store their variability information in a *Software Product Line* context [9]. Although RSPA generally allows for an arbitrary number of input models, in this paper we focus on pairwise comparisons which explicitly reflect a model evolution scenario. The basic workflow of RSPA is shown in Fig. 3.

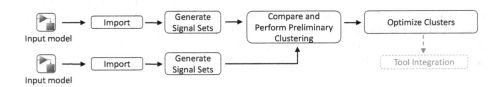

Fig. 3. Basic workflow of RSPA

RSPA requires preparatory work, for instance importing the models (cf. Sect. 3.1), and comprises a total of three sequentially processed phases[3]. First, we traverse each model separately from top to bottom. For each hierarchical layer, we generate a *Signal Set* to store the outgoing signals present on that layer (cf. Sect. 3.2). We then compare two signal sets of distinct models that

---

[2] Mathworks®- https://www.mathworks.com/products/stateflow/ - Nov. 2016.

[3] We provide further details and a screencast on our website:
https://www.isf.cs.tu-bs.de/cms/team/schlie/material/icsr17rspa/.

correspond to the same hierarchical depth. We do so in reverse, thus starting with the lowest hierarchical layer present in either model. Blocks associated with varying signals are clustered within preliminary sets (cf. Sect. 3.3). Between the preliminary sets, intersections may exist which need to be resolved. Hence, we iteratively chain together sets until no more intersections exist (cf. Sect. 3.4). The results are intersection-free sets, each one representing a complete and syntactically delimitable variation point. In other words, every final set itself comprises all blocks associated with a variation point but no two sets exist that contain the same block. Although not explicitly explained in this paper, RSPA automatically generates instructions to display variation points found in evolving models and categorize the comprised elements directly within the *MATLAB/Simulink* environment.

3.1 Preparatory Work

For RSPA to detect and cluster variation points in *MATLAB/Simulink* models, we utilize the FMF and its integrated *MATLAB/Simulink* importer. It is essential to RSPA for each signal set to only contain signals on the same hierarchical layer. To assure this, we assign a parameter H_D to each block during import. This parameter states the hierarchy layer the block and its associated outgoing signals reside on within the model and, thus, their hierarchical depth. The importer itself guarantees a valid assignment of the parameter H_D for a given block in both the presence and absence of a corresponding parent block.

Utilizing the *SID*s, we introduce a specification that allows for an outgoing signal φ_{out}, regardless of its hierarchical depth, to be traced and affiliated with its start block and target block. Specifically, we use the *SID*s of the start block and the target block as well as the signal label if present. Using the lifetime-persistent *SID*s, the specification of a signal also persists for the lifetime of a model. For the model shown in Fig. 4, an example of such specification is as follows:

$$\varphi_{out} = 4 - pass\_Value - 5$$

The parameters that are necessary for RSPA to function are listed in Table 1 and illustrated in Fig. 4. For simplicity reasons, the block names in Fig. 4 correspond with their *SID*s. The subsystem block resides on the top layer and, thus, is assigned '0' for its hierarchical depth. Consequently, the contained sub blocks are assigned '1' as their hierarchical depth. For both sub blocks, their SID_P is the *SID* of the subsystem block. We also store the *type* of a block during import. Both parameters, SID_P and the block type are important later on to capture variations that affect multiple hierarchical layers. With the parameters listed in Table 1, RSPA can explicitly distinguish between *local* variation points that reside on a single layer and variation points that affect multiple hierarchical layers.

Table 1. Parameters used by the RSPA

Name	Description
SID	Unique and unmodifiable identifier (cf. Sect. 2.4)
φ_{out}	An outgoing signal for a given block
H_D	The element's hierarchical depth
SID_P	SID of the parent block if present
type	Semantical function of a block

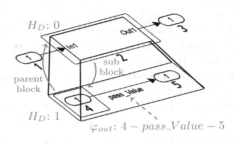

Fig. 4. Parameter illustration

3.2 Signal Set Generation

RSPA begins by generating the signal sets for each model. We start with the highest hierarchy layer present and traverse each model from top to bottom. For each hierarchical layer, we generate a signal set that only contains outgoing signals present on that specific layer. For the signal set generation shown in Algorithm 1, the following properties are of interest.

M_i Single *MATLAB/Simulink* model
K_i Result set holding all generated signal sets for the model M_i
δ_j Specific hierarchical layer of the current model, j ≥ 0
k_j Signal set holding all φ_{out} present on the current hierarchical layer δ_j
b *MATLAB/Simulink* block or *Stateflow* element
φ_{out} Outgoing signal of a *MATLAB/Simulink* block or *Stateflow* element

RSPA processes each input model separately and creates an individual result set to hold all generated signal sets for that specific model (line 1). We utilize the parameter H_D to associate a block's outgoing signal with its hierarchical depth and store the respective signal specification in a signal set k_j (line 6). With the procedure shown in Algorithm 1, we guarantee each signal specification to be placed in the signal set that represents the corresponding hierarchical depth.

For instance, the model M_1 shown in Fig. 5 contains a total of two hierarchical layers, δ_0 and δ_1. Consequently, processing M_1 results in two signal sets, k_0 representing the top layer itself and k_1 for the signals associated with the blocks contained in the two subsystems. Figure 6 represents the model M_1 from Fig. 5 as a graph to illustrate the hierarchical layers, the corresponding signal sets and the generated result set for that model.

When evaluating models that differ in their hierarchical depth, the total number of signal sets and, thus, the size of the result sets reflect this structural divergence.

Algorithm 1. Creating the Signal Sets

Input: M_i
Output: K_i | Iterate through all layers of the model |

1 $K_i \leftarrow \emptyset$
2 **forall** $\delta_j \in M_i$ **do**
3      $k_j \leftarrow \emptyset$
4   **foreach** $b \in \delta_j$ **do** | Store the block's outgoing signals in a set representing the current layer |
5   **forall** $\varphi_{out} \in b$ **do**
6              $k_j \leftarrow (k_j \cup \{\varphi_{out}\})$
7   **end**
8   **end**
9      $K_i \leftarrow (K_i \cup \{k_j\})$ | Store the generated signal set |
10 **end**
11 **return** K_i

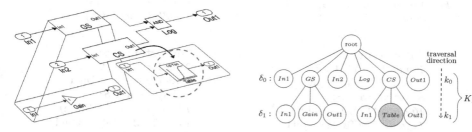

Fig. 5. *MATLAB/Simulink* model M_1 (Color figure online)

Fig. 6. Graph representation of M_1

The model M_2 displayed in Fig. 7 is created by copying the model M_1 from Fig. 5 and replacing the block circled in red with a new subsystem that comprises two *StateFlow* elements. In comparison to the model M_1, the additional third hierarchical layer introduced by this operation results in an additional signal set k_2. The graph representation for M_2 shown in Fig. 8 illustrates the additional hierarchical layer present in M_2 and highlights in gray the modified parts.

In Table 2, we show an excerpt from the generated signal sets for the models M_1 and M_2 from Figs. 5 and 7 along with their result sets K_1 and K_2. Marked gray are the varying signal specifications that correspond to the highlighted parts in Figs. 6 and 8 and that represent a delimitable variation point between the models.

With the signal specification we are able to identify varying parts. For instance for the first entry for the subsystem CS in Table 2, the target block *Table* and, thus, its $SID = 11$ have changed to *State* with $SID = 13$. However, RSPA also identifies the common part for this specification, the start block *In1* with $SID = 10$.

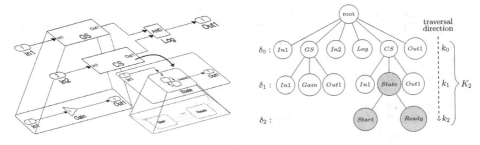

Fig. 7. *MATLAB/Simulink* model M_2 **Fig. 8.** Graph representation of M_2

Table 2. Excerpt from the signal sets for models from Fig. 5 (left) and Fig. 7 (right)

Set	Contained Signals	Set	Contained Signals
k_0	*1–null–2* (In1 – GS) *3–null–4* (In2 – CS) ⋮	k_0	*1–null–2* (In1 – GS) *3–null–4* (In2 – CS) ⋮
k_1	**Subsystem GS:** *7–null–8* (In1 – Gain) *8–null–9* (Gain – Out1) **Subsystem CS:** *10–null–11* (In1 – Table) *11–null–12* (Table – Out1)	k_1	**Subsystem GS:** *7–null–8* (In1 – Gain) *8–null–9* (Gain – Out1) **Subsystem CS:** *10–null–13* (In1 – State) *13–null–12* (State – Out1)
	The listed signal specifications contain consistent but example SIDs only	k_2	**Subsystem State:** *14–pass–15* (Start – Ready) *15–null–14* (Ready – Start)

$K_1 = \{k_0, k_1\}$ $K_2 = \{k_0, k_1, k_2\}$

3.3 Comparison and Preliminary Clustering

After the result sets have been generated, RSPA compares the contained signal sets and preliminarily clusters blocks associated with varying signal specifications. We explicitly exploit the upward signal propagation in *MATLAB/Simulink* models (cf. Sect. 2.3) and start the comparison and clustering procedure shown in Algorithm 2 by processing the signal sets with the highest index, i.e., deepest in the hierarchy first. Hence, we guarantee a sub block to be analyzed prior to its respective parent block and ensure both to be validly grouped within one cluster. In addition to the previously provided parameters, the following properties are of interest for the signal set analysis.

$\hat{P}$ Set to hold the preliminary results prior to optimization
k_j, f_j Signal set, each from a different input model and corresponding to their respective hierarchy layer δ_j, generated in Algorithm 1
s Disjoint set holding the varying signals between k_j and f_j

b_{start} Start block for the varying and currently evaluated outgoing signal
b_{target} Target block for the varying and currently evaluated outgoing signal
$f_N(\varphi_{out})$ Successor function, thus, target block of φ_{out}
τ Set holding b_{start} and b_{target}
VS Variance Set clustering blocks associated with varying signals

We only compare two signal sets k_i and f_i from different input models that correspond to the same hierarchical depth. This might seem like a strong limitation but we argue that it suffices for an evolution scenario and that it also drastically reduces overhead. Moreover, by exploiting the upward signal propagation, RSPA not only reliably detects local variations but also large-scale structural relocations across hierarchical layers. We only consider two signals equal if their specification is identical (cf. Sect. 3.1).

For the signal sets $k_1 \in K_1$ and $k_1 \in K_2$ in Table 2, the signals for the subsystem CS are all considered varying because their specification does not match. Every varying signal is evaluated separately and the respective start block and target block are grouped in a set τ (line 16). To cluster blocks associated with varying signals, we look for an existing *Variance Set (VS)* that already contains one of the two blocks within τ (line 17). We refer to these sets as *VS*s as they hold and cluster blocks associated with varying signals. During the procedure depicted in Algorithm 2, *VS*s can grow in size and in the number of hierarchical layers they comprise. When evaluating the signal sets k_1 for our example, we would create a new *VS* (line 21) for the specification *10-null-11* from Table 2. However, when analyzing *10-null-13*, a *VS* now exists that already contains the *SID* 10. Thus, the block *State* with *SID* 13 is added to that *VS*. Although not explicitly shown in line 17 of Algorithm 2, we also evaluate the SID_P and the *type* of every element within an existing *VS* to capture variation points that comprise multiple hierarchical layers. For the type, we specifically focus on certain blocks that introduce (i.e., *Inport*) or forward (i.e., *Outport*) data between layers or systems and, thus, can establish a syntactical connection between them.

For instance in Fig. 1, the added *Outport* requires the parent block shown in Fig. 2 to relay the signal. We recognize this syntactical connection and, thus, cluster both blocks within one *VS*. With the procedure shown in Algorithm 2, we allow for a precise distinction between variations that propagate between hierarchical layers and local variations that do not affect other layers. With RSPA, we aim for each single *VS* to represent a syntactically delimitable variation point and for each *VS* to contain all elements that variation point comprises.

However, within the preliminary result set $\hat{P}$, the contained *VS*s may share elements. These intersections between the *VS*s need to be resolved for each *VS* to represent a clearly delimitable variation point. To assure this, we initiate the procedure shown in Algorithm 3, which we explain in Sect. 3.4.

Algorithm 2. Analyzing Signals and creating Preliminary Variance Sets

---

    Input: K_1, K_2, M_1, M_2
    Output: $\hat{P}$

1 $\hat{P} \leftarrow \emptyset$
2 $j \leftarrow max(|K_1|, |K_2|)$
3 **while** $j \geq 0$ **do**
4   **if** $k_j \notin K_1$ **then**
5        $k_j \leftarrow \emptyset$
6   **end**
7   **else if** $f_j \notin K_2$ **then**
8        $f_j \leftarrow \emptyset$

> Store the varying signals

> For each varying signal, get the respective start and target block from the original input model

9   **end**
10   **for** $k_j \in K_1,\ f_j \in K_2$ **do**
11        $s \leftarrow (k_j \cup f_j) \setminus (k_j \cap f_j)$
12   **if** $s \neq \emptyset$ **then**
13   **foreach** $\varphi_{out} \in s$ **do**
14             $b_{start} \leftarrow \left\{ b_x \in M_i : b_x \xrightarrow{f_N(\varphi_{out})} b_y, b_x \neq b_y, i \in \{1,2\} \right\}$
15             $b_{target} \leftarrow \left\{ b_y \in M_i : b_x \xrightarrow{f_N(\varphi_{out})} b_y, b_x \neq b_y, i \in \{1,2\} \right\}$
16             $\tau \leftarrow \{b_{start}, b_{target}\}$
17   **if** $\exists VS \in \hat{P} : (\tau \cap VS) \neq \emptyset$ **then**
18                $VS \leftarrow (VS \cup \tau)$

> If there is a subset containing either the start or target block

> Add both to the current subset

19   **end**
20   **else**
21                $VS \leftarrow \tau$
22   **end**
23             $\hat{P} \leftarrow \hat{P} \cup \{VS\}$

> Create a new subset to store both blocks

24   **end**
25   **end**
26   **end**
27     $j \leftarrow (j - 1)$
28 **end**
29 **return** $\hat{P}$

3.4   Cluster Optimization

Depending on the order in which signals are analyzed in Algorithm 2, the VSs within $\hat{P}$ may share elements and, thus, an intersection exists between them. To resolve these intersections, we use the procedure shown in Algorithm 3 to chain VSs together. If, for instance, two VSs share a block, thus an intersection exists, both VSs really correspond to the same variation point. Hence, we chain them together.

The procedure shown in Algorithm 3 runs iteratively. In each iteration, we transfer VSs from $\hat{P}$ to the new set $\hat{L}$. Within $\hat{L}$, VSs are either chained together (line 7) or simply stored for further iterations (line 10). We can easily find out if an optimization was possible, by storing the set's size before chaining (line 3) and after chaining (line 14). If the total number of *VS*s decreased, an optimization was possible. However, further chaining might still be possible and, thus, we initiate the next iteration. If no chaining was possible, the procedure terminates (line 17).

Algorithm 3. Optimization of the Preliminary Variance Sets

Input: $\hat{P}$
Output: $\hat{L}$ ⟵ Result set holding all final, intersection-free *Variance Sets*

1 $optimized \leftarrow false$
2 **while** $\neg optimized$ **do**
3      $VS_{old} \leftarrow |\hat{P}|$ ⟵ Store the preliminary set's size before chaining, and reset the final result set
4      $\hat{L} \leftarrow \emptyset$
5   **foreach** $VS \in \hat{P}$ **do**
6   **if** $\exists l \in \hat{L} : (l \cap VS) \neq \emptyset$ **then**
7              $l \leftarrow (l \cup VS)$
8   **end**
9   **else**   Iterate through all elements of the original set $\hat{P}$ and try to chain them together with elements of $\hat{L}$
10              $l \leftarrow VS$
11   **end**
12          $\hat{L} \leftarrow \hat{L} \cup \{l\}$ Store the size of the set $\hat{L}$ after chaining
13   **end**   and set $\hat{P}$ to $\hat{L}$ for the next iteration
14      $l_{current} \leftarrow |\hat{L}|$
15      $\hat{P} \leftarrow \hat{L}$
16   **if** $l_{current} = VS_{old}$ **then**
17          $optimized \leftarrow true$ ⟵ If no improvement, break the procedure
18   **end**
19 **end**
20 **return** $\hat{L}$

The resulting set $\hat{L}$ contains the final *VS*s and the intersections, if present, have been resolved. Each of the contained *VS*s may contain large numbers of blocks and comprise multiple hierarchical layers. However, essential to RSPA, each *VS* itself represents a clearly delimitable variation point between the input models. The *VS*s themselves contain the *SID*s of all blocks associated with varying signals for both input models. This information can be used to further process or to classify the findings, for instance by the model engineer, and we provide more information on our website (See footnote 3) and in the screencast respectively.

We implemented our technique in *Java*[4] using *Eclipse*[5] and its *Modeling Framework*[6]. Our approach automatically generates *MATLAB/Simulink* instructions. The instructions allow for each *VS* to specifically highlight the contained blocks directly within the *MATLAB/Simulink* environment. We post-process the information contained in the *VS*s and use color schemes to explicitly

---

[4] Oracle Systems®- https://www.java.com/en/ - Nov. 2016.
[5] Eclipse Foundation®- https://eclipse.org/ - Nov. 2016.
[6] Eclipse Foundation®- https://www.eclipse.org/modeling/emf/ - Nov. 2016.

distinguish between blocks that are present in both input models and blocks that are only present in one input model. With the generated instructions and the possibility to further utilize them, we allow model engineers to directly validate the results of our technique without using any intermediate or abstracted representation.

4   Evaluation

To assess the feasibility of our proposed technique, we conducted a case study with real-world models from the automotive domain. In this section, we provide our objectives, information about the analyzed models, the methodology we used for the evaluation and the results we were able to achieve. With RSPA, we want to support model engineers in developing and maintaining large-scale systems by automatically and reliably identifying variations within models as they evolve. We focus on the following research questions:

RQ1: *What level of precision and recall can our technique achieve?*
The level of precision is substantially important for our technique to be accepted by model engineers. We refer to precision as the extent to which each of the generated *VS*s reflects a syntactically delimitable variation point. We refer to recall as the extent to which each *VS* only contains blocks associated with varying signals.
RQ2: *Is the performance reasonable when scaling up?*
Especially in an industrial environment, an acceptable runtime is essential for our proposed technique to be applicable in practice. We refer to performance as the total runtime required and its distribution over RSPA's three, non-concurrent phases: *Signal Set Generation, Comparison and Preliminary Clustering* and *Cluster Optimization* (cf. Sect. 3).

4.1   Analyzed Models

We identified delimitable parts within an exemplary *Driver Assistance System (DAS)* from the publicly available *SPES_XT*[7] project and extracted them as *Sub Models (SMs)*. The SMs are listed in Table 3, along with information on their size and complexity. We combined the SMs in various ways to constitute a total of 18 large-scale models that specifically address structural changes reflecting a system evolution. For instance, systems contain only one SM, e.g., *EmergencyBrake (EB)*, or two SMs respectively, e.g., *SpeedLimiter (SL)* and *CruiseControl (CC)*. The largest generated model contains all SMs listed in Table 3. Using the project documentation, we identified constraints that prohibit certain SMs to be used in isolation and we list those constraints in Table 3. Further information on the models can be found on our website (See footnote 3).

---

[7] http://spes2020.informatik.tu-muenchen.de/spes_xt-home.html - Nov. 2016.

Table 3. Basic properties of the analyzed models

Model name & *Abbreviation*	#blocks	#B_{Sub}	$maxH_D$
EmergencyBreak *'EB'*	409	43	7
FollowToStop *(req.* CC) *'FTS'*	699	77	11
SpeedLimiter *'SL'*	497	57	10
CruiseControl *'CC'*	671	74	11
Distronic *(req.* CC) *'DT'*	728	78	11

B_{Sub} – *Subsystem* blocks, $maxH_D$ – max. hierarchical depth, *req.–* requires

4.2 Methodology

To assess the feasibility of our proposed technique regarding its potential usage in an industrial environment, we focus on analyzing performance, precision and recall. For the 18 generated models, all possible 153 pairwise comparisons[8] were performed twenty times each to account for runtime deviations inherently present in a non-closed system.

For precision and recall, manually analyzing all combinations is infeasible due to their size and complexity. Hence, we focused on two subsets, covering a total of 50 models ($\approx$ 33%) that explicitly reflect a development process as follows:

1: Model evolution, for instance, *SL* and *SL-CC*. From an evolutionary standpoint, the latter can be considered an extension. For this, we analyzed a total of 30 combinations.
2: Model modification, for instance, *SL-CC* and *EB-CC*. The latter can be considered a modification of the former by replacing a certain part of the model. For this, we analyzed a total of 20 combinations.

For the 50 combinations mentioned above, we manually identified the variation points *before* applying our technique to compare the results with our initial findings. The combinations were examined by an expert well familiar with the analyzed *MATLAB/Simulink* models. Using the generated instructions, the variability information clustered within the produced *VS*s was assessed directly within the *MATLAB/Simulink* environment.

The case study was evaluated on a Dual-Core i7 processor with 12GB of RAM, running Windows 10 on 64bit. All runtime measurements were performed using Java's *System.nanoTime()* [10].

4.3 Results and Interpretation

The results we provide in this section show aggregated data. Detailed information on the models used for the analysis and the data collected during the process can be found on our website (See footnote 3). We further provide all

---

[8] $153 = 18 * (17/2)$, since the input order does not matter.

generated instruction sets for the evaluated combinations to allow the results to be reproduced.

Precision and Recall (RQ1): To evaluate RSPA regarding precision and recall for the feasibility study, we manually inspected the results of 50 comparisons as described in Sect. 4.2. Using the automatically generated instructions, we assessed the results directly within the *MATLAB/Simulink* environment.

For all evaluated combinations, RSPA identified all variation points present within the compared models. Each variation point was clustered within a single *VS* and we found all *VS*s to represent a syntactically delimitable variation point. Hence, we consider our RSPA to operate with absolute precision for the evaluated models. For recall, we analyzed each of the generated *VS*s with regard to the presence of blocks that are associated with non-varying signals and, thus, are incorrectly clustered within the *VS*. For all generated *VS*, we did not find such elements but only blocks associated with varying signals. Hence, we claim our RSPA to exhibit total recall for the evaluated models.

Performance (RQ2): For all possible 153 combinations (cf. Sect. 4.1), we measured the total runtime required and its distribution over the involved phases. The import of the models and the generation of the *MATLAB/Simulink* instructions were omitted for the runtime as they are not part of the algorithm itself.

Figure 9 depicts the performance results of our proposed technique. We show the total runtime required in relation to the combined model size, measured by the number of contained blocks, and highlight the combinations we selected for our two evolution scenarios (cf. Sect. 4.2). Each data point shown in Fig. 9 represents the average over the 20 runs performed for every comparison.

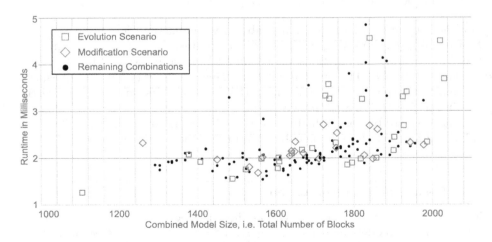

Fig. 9. Performance results of the RSPA

Our proposed RSPA requires an average of approximately 2.5 ms to compare two models from our case study. The longest runtime is just shy of 5 ms. Although not shown in Fig. 9, we experimentally enlarged the models up to a combined size for both compared models of 15.000 blocks and 62.000 blocks respectively. For these two comparisons, RSPA required an average of $\approx$ 44 ms and $\approx$ 720 ms and precisely identified all artificially placed variation points. For the 50 evaluated combinations, we measured the time for each of RSPA's three sequentially processed phases separately to asses the runtime distribution. *Signal Set Generation* requires $\approx$ 60%, *Comparison and Preliminary Clustering* makes up for $\approx$ 37% and *Cluster Optimization* accounts for $\approx$ 3% of the total runtime.

Considering the runtime RSPA exhibits, we argue that models can be processed almost instantly so that we consider performance acceptable. Without confirmation from industrial experts, we conservatively consider our technique to be applicable in an industrial environment. Overall, the results strengthen the confidence we have in our approach to effectively support engineers in developing and maintaining models by precisely and fully identifying variation points within evolving systems.

Threats to Validity: Although we designed, implemented and evaluated our technique with great care, a variety of threats to validity are inherently present. For our evaluation, we used a single case study with models from one domain. We argue that the analyzed models exhibit a relatively high complexity and that they are to some extent representative for models used in the automotive industry. We kept ourselves from being biased and developed and implemented RSPA without specific domains in mind. We acknowledge that other domains might have different development procedures and their systems could entail peculiarities that impinge the results produced by our approach and the results' usability in general. We recognize that certain development processes may exist that adversely affect RSPA's dependency on the *SID*. For several cases, a non-volatile, unique and persistent identifier might be a too strong restriction. We also analyze syntactical properties only and do not consider semantic properties.

5 Related Work

A variety of approaches exists in the literature to identify variability in models. The two most prominent techniques are *Clone Detection* and *Model Differencing*. Deissenboeck et al. [1] transform models into graphs to perform clone detection. Their *CloneDetective* approach is integrated into the *ConQAT* tool[9]. In contrast to RSPA, the models are flattened and certain blocks are removed prior to the analysis. Based on *ConQAT*, Al-Batran et al. [11] describe an approach which is able to detect syntactic clones in *MATLAB/Simulink* models but also to identify semantic clones by normalizing the compared models with semantic-preserving graph transformations. With RSPA, we do not use graph transformations but

---

[9] https://www.conqat.org.

explicitly exploit the upward signal propagation in *MATLAB/Simulink* models as they evolve to realize a lightweight analysis. Alafi et al. [12] use *SIMONE* to analyze and cluster subsystem clones within *MATLAB/Simulink* models. They aim to detect clone patterns and to visualize clones. In contrast to their approach and clone-detection in general, we aim to precisely detect variation points rather than clones and their distribution. Kelter et al. [13] propose a generic algorithm to detect model differences. They use a special data model to store properties of *Unified Modeling Language (UML)* [14] class-diagrams for comparison. Based on [13], Treude et al. [15] introduce *SiDiff* and allow for various types of UML models and also *MATLAB/Simulink* models to be compared. Kelter et al. and Treude et al. both use an internal data model and semantically lift retrieved information. Our technique does not use any intermediate or abstracted model. Similar to Treude et al., Könemann [16] also uses model differencing to detect and semantically lift performed changes. Könemann's approach aims to generate model-independent differences and to apply them as patches to other models. Unlike RSPA, he assesses the approach with UML class-diagrams with only one hierarchical layer. Ryssel et al. [17] propose a technique to identify variation points in multiple *MATLAB/Simulink* models. In contrast to RSPA, they use a metric to calculate the similarity of blocks and use graph transformations to identify variation points.

6   Conclusion and Future Work

In this paper, we propose RSPA to automatically detect and cluster variation points within evolved and related *MATLAB/Simulink* models. With RSPA, we allow model engineers to capture performed modifications in their entirety and by using their domain knowledge, to also validate them. By precisely identifying variation points within evolving systems and visualizing them within *Matlab/Simulink* we offer assistance that is potentially helpful for the entire development process. We provide a feasibility study with models from the automotive domain that reflect an evolution scenario and show our technique's capability to identify variation points rapidly and precisely.

In the future, we plan to assess our technique with models used in the industry to identify both specific use cases and limitations for the RSPA in an industrial environment. Currently, the generated instructions need to be copied to *MATLAB/Simulink* manually. To increase RSPA's user-friendliness, we further intend to integrate RSPA directly within the *MATLAB/Simulink* environment. Ultimately, we plan to evaluate the applicability of RSPA for other model-based languages, for instance *State Charts*.

Acknowledgments. We would like to thank Remo Lachmann and Christoph Seidl for their strong support and guidance on this paper.

References

1. Deissenboeck, F., Hummel, B., Jürgens, E., Schätz, B., Wagner, S., Girard, J.F., Teuchert, S.: Clone detection in automotive model-based development. In: Proceedings of the International Conference on Software Engineering (ICSE), pp. 603–612. ACM (2008)
2. Grönniger, H., Krahn, H., Pinkernell, C., Rumpe, B.: Modeling variants of automotive systems using views. CoRR abs/1409.6629 (2014)
3. Eckl, C., Brandstätter, M., Stjepandic, J.: Using the "model-based systems engineering" technique for multidisciplinary system development. In: Transdisciplinary Lifecycle Analysis of Systems - Proceedings of the 22nd ISPE Inc., International Conference on Concurrent Engineering, Delft, The Netherlands, July 20–23, 2015, pp. 100–109 (2015)
4. Kolovos, D.S., Di Ruscio, D., Pierantonio, A., Paige, R.F.: Different models for model matching: an analysis of approaches to support model differencing. In: Proceedings of the 2009 ICSE Workshop on Comparison and Versioning of Software Models. CVSM 2009, Washington, DC, pp. 1–6. IEEE Computer Society (2009)
5. Deissenboeck, F., Hummel, B., Juergens, E., Pfaehler, M., Schaetz, B.: Model clone detection in practice. In: Proceedings of the 4th International Workshop on Software Clones. IWSC 2010, pp. 57–64. ACM, New York (2010)
6. Wille, D., Holthusen, S., Schulze, S., Schaefer, I.: Interface variability in family model mining. In: Proceedings of the International Workshop on Model-Driven Approaches in Software Product Line Engineering (MAPLE), pp. 44–51. ACM (2013)
7. Holthusen, S., Wille, D., Legat, C., Beddig, S., Schaefer, I., Vogel-Heuser, B.: Family model mining for function block diagrams in automation software. In: Proceedings of the International Workshop on Reverse Variability Engineering (REVE), pp. 36–43. ACM (2014)
8. Wille, D.: Managing lots of models: the famine approach. In: Proceedings of the International Symposium on the Foundations of Software Engineering (FSE), pp. 817–819. ACM (2014)
9. Pohl, K., Böckle, G., van der Linden, F.J.: Software Product Line Engineering: Foundations Principles and Techniques. Springer-Verlag New York, Inc., Secaucus (2005)
10. Kuperberg, M., Reussner, R.: Analysing the fidelity of measurements performed with hardware performance counters. In: Proceedings of the 2nd ACM/SPEC International Conference on Performance Engineering. ICPE 2011, pp. 413–414. ACM, New York (2011)
11. Al-Batran, B., Schätz, B., Hummel, B.: Semantic clone detection for model-based development of embedded systems. In: Whittle, J., Clark, T., Kühne, T. (eds.) MODELS 2011. LNCS, vol. 6981, pp. 258–272. Springer, Heidelberg (2011). doi:10. 1007/978-3-642-24485-8_19
12. Alalfi, M., Cordy, J.R., Dean, T.R.: Analysis and clustering of model clones: an automotive industrial experience, pp. 375–378. IEEE (2014)
13. Kelter, U., Wehren, J., Niere, J.: A generic difference algorithm for UML models. Softw. Eng. **64**(105–116), 4–9 (2005)
14. The Object Management Group: Unified Modeling Language (UML). Technical report, OMG Version 2.4.1. (2011)

15. Treude, C., Berlik, S., Wenzel, S., Kelter, U.: Difference computation of large mod-
    els. In: Proceedings of the 6th Joint Meeting of the European Software Engineering
    Conference and the ACM SIGSOFT Symposium on The Foundations of Software
    Engineering. ESEC-FSE 2007, pp. 295–304. ACM, New York (2007)
16. Könemann, P.: Semantic grouping of model changes. In: Proceedings of the 1st
    International Workshop on Model Comparison in Practice. IWMCP 2010, pp. 50–
    55. ACM, New York (2010)
17. Ryssel, U., Ploennigs, J., Kabitzsch, K.: Automatic variation-point identification
    in function-block-based models. In: Proceedings of the International Conference on
    Generative Programming and Component Engineering (GPCE), pp. 23–32. ACM
    (2010)

Discovering Software Architectures with Search-Based Merge of UML Model Variants

Wesley K.G. Assunção[1,2(✉)], Silvia R. Vergilio[2],
and Roberto E. Lopez-Herrejon[3]

[1] DInf, Federal University of Paraná, CP: 19081, Curitiba 81531-980, Brazil
[2] COINF, Federal University of Technology - Paraná, Toledo 85902-490, Brazil
{wesleyk,silvia}@inf.ufpr.br
[3] ÉTS, University of Quebec, Notre-Dame Ouest 1100, Montreal H3C 1K3, Canada
roberto.lopez@etsmtl.ca

Abstract. Software reuse is a way to reduce costs and improve quality. However, in industry, the reuse of existing software artifacts is commonly done by ad hoc strategies such as clone-and-own. Clone-and-own leads to a set of system variants developed independently, despite of having similar parts. The maintenance of these independent variants is a difficult task, because of duplication and spread functionalities. One problem faced by developers and engineers is the lack of a global view of such variants, providing a better understanding of the actual state of the systems. In this paper we present an approach to discover the architecture of system variants using a search-based technique. Our approach identifies differences between models and uses these differences to generate candidate architectures. The goal is to find a candidate architecture most similar to a set of UML model variants. Our contribution is threefold: (i) we proposed an approach to discover model-based software architecture, (ii) we deal with the merging of multiple UML model variants; and (iii) our approach applies a search-based technique considering state-based merging of models. We evaluate our approach with four case studies and the results show that it is able to find good candidate architectures even when different features are spread among model variants.

Keywords: Model merging · UML models · Model-based architectures · Search-based techniques

1 Introduction

Developing software systems from scratch is a complex and high cost activity. A well established strategy to reduce costs, improve productivity and increase quality is software reuse, which is based on the use of existing artifacts to develop

S.R. Vergilio—This work was supported by the Brazilian Agencies CAPES: 7126/2014-00 and CNPq: 453678/2014-9 and 305358/2012-0.

© Springer International Publishing AG 2017
G. Botterweck and C. Werner (Eds.): ICSR 2017, LNCS 10221, pp. 95–111, 2017.
DOI: 10.1007/978-3-319-56856-0_7

new software systems [14]. Any artifact built during software development can be reused, including source code, design models, test cases, etc.

Software reuse is generally carried out using an ad hoc strategy, called "clone-and-own" [20]. In this strategy, existing software artifacts are cloned/copied and adapted to fulfill the new requirements. The clone-and-own strategy is an easy way to reuse software, does not require an upfront investment, while obtaining good results quickly. However, the simultaneous maintenance and evolution of a typically large number of individual system variants is a complex activity because different variants can provide the same functionalities, but at the same time modify or add others. These duplicated functionalities must be maintained individually [6]. Furthermore, engineers commonly do not have a global view on how the different implementations are spread over the variants.

There exists extensive work on migration of multiple variants into SPLs [1]. However, this task demands high levels of investment and human resources [19]. There is a lack of effective ways to support the maintenance and evolution of multiple variants. One way to deal with this problem is the creation of a documented architecture. Software architectures are artifacts that provide a high-level view of functional parts of systems and allow analysis of their structure [4]. An architecture supports design decisions and eases software reuse. Currently, majority of the work on software architecture recovery/discovery is based on source code [7,10,11].

In this paper, we present an approach to automatically merge multiple UML model variants to obtain a documented software architecture. The goal is to discover a global model that contains all the features spread across the different variants. A *feature* is a user-visible aspect, functionality, or characteristic of a system [12]. The input of our approach is a set of UML model variants and the output is a complete model, the most similar to all variants. The proposed merging process relies on a search-based technique to avoid having to deal with domain specific constraints of systems under consideration and possible conflicts among models. In other words, we delegate to the evolutionary process the solution of problems regarding constraints and conflicts [9]. We implemented our approach with a genetic algorithm, and evaluated it using four case studies from different domains and with different sizes. Our evaluation showed that good candidate architectures can be found.

The main contributions of our work are:

- Our study relies on the discovery of model-based architectures from different UML model variants. In the literature there are few pieces of work with focus on discovery of architectures from diagrams/models [15,17].
- The proposed search-based merging approach deals with multiple UML models variants, whereas the majority of studies on model merging considers only two or three models at once [3,13,16].
- Our approach performs state-based merging of models, i.e. we consider the model itself during the evolutionary process. Other pieces of work that merge models are operation-based, which means they work mainly considering the history of operations applied to the different models created [13,16].

The remainder of this paper is as follows. In Sect. 2 we describe in detail the proposed search-based approach. The evaluation of the proposed approach and the results are presented in Sect. 3. Section 4 reviews related work. Section 5 contains conclusions and future work.

2 Proposed Approach

In this section we present details of our search-based approach to discover software architectures. According to Harman et al. [9], three ingredients are necessary to implement a search-based approach: (i) an appropriate way to represent solutions, (ii) a function designed to evaluate the quality of a solution, and (iii) a set of operators to generate new solutions and explore the search space.

In this section we describe such ingredients of our approach. To illustrate how it works, we rely on three variants of a Banking System [17]. These variants[1] are presented in Fig. 1. The goal of our approach is to obtain a global UML model with the greatest similarity to the variants of our example. To reach this greatest similarity, the global UML model must have as many as possible of the features contained across the variants.

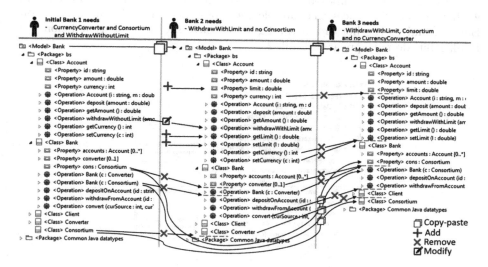

Fig. 1. Three banking system model variants, extracted from [17]

2.1 Representation

Our approach deals with models created with the Eclipse Modeling Framework (EMF). EMF is a well-known and widely used set of modeling tools [22]. We represent the models using EMF-based UML2[2] implementation of the UML[TM]

---

[1] Available at: https://github.com/but4reuse/but4reuse/wiki/Examples.
[2] http://wiki.eclipse.org/MDT/UML2.

2.x metamodel for the Eclipse platform. When models are represented using EMF-based UML2 data types, they can be compared, modified, and saved. These operations enabled by EMF tools are the basis to our search-based approach.

2.2   Fitness Function

The fitness function of our approach is based on differences among UML models of system variants. To compute these differences we use the Eclipse EMF Diff/Merge tool[3]. EMF Diff/Merge compares two models and returns the differences between them. EMF Diff/Merge computes three essential types of differences between models: (i) presence of an unmatched element, which refers to an element in a model that has no match in the opposite model; (ii) presence of an unmatched reference value, which means that a matched element references another element in only one model; (iii) presence of an unmatched attribute value, where a matched element owns a certain attribute value in only one model.

Figure 2 presents the output of EMF Diff/Merge when comparing differences between the variants Bank 1 and Bank 2 (Fig. 1). The total number of differences is thirteen, but it is composed of two sets of differences. At the top of the figure we have seven differences that are elements present in Bank 2 but missing on Bank 1, and at the bottom of the figure we have six elements that belong to Bank 1 but do not appear in Bank 2.

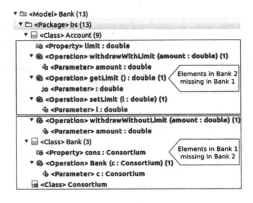

Fig. 2. Differences between variants Bank 1 and Bank 2

EMF Diff/Merge tool is able to compare only two or three models at once. However, to evaluate a candidate architecture we have to compute differences from one model to many model variants. Considering this, the proposed fitness function is composed of the sum of differences from one model to all input model variants. Definition 1 presents the fitness function called here *Model Similarity*.

---

[3] http://www.eclipse.org/diffmerge/.

The function *diff* represents the number of differences found by using EMF Diff/Merge, but here we sum only the set of differences that indicate the elements that exist in the variant *v* but are missing on the *candidate_model*. There are no distinctions among the three essential types of differences.

Definition 1. *Model Similarity (MS).* *Model Similarity expresses the degree of similarity of the candidate architecture model to a set of model variants.*

$$MS = \sum_{v\ \in\ Variants} diff(candidate\_model, v) \qquad (1)$$

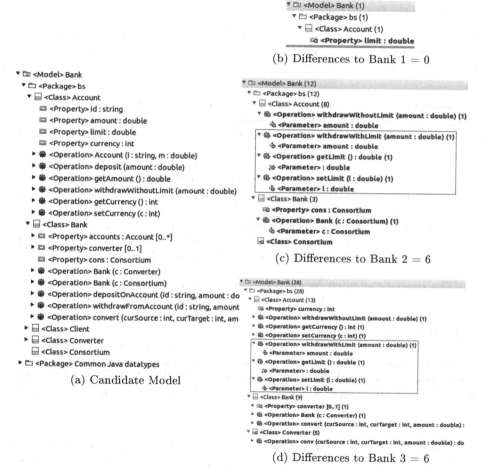

(a) Candidate Model

(b) Differences to Bank 1 = 0

(c) Differences to Bank 2 = 6

(d) Differences to Bank 3 = 6

Fig. 3. Example of fitness evaluation

To illustrate the computation of MS we consider the candidate architecture model presented in Fig. 3(a) and the input models in Fig. 1. Using EMF Diff/Merge tool we have obtained the sets of differences presented in Figs. 3(b), 3(c) and 3(d), respectively to Bank 1, Bank 2 and Bank 3. For our fitness function only the differences from the candidate architecture to each variant are relevant, they are highlighted in the figures. There are no differences from the candidate model to Bank 1. From candidate model to Bank 2 there exist six differences. From candidate model to Bank 3 we have also six differences. We can observe twelve differences from the candidate model to all input variants, then MS = 12. The goal is to minimize the value of MS. An ideal solution has MS equal to zero, which indicates that the candidate architecture has all elements from the variants for which we want to discover the corresponding architecture.

2.3   Genetic Operators

The set of differences returned by EMF Diff/Merge is used to perform crossover and mutation and it also allows duplication/modification of models to incorporate the changes done by the operators.

Crossover. The start point of our crossover operator is two candidate architectures. From these two models we generate two children: one with the differences merged and one without the differences. For instance, let us consider any parent models X and Y. The children will be:

– *Crossover Child Model 1*: this model has the differences between its parents merged. For example, the elements of X that are missing on Y are merged in this later, or vice versa. Both ways will produce the same child.
– *Crossover Child Model 2*: this child is generated by removing the differences between the parents. For example, the differences of X that are missing on Y are removed, or vice versa. Both ways will produce the same child.

The strategy adopted by child model 1 aims at creating a model that has more elements, going to the direction of the system architecture. On the other hand, the strategy used by child model 2 has the goal of eliminating possible conflicting elements from a candidate architecture.

To illustrate the crossover operator let us consider as parents Bank 1 and Bank 2 presented in Fig. 1 and the differences between them, presented in Fig. 2. The offspring generated by crossover is presented in Fig. 4. In Fig. 4(a) we have the child with all differences merged (highlighted) and in Fig. 4(b) the child with the differences removed.

Mutation. Mutation operator aims at applying only one modification in each model parent. The start point of mutation operator is two candidate architectures, and the result is also two children. Let us again consider any parent models X and Y. The children are:

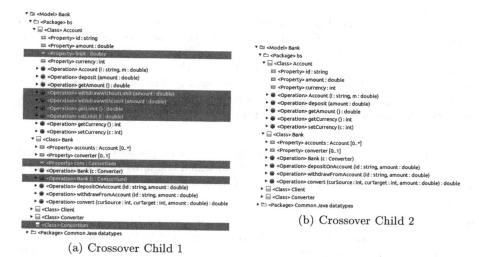

(a) Crossover Child 1

(b) Crossover Child 2

Fig. 4. Example of crossover between Bank 1 and Bank 2

– *Mutation Child Model 1*: the first child is created by merging one difference of the model Y in the model X. After randomly selecting one element of the model Y, but missing on the model X, this element is added in the model X.
– *Mutation Child Model 2*: the same process described above is performed but including one element of the model X in the model Y.

An example of mutation between Bank 1 and Bank 2 (Fig. 1) is presented in Fig. 5. Considering the differences shown in Fig. 2, we have have seven differences to select one to include in Bank 1, and six differences to select one to include in

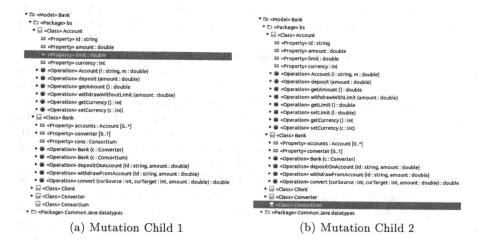

(a) Mutation Child 1

(b) Mutation Child 2

Fig. 5. Example of mutation between Bank 1 and Bank 2

Bank 2. As highlighted in Fig. 5(a), the attribute limit was chosen to be included in Bank 1. In the child of Fig. 5(b) we can see that the class Consortium was selected to be included in Bank 2.

The mutation process can select a difference that is owned (i.e. is part of) another difference. In such cases, the entire owning difference is moved to the child. For example, when a mutation selects a parameter owned by an operation, the entire operation is moved to the child.

Selection. We use binary tournament strategy whereby a set of individuals are randomly selected from the population, from which the individual with the best fitness is chosen to undergo crossover and mutation [8].

Initial Population. The initial population is created by copying the input UML models variants. All variants should be included in the initial population at least once. Each copied variant is an individual. More than one copy of each variant is allowed to reach the population size.

3   Evaluation

In this section we present the setup and case studies used to evaluate the proposed approach, along with the results obtained and their analysis.

3.1   Implementation Aspects and Experimental Setup

We implemented our work using JMetal framework which provides several algorithms for multi-objective and mono-objective optimization [5]. We selected the mono-objective generational Genetic Algorithm (GA) [8]. Our GA was designed to deal with an minimization problem, recall that an ideal solution for our architecture recovery problem is an individual (i.e. candidate architecture) with fitness equal to zero (0).

As mentioned before, in our implementation we handle the UML models using EMF framework. This framework was used mainly to load and save models. For the evolutionary process, where we compare and modify models, we used EMF Diff/Merge. Despite of EMF Diff/Merge having many functionalities, we needed to develop a customized match policy. The default match policies of EMF Diff/Merge only perform comparisons based on XMI:ids. However, model variants could have similar semantic even with different structures. Our customized match police considers qualified names, data types, and relationship types.

The GA parameters were: population size = 200, crossover probability = 0.95, mutation probability = 0.2, and number of fitness evaluations = 8000. We have set the parameters of crossover and mutation based on default values used in other discrete problems on JMetal. Population size and number of evaluations were set based on hardware limitation. When we tried to use greater values for these two latter parameters it caused limit memory exception. The elitism strategy for the generation GA was copying the best four individuals of one generation for the next generation. The number of fitness evaluations is the stop criteria. The experiments were run on a machine with an Intel® Core^{TM} i7-4900MQ CPU with 2.80 GHz, 16 GB of memory, and running a Linux platform.

3.2   Case Studies

In our experiment we used four case studies. Each case study is a set of different UML model variants where each variant implements different system features, and is composed of classes, attributes, operations and relationships. The case studies are: Banking System (BS), a small banking application composed of four features [18]; Draw Product Line (DPL), a system to draw lines and rectangles with six features [2]; Video On Demand (VOD) implements eleven features for video-on-demand streaming [2]; and ZipMe (ZM), a set of tools to files compression with seven features [2]. The variants are presented in Tables 1, 2, 3 and 4, respectively. These tables show the features, number of classes (#Cl), number of attributes (#Attr), number of operations (#Op), and number of relationships (#Rel) for each variant. This information was computed using SDMetrics[4]. Only BS is originally a set of UML model variants, for the other case studies we reverse engineered the models from Java code using the Eclipse MoDisco[5].

Table 1. Banking system

Variant	Features				#Cl	#Attr	#Op	#Rel
	BS	WL	CON	CC				
1	✓				3	5	6	1
2	✓		✓		4	6	7	3
3	✓	✓			3	6	8	1
4	✓			✓	4	7	11	2
Baseline	✓	✓	✓	✓	5	9	14	4

BS: Base, WL: Withdraw Limit, CON: Consortium, CC: Currency Converter

For the four case studies we have variants with all possible features combinations. However, we selected only variants that implement at most half of the non-mandatory features. To select these variants we follow the rule:

$$threshold = \left(RoundUp\left(\frac{\#all\_features - \#mandatory\_features}{2}\right) + \#mandatory\_features\right)$$

We selected for our experiment only variants that implement a number of features below the threshold. The reason to select only a sub-set of variants is to have the combinations of features spread on different variants, to assess the ability of our

---

[4] http://www.sdmetrics.com.
[5] https://eclipse.org/MoDisco.

approach to merge the models and get good system architectures. For each case study we also had a variant that implements all features, i.e. the most complete variants. We use this variant as a baseline for our analysis, since we consider this variant as the most similar model to a known system architecture. In the last line of Tables 1, 2, 3 and 4 there is information about the baseline.

Table 2. Draw product line

Variant	Features						#Cl	#Attr	#Op	#Rel
	DPL	L	R	C	W	F				
1	✓	✓					4	13	26	3
2	✓	✓	✓				5	24	37	4
3	✓		✓				4	18	29	3
4	✓	✓		✓			4	22	27	3
5	✓		✓	✓			4	27	30	3
6	✓	✓			✓		4	15	27	3
7	✓		✓		✓		4	20	30	3
8	✓		✓	✓		✓	4	33	32	3
Baseline	✓	✓	✓	✓	✓	✓	5	42	41	4

DPL: Base, L: Line, R: Rectangle, C: Color, W: Wipe, F: Fill

Table 3. Video on demand

Variant	Features											#Cl	#Attr	#Op	#Rel
	VOD	SP	SelM	StaM	PI	VRC	P	StoM	QP	CS	D				
1	✓	✓	✓	✓	✓	✓						32	362	217	75
2	✓	✓	✓	✓	✓	✓	✓					32	362	217	75
3	✓	✓	✓	✓	✓	✓		✓				33	364	221	77
4	✓	✓	✓	✓	✓	✓	✓	✓				33	364	221	77
5	✓	✓	✓	✓	✓	✓			✓			33	364	221	77
6	✓	✓	✓	✓	✓	✓	✓		✓			33	364	221	77
7	✓	✓	✓	✓	✓	✓		✓	✓			34	366	225	79
8	✓	✓	✓	✓	✓	✓				✓		37	377	232	87
9	✓	✓	✓	✓	✓	✓	✓			✓		37	377	232	87
10	✓	✓	✓	✓	✓	✓		✓		✓		38	379	236	89
11	✓	✓	✓	✓	✓	✓	✓	✓		✓		38	379	236	89
12	✓	✓	✓	✓	✓	✓					✓	35	374	226	82
13	✓	✓	✓	✓	✓	✓	✓				✓	35	374	226	82
14	✓	✓	✓	✓	✓	✓		✓			✓	36	376	230	84
15	✓	✓	✓	✓	✓	✓	✓	✓			✓	36	376	230	84
16	✓	✓	✓	✓	✓	✓				✓	✓	40	389	241	94
Baseline	✓	✓	✓	✓	✓	✓	✓	✓	✓	✓	✓	42	393	249	98

VOD: Base, SP: Start Player, SelM: Select Movie, StaM: Start Movie, PI: Play Imm, VRC: VRC Interface, P: Pause, StoM: Stop Movie, QP: Quit Player, CS: Change Server, D: Details

Table 4. ZipMe

Variant	Features							#Cl	#Attr	#Op	#Rel
	ZM	C	CRC	AC	GZIP	A32	E				
1	✓	✓						22	212	241	64
2	✓	✓	✓					23	215	251	66
3	✓	✓		✓				22	212	243	66
4	✓	✓	✓	✓				23	215	253	68
5	✓	✓			✓			25	223	263	68
6	✓	✓	✓		✓			26	229	282	72
7	✓	✓		✓	✓			25	223	265	70
8	✓	✓				✓		23	216	263	69
9	✓	✓	✓			✓		24	219	273	71
10	✓	✓		✓		✓		23	216	265	71
11	✓	✓		✓	✓	✓		26	227	285	73
12	✓	✓					✓	23	219	262	70
13	✓	✓	✓				✓	24	223	279	74
14	✓	✓		✓			✓	23	219	264	72
15	✓	✓			✓		✓	26	230	284	74
16	✓	✓				✓	✓	24	223	284	75
Baseline	✓	✓	✓	✓	✓	✓	✓	28	241	334	87

ZM: ZipMe, C: Compress, CRC: CRC-32 checksum, AC: Archive Check, GZIP: GZIP format support, A32: Adler32 checksum, E: Extract

Observing the information in case studies tables (Tables 1, 2, 3 and 4) we can see that there are no variants with as many features as the baselines. Furthermore, the number of classes, attributes, operations, and relationships in the variants of all case studies are smaller than the baselines.

3.3 Results and Analysis

Figure 6 shows the evolution of the best candidate architecture in each GA generation. As mentioned before, the initial population is composed of copied the input models. The best individual of each case study after the first 200 fitness evaluations is an input model from the initial population that has the least difference from the other input models. For BS the best individual is Variant 4 that has 25 differences from the input. For DPL the best initial individual is Variant 2 with 127 differences. For VOD the best initial candidate architecture is Variant 16 with 315 differences. Finally, Variant 11 of ZM is the best individual of the initial population having 854 differences from the input. These individuals are the first solutions presented in the charts of Fig. 6. Observing the figures we can see how the evolutionary process is able to find better candidate architectures by reducing the number of differences. On average the best solution is found after

1400 fitness evaluations. VOD is the simplest case study, since the best solution was reached with approximately 1000 fitness evaluations. On the other hand, ZM is the most complex case study, needing approximately 1800 fitness evaluations to reach the best solution. As expected for a GA, in all case studies there is a great improvement in the number of found solutions in the initial generations, and then the search remains stable.

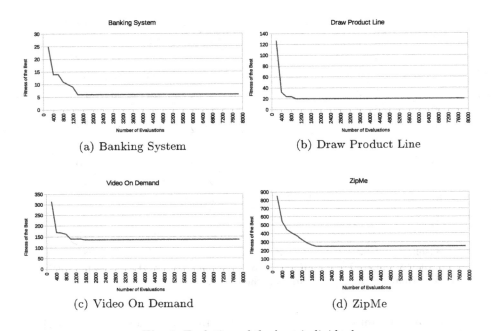

(a) Banking System

(b) Draw Product Line

(c) Video On Demand

(d) ZipMe

Fig. 6. Evolution of the best individual

Another information gathered during the experimentation is the runtime. The amount of time spent by the GA to perform the entire evolutionary process was: BS = 55s 740ms, DPL = 6m 13s 17ms, VOD = 1h 46m 55s 698ms, and ZM = 2h 10m 29s 267ms. GA ran very fast for BS, that has the smallest number of features, classes, attributes, operations, and relationships. DPL has more features and model elements (Table 2) than BS, and for this case study, the GA took a little more than 6 min. A huge difference on the runtime is observed for VOD and ZM. VOD needed almost 2 h to be finished. ZM is the case study which required the biggest amount of time, it took more than 2 h.

Now let us consider the details of the best solutions found. Table 5 shows the information of candidate architectures and baseline models. The values of MS presented in the third column is in relation to the input models. Regarding the number of classes, attributes, operations and relationships, the baseline model and the best individual model are very similar. For BS there is only a single difference in the number of relationships, where the best individual has one relationship less. In DPL and VOD the number of model elements are the same. For ZM the number of model elements is different in operations and relationships. Despite having a similar number of model elements, we can observe that the values of MS are not similar. As mentioned before in Sect. 2.2, the fitness function EMF Diff/Merge computes the presence of elements, presence of attributes values, and presence of reference values. This latter difference happens when a model element references to, or belongs to, different model elements. This explains the reason why baselines and best individuals have similar number of model elements but different values of MS.

Table 5. Candidate architectures

Case Study	Model	MS	#Cl	#Attr	#Op	#Rel
BS	Baseline	20	5	9	14	4
	Best Individual	6	5	9	14	3
DPL	Baseline	40	5	42	41	4
	Best Individual	20	5	42	41	4
VOD	Baseline	162	42	393	249	98
	Best Individual	136	42	393	249	98
ZM	Baseline	633	28	241	334	87
	Best Individual	250	28	241	381	79

#Cl: Number of classes, #Attr: Number of attributes,
#Op: Number of operations, #Rel: Number of relationships

Table 6 presents the differences between baseline and the best individuals for each case study. Since the comparison of EMF Diff/merge has two directions, we show the number of differences existing from baseline to the best individual (candidate architecture), and vice versa. For example, considering BS, there are seven differences needed for baseline having all elements of the candidate architecture. On the other hand, candidate architecture needs fourteen existing differences to have all elements of baseline. In the values of Table 6 we can observe that the baseline is the less different for the case studies BS, DPL and VOD. This means that it is easier to transform baseline in the best than vice versa. For ZM, the solution obtained by the GA is the most similar to the baseline.

The analysis of Tables 5 and 6 reveals that a model having all features does not imply that it is the most similar to a set of model variants. We can infer this by considering that the best individual obtained by the GA for each case study is the most similar to the model variants than the baseline (third column in Table 5), and on the other hand baseline is more similar to the best individual when comparing these two models (second and third columns of Table 6). To illustrate this situation, let us use the models of BS presented in Fig. 7. In Fig. 7(a) the baseline has all features implemented and in Fig. 7(b) the best solution found is the most similar to the input models. Observe that in the best solution there exists an operation `withdrawWithoutLimit(amount: double)`.

Table 6. Differences between baseline and candidate architectures

Case study	From baseline to best	From best to baseline
BS	7	14
DPL	5	451
VOD	20	3425
ZM	4155	200

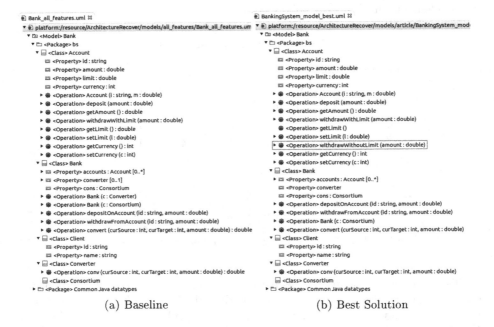

(a) Baseline   (b) Best Solution

Fig. 7. Baseline and best solution for banking system

This operation is present in the variants that do not implement the feature WL (see Fig. 1), i.e., it is present in three out of four variants. This operation is not present in the baseline model, so this baseline model does not provide a global overview of the variants. The baseline would not serve as reference for maintaining variants that do not have feature WL. However, in the architecture we can find out where the operation withdrawWithoutLimit is located.

3.4 Threats to Validity

The first threat to validity regards the parameter setting for the GA. We addressed this threat by adopting default values for crossover and mutation and set the values of population size and number of evaluations as big as possible. The second threat is the influence of the case studies. Despite of using only four case studies these systems are from different domains, and have different sizes. They can provide evidence about the usage of our approach. But nonetheless further studies should be conducted in the future. The third threat concerns the comparison to other approaches. To the best of our knowledge, there are no other studies with the exact same focus as ours. As baseline we used models known in advance that implement all features that compose the systems, assuming these models are the closest to an ideal solution.

4 Related Work

A detailed study on comparative techniques to architecture recovery is presented by Garcia et al. [7]. The authors observed that most techniques identify software components by using structural information from source code and do not present any technique based on UML models to recovery system architecture.

Hussain et al. apply a search-based technique to recovery software architecture using Particle Swarm Optimization that clusters system units based on cohesion and coupling of the source code [10], while Jeet and Dhir use a Genetic Black Hole to also perform clustering in the source code considering dependencies between system units [11]. Differently from our approach, none of them include UML models in the evolutionary process.

A search-based model merge approach is presented by Debreceni et al. who support collaborative model-driven engineering by merging models developed by different collaborators [3]. They propose a guided rule-based design space exploration where candidate models are generated to reach a conflict-free merged model. This approach also performs comparison in model states (state-based approach). However, it applies only a three-way model merge. In contrast, in our study we deal with the merging of multiple models. Kessentini et al. propose a search-based technique to merge models based on sequences of operations that originate different models [13,16]. Operation-based merge considers the operations that perform modifications in a model, instead of the state of the model. Their goal is to find a sequence of operations to generate a merged model in order to minimize the number of conflicts and maximize the number of successfully applied operations. In both pieces of work the authors apply only three-way model merge. Our work differs from theirs in two points. First, we consider the state of the models (state-base) instead of the operations used to generate each variants (operation-based). Second, we deal with more than three models at once.

Maazoun et al. propose an approach to construct an SPL design from a set of class diagrams that are merged and then enriched with information from a Feature Model [15]. Martinez et al. create a model-based SPL by discovering variabilities and commonalities from model variants, which are then described using Common Variability Language [17]. Even though they deal with model variants, in contrast with us their focus on SPLs imply another upfront investment to implement the benefits of systematic reuse, which is outside of our scope.

Rubin and Chechik propose an algorithm, named *NwM*, to merge multiple models simultaneously [21]. Their algorithm starts from a common set of model elements, the most frequent in the variants, and analyses all possible combination of remaining elements among the variants to find the best merging operations. This process is a polynomial-time approximation, since the problem is NP-Hard. It works for a limited number of models. Our approach differs from *NwM* because we do not need to identify the initial set of common elements and our search-based approach can deal with many model variants.

5 Conclusions

We presented in this paper an approach to discover model-based software architecture by merging UML model variants. Our approach relies on a search-based technique that does not require information regarding domain constrains or conflicting models elements in advance. The candidate architectures are evaluated by a measure called Model Similarity.

To evaluate our approach we performed an experiment with four case studies from different domains and with different sizes. The results show that our approach is able to find good candidate architectures even when features are implemented in multiple variants. Furthermore, we could observe that having a variant that implements all features of a system does not imply that this variant has all model elements spread in other variants.

We acknowledge that some results could be influenced by internal aspects of the case studies, however our approach is an easy way to support the discovery of a documented architecture. This architecture helps maintenance by (i) providing a global view of a set of variants that supports the identification of bad smells and refactoring activities; (ii) allowing reconciling design of different variants (potentially inconsistent) implemented by many designers; (iii) when a bug is fixed in one variant, the architecture helps to replicate the changes to other variants that also have the same model elements. The documented architecture supports evolution by (i) being a starting point to combine variants into an SPL, and (ii) reducing the time to produce variants with new combination of features.

For future work we plan to improve the match policy to include more detailed information regarding the semantics of the model variants. Furthermore, we want to evaluate our approach with more case studies to infer how model elements, i.e. implementation aspects, can have influence on getting good architectures.

References

1. Assunção, W.K.G., Lopez-Herrejon, R.E., Linsbauer, L., Vergilio, S.R., Egyed, A.: Reengineering legacy applications into software product lines: A systematic mapping. Empirical Softw. Eng. 1–45 (2017)
2. Assunção, W.K.G., Lopez-Herrejon, R.E., Linsbauer, L., Vergilio, S.R., Egyed, A.: Extracting variability-safe feature models from source code dependencies in system variants. In: Genetic and Evolutionary Computation Conference (GECCO), pp. 1303–1310. ACM (2015)

3. Debreceni, C., Ráth, I., Varró, D., Carlos, X., Mendialdua, X., Trujillo, S.: Automated model merge by design space exploration. In: Stevens, P., Wąsowski, A. (eds.) FASE 2016. LNCS, vol. 9633, pp. 104–121. Springer, Heidelberg (2016). doi:10.1007/978-3-662-49665-7_7

4. Dobrica, L., Niemela, E.: A survey on software architecture analysis methods. IEEE Trans. Softw. Eng. **28**(7), 638–653 (2002)

5. Durillo, J.J., Nebro, A.J.: jMetal: A java framework for multi-objective optimization. Adv. Eng. Softw. **42**, 760–771 (2011). http://jmetal.sourceforge.net/

6. Faust, D., Verhoef, C.: Software product line migration and deployment. Softw. Pract. Experience **33**(10), 933–955 (2003)

7. Garcia, J., Ivkovic, I., Medvidovic, N.: A comparative analysis of software architecture recovery techniques. In: International Conference on Automated Software Engineering (ASE), pp. 486–496. IEEE (2013)

8. Goldberg, D.E., Deb, K., Clark, J.H.: Genetic algorithms, noise, and the sizing of populations. Complex Syst. **6**, 333–362 (1992)

9. Harman, M., Mansouri, S.A., Zhang, Y.: Search-based software engineering: Trends, techniques and applications. ACM Comput. Surv. **45**(1), 1–61 (2012)

10. Hussain, I., Khanum, A., Abbasi, A.Q., Javed, M.Y.: A novel approach for software architecture recovery using particle swarm optimization. Int. Arab J. Inf. Technol. **12**(1), 32–41 (2015)

11. Jeet, K., Dhir, R.: Software architecture recovery using genetic black hole algorithm. ACM SIGSOFT Softw. Eng. Notes **40**(1), 1–5 (2015)

12. Kang, K.C., Cohen, S.G., Hess, J.A., Novak, W.E., Peterson, A.S.: Feature-Oriented Domain Analysis (FODA) feasibility study. Technical report, SEI - CMU (1990)

13. Kessentini, M., Werda, W., Langer, P., Wimmer, M.: Search-based model merging. In: Genetic and Evolutionary Computation Conference, pp. 1453–1460 (2013)

14. Krueger, C.W.: Software reuse. ACM Comput. Surv. **24**(2), 131–183 (1992)

15. Maazoun, J., Bouassida, N., Ben-Abdallah, H.: A bottom up SPL design method. In: 2014 2nd International Conference on Model-Driven Engineering and Software Development (MODELSWARD), pp. 309–316, January 2014

16. Mansoor, U., Kessentini, M., Langer, P., Wimmer, M., Bechikh, S., Deb, K.: Momm: Multi-objective model merging. J. Syst. Softw. **103**, 423–439 (2015)

17. Martinez, J., Ziadi, T., Bissyandé, T.F., Klein, J., Traon, Y.: Automating the extraction of model-based software product lines from model variants. In: International Conference on Automated Software Engineering (ASE), pp. 396–406 (2015)

18. Martinez, J., Ziadi, T., Klein, J., Traon, Y.: Identifying and visualising commonality and variability in model variants. In: Cabot, J., Rubin, J. (eds.) ECMFA 2014. LNCS, vol. 8569, pp. 117–131. Springer, Heidelberg (2014). doi:10.1007/978-3-319-09195-2_8

19. Pohl, K., Böckle, G., van Der Linden, F.J.: Software Product Line Engineering: Foundations, Principles and Techniques. Springer, Heidelberg (2005)

20. Riva, C., Del Rosso, C.: Experiences with software product family evolution. In: International Workshop on Principles of Software Evolution, pp. 161–169 (2003)

21. Rubin, J., Chechik, M.: N-way model merging. In: 9th Joint Meeting on Foundations of Software Engineering (ESEC/FSE), pp. 301–311. ACM (2013)

22. Steinberg, D., Budinsky, F., Merks, E., Paternostro, M.: EMF: Eclipse Modeling Framework. Pearson Education, Boston (2008)

Tracing Imperfectly Modular Variability in Software Product Line Implementation

Xhevahire Tërnava$^{(\boxtimes)}$ and Philippe Collet

Université Côte d'Azur, CNRS, I3S, Sophia Antipolis, France
{ternava,collet}@i3s.unice.fr

Abstract. When large software product lines are engineered, a combined set of traditional techniques, *e.g.*, inheritance, design patterns, generic types, is likely to be used for realizing the variability at the implementation level. In these techniques the concept of feature, as a reusable unit, does not have a first-class representation in implementation, but still an imperfect form of modularization of variability can be achieved. We present in this paper a framework (*i*) to explicitly capture and document this imperfectly modular variability – by several combined techniques – in a dedicated variability model, and (*ii*) to establish trace links between this model and the variability model at the specification level. We report on the implementation of the framework through a domain specific language, and show the feasibility of the approach on a real feature-rich system.

1 Introduction

In *Software Product Line Engineering* (SPLE), the core software assets are developed during the domain engineering phase [13] and represent those reusable artifacts and resources that form the basis for eliciting the single software products during the application engineering phase. Core assets are made reusable by modeling and realizing what is common and what is going to vary, *i.e.*, the commonality and the variability, between the related products in a methodological way. In realistic SPLs, where variability is extensive, a crucial issue is the ability to manage it in these different core assets among different abstraction levels [5]. An important aspect of the variability management activity is then the ability to trace a variable unit, commonly known as a *feature* [10], along the SPLE phases.

Traceability is defined as the ability to describe and follow the life of a software artifact forward and backward along the software lifecycle [2,7]. In SPLE there are four main dimensions of traceability: refinement, similarity, variability, and versioning traceability [2,13]. Variability traceability *"is dealt by capturing variability information explicitly and modeling the dependencies and relationships separate from other development artifacts"* [4]. In this work we focus on an analysis of the variability traceability between the specification and implementation level, *i.e.*, on the *realization* trace links [2,13] to the core-code assets.

The results of a recent survey on SPLE traceability, by Kim et al. [12], show that none of the current approaches fully support end–to–end traceability,

© Springer International Publishing AG 2017
G. Botterweck and C. Werner (Eds.): ICSR 2017, LNCS 10221, pp. 112–120, 2017.
DOI: 10.1007/978-3-319-56856-0_8

and there are unexplored research areas in these approaches. To the best of our knowledge, no variability traceability and management approach at the implementation level, *e.g.*, [3,4,6,9,13,14], is currently addressing the early steps of capturing and modeling the variability when a subset of traditional techniques (*e.g.*, inheritance, design patterns, generic types) are used in combination, as in many realistic SPL settings [3,8,9].

In this paper, we propose an approach for tracing variability between the specification level and, what we name *imperfectly modular variability*[1] at the implementation level. We distinguish both levels in a way similar to Becker [3]. Our contribution is a tooled framework (Sect. 3) that gives support from the early steps of variability traceability, *i.e.*, from the capturing and modeling of the variability in core-code assets. Unlike other works that tackled similar issues [6,9,14] we show how to capture and model the variability when it is implemented by several traditional techniques in combination. We keep the variability information separated from the core code assets as by Berger et al. [4] and Pohl et al. [13]. Further, as the variability to be represented may be large [13], our framework fosters the documentation of the implemented variability in a fragmented and flexible way, inspired by Kästner et al. [11]. We also report on our implementation of the framework by a *Domain Specific Language* (DSL), and on its application to a feature-rich system, showing its feasibility (Sect. 4).

2   Motivations

Background. We consider that the variability of an SPL is documented in a Variability Model (VM), which is commonly expressed as a Feature Model (FM) [10]. An FM is mainly used at the specification level for scoping the software products within an SPL in terms of *features*. On the other hand variation points (*vp*-s) are places in a design or implementation that identify locations at which the variation occurs [9], and the way that a *vp* is going to vary is expressed by its *variants*.

Variability traceability can be established and used for different reasons, and by different stakeholders [2,7]. It is mainly used for (semi)automating different processes in SPLE, *e.g.*, for resolving the variability (product derivation), evolving, checking consistency, addressing, or comprehending the variability.

Imperfectly Modular Variability. For illustration and validation we use *JavaGeom*[2], an open source geometry library for Java that is architected around well identified features. Although not presented as an SPL, JavaGeom is a relevant and easily understandable case for demonstrating the applicability of our framework on the equivalent of a medium-size SPL. Let us consider the implementation of a set of features as depicted in the FM on Fig. 1. StraightCurve2D is a mandatory feature with three shown alternative features: Line2D, Segment2D, and Ray2D. Focusing on the realization techniques (*cf.* Fig. 2), the abstract class

---

[1] This notion is defined in Sect. 2 using a real feature-rich system.
[2] http://geom-java.sourceforge.net/index.html.

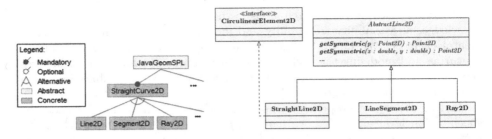

Fig. 1. Features from *JavaGeom*   **Fig. 2.** A detailed design excerpt of *JavaGeom*

AbstractLine2D is a *vp* and its three variants, *i.e.*, StraightLine2D, LineSegment2D, and Ray2D, are created by generalizing/specializing its implementation. Features from Fig. 1 seem to have a direct and perfect modular mapping in implementation (*cf.* Fig. 2), *e.g.*, «StraightCurve2D implemented by AbstractLine2D», or «Line2D implemented by StraightLine2D». But actually, this perfect modularity hardly exists.

Imperfect modularity comes from the fact that a feature is a domain concept and its refinement in core-code assets is *a set* of *vp*-s and *variants* (even if they are modular), *i.e.*, it does not have a direct and single mapping. For example, the feature Line2D uses several *vp*-s, such as AbstractLine2D and CirculinearElement2D (other *vp*-s are not shown), the variant StraightLine2D (*cf.* Fig. 2), plus their technical *vp*-s (Sect. 3.2), as the getSymmetric() *vp* of the AbstractLine2D. When a combined set of traditional techniques are used for implementing the variability, *e.g.*, inheritance for StraightCurve2D, overloading for getSymmetric(), the code is not shaped in terms of features. Therefore, the trace relation is *n–to–m* between the specified features to the *vp*-s and *variants* at the implementation. Moreover an SPL architect has to deal with a variety of *vp*-s and *variants*.

Our approach addresses the ability to trace this imperfectly modular variability in implementation, which we define as follows: *An imperfectly modular variability in implementation occurs when some variability is implemented in a methodological way, with several implementation techniques used in combination, the code being not necessarily shaped in terms of features, but still structured with the variability traceability in mind.*

3   A Three Step Traceability Approach

To trace imperfectly modular variability in implementation, we propose an approach that follows three main steps (*cf.* Fig. 3): ① capturing the implemented variability in terms of *vp*-s and *variants*, as abstract concepts, ② modeling (documenting) the variability in terms of *vp*-s and *variants*, while keeping the consistency with their implementation in core-code assets, and ③ establishing the trace links between the specified and implemented variabilities.

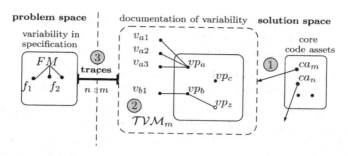

Fig. 3. Proposed traceability approach ($\mathcal{TVM}_m$ *stands for Technical Variability Model* *(cf. Sect. 3.2) of the core-code asset* ca_m, *with vp-s* $\{vp_a, vp_b, ...\}$ *and their respective variants* $\{v_{a1}, v_{a2}, ...\}$. *While,* $\{f_1, f_2, ...\}$ *are features in the FM.)*

3.1   Capturing the Variability of Core-Code Assets (Step ①)

The core-code assets that realize variability usually consist of a common part and a variable part. It can happen that a whole asset is also a variable asset. A core-code asset can be, *e.g.*, a source file, package, class. The variable part consists of a mechanism (*i.e.*, technique) for creating the variants, a way for resolving the variants, and the variants themselves. They are abstracted using the concepts of *variation points* (*vp*-s), *variants*, and their dependencies.

Let the set of all *vp*-s in an SPL be $\mathcal{VP} = \{vp_a, vp_b, vp_c, ...\}$ for the set of core-code assets, with variability or variable, $\mathcal{CA} = \{ca_m, ca_n, ca_o, ...\}$. We assume that a $vp_x \in \mathcal{VP}$ is implemented by a single traditional technique $t_x \in \mathcal{T}$. The set $\mathcal{T}$ of possible techniques for vp_x is then made explicit in our framework,

$\mathcal{T}$ = {Inheritance, Generic Type, Overriding, Strategy
        pattern, Template pattern,...}

A *vp* is not a by-product of an implementation technique [5], therefore we have to tag it in some way. "Tagging a *vp*" means to map the $vp_x \in \mathcal{VP}$ concept to its concrete varying element of any $ca_x \in \mathcal{CA}$. For example, we abstract/tag the superclass `AbstractLine2D` (*cf.* Fig. 2) with `vp_AbsLine2D`, and its subclasses as variants `v_Line2D`, `v_Segment2D`, and `v_Ray2D`, respectively. Depending on the size of variability and the used technique, the nature of a core asset element that represents a *vp* varies. We gathered their variety as *characteristic properties of* *vp*-s. Their properties that are important to be captured are: granularity, relation logic, binding time, evolution, and resolution.

Granularity. A *vp* in a core-code asset can represent a coarse-grained element that is going to vary, *e.g.*, a file, package, class, interface; a medium-grained element *e.g.*, a method, a field inside a class; or a fine-grained element *e.g.*, an expression, statement, or block of code.

Logic Relation ($\mathcal{LG}$). The set of the logic relations between variants in a *vp*, that are commonly faced in practice, is similar to the possible relations between features in an FM. Thus, a $t_x \in \mathcal{T}$ offers at least one of these logic relations,

$\mathcal{LG}$ = {Mandatory, Optional, Alternative, Multi-Coexisting}

Binding Time (*BT*). Each *vp* is associated with a binding time, *i.e.*, the time when is decided for its variants, or when they are resolved. Based on the available taxonomies [6], the possible binding times for the vp_x are:

BT = {Compilation, Assembly, Programming time,
          Configuration, Deploy, StartUp, Runtime}

Evolution (*EV*). Depending on whether a *vp* is meant to be evolved in the future with new variants or not, it can be EV = {Open, Close}.

For example, the vp_AbsLine2D has a class level granularity (*cf.* Fig. 2). It is resolved at runtime to one of its alternative variants, v_Line2D, v_Segment2D, or v_Ray2D, and we tag it as open as it is implemented as an abstract class.

Another characteristic property of a *vp* is how it is resolved, *i.e.*, whether a variant is added, removed or replaced by another variant. This matters during the process of product derivation, which is a possible usage of our framework.

3.2 Modeling the Implemented Variability (Step ②)

During this phase, the variability of a core-code asset ca_x is modeled in terms of *vp*-s and *variants* as abstractions (*cf.* Fig. 3, step ②). We distinguish five types of *vp*-s that can be chosen from:

X = {vp, vp_unimpl., vp_technical, vp_optional, vp_nested}

A resolution for each of them is given in Table 1. The implementation technique $t_x \in T$ of the $vp_x \in VP$, which relation we write as (vp_x, t_x), describes three main properties of the vp_x: the relation logic for its variants, the evolution, and the binding time. Possibly, other properties can also be abstracted and attached. Then, $t_x = \{lg_x, ev_x, bt_x, ...\}$, where $lg_x \in LG$, $ev_x \in EV$, and $bt_x \in BT$. So, when the vp_x is an ordinary *vp* (*cf.* Table 1) we model the variability in a core-code asset as a set of its *variants* $V = \{v_{x1}, v_{x2}, v_{x3}, ...\}$, and the characteristic properties derived from the vp_x's implementation technique t_x. This leads to the following definition:

$$vp_x = \{V, t_x\} = \{\{v_{x1}, v_{x2}, v_{x3}, ...\}, t_x\} \qquad (1)$$

As an illustration we present the ordinary vp_x (*cf.* Table 1) as in Fig. 4, numbered with ⬛1. Similarly, a technical *vp*, *e.g.*, the technical vp_a of vp_y, is represented as in ⬛2. An optional *vp* is modeled as the vp_z in ⬛3. We use the acronym *opt* here in order to distinguish between the optional relations between variants in a *vp* and the optionality of the *vp* itself. Moreover a nested *vp* is illustrated as the nested vp_b of vp_z, where the variant v_{z2} of vp_z represents a common part for its three variants $\{v_{b1}, v_{b2}, v_{b3}\}$. Finally, the $vp_c = \{\{\varnothing\}, t_c\}$ in ⬛4 is an unimplemented *vp*. These types of *vp*-s can be combined, *e.g.*, an optional *vp* can be ordinary, unimplemented, or can have other nested or technical *vp*-s.

Instead of modeling the whole implemented variability at once and in one place, we model it in a fragmented way. A fragment can be any unit (*i.e.*, a package, a file, or a class) that has its inner variability and that is worth to

Table 1. Types of variation points that are commonly faced in practice

Types	Description
Ordinary	A vp is introduced and implemented (i.e., its variants are realized) by a specific technique
Unimplemented	A vp is introduced but is without predefined variants (i.e., its variants are unknown during the domain engineering)
Technical	A vp is introduced and implemented only for supporting internally the implementation of another vp, which realizes some of the variability at the specification level
Optional	The vp itself, not its variants, is optional (i.e., when it is included or excluded in a product, so are its variants)
Nested vp	When some variable part in a core-code asset becomes the common part for some other variants

be separately modeled. For this reason, we designed specific models, named as *Technical Variability Models* ($\mathcal{TVM}$), which are created and maintained locally, *i.e.*, closer to the core-code assets (*cf.* Fig. 3). They contain the abstractions of *vp*-s and *variants*, their tags with core asset elements, and describe the variability of a specific core-code asset. For example, the variability of a ca_m with six different *vp*-s is modeled by the $\mathcal{TVM}_m$ as in Fig. 4.

All the $\mathcal{TVM}$s together constitute the *Main Technical Variability Model* ($\mathcal{MTVM}$). Unlike the organization of features in an FM as a tree structure, in $\mathcal{MTVM}$ the *vp*-s reside in a forest-like structure. Moreover, the meaning of a *vp* is extended, *i.e.*, it is the place at which the variation occurs [9], and represents the used technique to realize the variability.

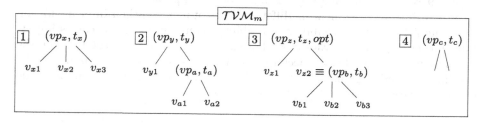

Fig. 4. An example of the Technical Variability Model ($\mathcal{TVM}_m$) for a ca_m

3.3 Establishing the Trace Links (Step ③)

The last step of our approach (*cf.* Fig. 3, step ③) is to map the variability between the VM at specification level (*i.e.*, features in an FM) and the $\mathcal{MTVM}$ at implementation level (*i.e.*, *vp*-s and *variants*), by establishing the trace links between them.

Let us suppose that $f_x \in \mathcal{FM}$ is a variable feature at specification level, where $\mathcal{FM} = \{f_1, f_2, f_3, ...\}$. For mapping features to vp-s, we use a single bidirectional type of trace links implementedBy ($\longmapsto$) or implements ($\longleftarrow$), which presents the *variability realization* trace link in implementation. When f_x is implemented ideally by a single variation point vp_x, or conversely, we write: $f_x \longmapsto vp_x$, or implementedBy(f_x, vp_x). Similarly, f_x can be implemented by a single variant $v_{xn} \in \mathcal{V}$ (*cf.* Sect. 3.2), *i.e.*, $f_x \longmapsto v_{xn}$. For example, the feature StraightCurve2D (*cf.* Fig. 1) is implemented by vp_AbsLine2D (*cf.* Fig. 2), *i.e.*, StraightCurve2D $\longmapsto$ vp_AbsLine2D, or Ray2D $\longmapsto$ v_Ray2D. When f_x is implemented by several vp-s, which can be from the same core-code asset or not, then $f_x \longmapsto \{vp_x, vp_y, vp_z, ...\}$.

The mapping between features and vp-s is a partial mapping, as some features in $\mathcal{FM}$ are abstract features (*i.e.*, do not require an implementation), or they can be deferred to be implemented later.

4   Implementation and Application

We implemented the proposed framework as an internal DSL in Scala. The interoperability between Java and Scala enabled us to use the DSL in JavaGeom. To document and trace variability, the DSL provides two modules **fragment** and **traces**, respectively. We used them to analyse 92% of the 35,456 lines of code from JavaGeom. The successful documentation phase resulted in 11 $\mathcal{TVM}_s$, all of them being at the package level. We observed that vp-s in JavaGeom are implemented using up to three techniques, inheritance, overloading, and generic types. Then, we established the trace links between the specified features (*cf.* Fig. 1, which consist of 110 features extracted from its documentation) to the vp-s and *variants* in implementation (*cf.* Fig. 2). We successfully traced 199 vp-s, with 269 *variants*, showing the feasibility of our approach.

Capturing and documenting different types of vp-s and their implementation techniques during the variability traceability, as in JavaGeom, becomes important during the usage of trace links. For example, the relation logic between the variants in a vp is needed to check the consistency between the variability at the specification and implementation level. Similarly, knowledge of the binding time of vp-s is necessary during the product derivation.

5   Conclusion

Tracing the variability between the specification and implementation levels is an important part of the development process in SPL engineering. At the implementation level, a combination of traditional variability implementation techniques are actually used in many realistic SPLs, thus leading to a form of *imperfectly modular variability* in implementation. The key contribution of our approach is a three-step framework for capturing, documenting, and tracing this imperfectly modular variability, together with some DSL-based tool support.

A limitation of the DSL, but not of the framework itself, is that we could not apply it for tracing the variability at the finest granularity level, *e.g.*, at the expression level, as our internal DSL in Scala uses reflection for tagging the variability. Although using reflection is not mandatory, this helps to keep the strong consistency between the abstractions of *vp*-s and *variants* with the core-code assets themselves. Although we used the DSL successfully in a real feature-rich system, we plan to extend this framework in supporting the documentation of the dependencies between the *vp*-s themselves and to integrate the DSL with another DSL that models the variability specifically at the specification level, such as FAMILIAR [1]. With these two extensions, we plan to apply our variability traceability framework to (semi)automated consistency checking of variability between the specification and implementation levels on several case studies.

References

1. Acher, M., Collet, P., Lahire, P., France, R.B.: FAMILIAR: a domain-specific language for large scale management of feature models. Sci. Comput. Program. (SCP) **78**(6), 657–681 (2013)
2. Anquetil, N., Kulesza, U., Mitschke, R., Moreira, A., Royer, J.C., Rummler, A., Sousa, A.: A model-driven traceability framework for software product lines. Software and Systems Modeling **9**(4), 427–451 (2010)
3. Becker, M.: Towards a general model of variability in product families. In: van Gurp, J., Bosch, J. (eds.) Workshop on Software Variability Management, Groningen, The Netherlands, pp. 19–27 (2003). http://www.cs.rug.nl/Research/SE/svm/proceedingsSVM2003Groningen.pdf
4. Berg, K., Bishop, J., Muthig, D.: Tracing software product line variability: from problem to solution space. In: Proceedings of the 2005 Annual Research Conference of the South African Institute of Computer Scientists and Information Technologists on IT Research in Developing Countries, pp. 182–191. South African Institute for Computer Scientists and Information Technologists (2005)
5. Bosch, J., Florijn, G., Greefhorst, D., Kuusela, J., Obbink, J.H., Pohl, K.: Variability issues in software product lines. In: Linden, F. (ed.) PFE 2001. LNCS, vol. 2290, pp. 13–21. Springer, Heidelberg (2002). doi:10.1007/3-540-47833-7_3
6. Capilla, R., Bosch, J., Kang, K.C.: Systems and Software Variability Management. Springer, Heidelberg (2013)
7. Cleland-Huang, J., Gotel, O., Zisman, A.: Software and Systems Traceability, vol. 2. Springer, London (2012)
8. Coplien, J.O.: Multi-paradigm Design for C+. Addison-Wesley, Reading (1999)
9. Jacobson, I., Griss, M., Jonsson, P.: Software Reuse: Architecture, Process and Organization for Business Success. ACM Press/Addison-Wesley Publishing Co., New York (1997)
10. Kang, K.C., Kim, S., Lee, J., Kim, K., Shin, E., Huh, M.: FORM: a feature-oriented reuse method with domain-specific reference architectures. Ann. Softw. Eng. **5**(1), 143–168 (1998)
11. Kästner, C., Ostermann, K., Erdweg, S.: A variability-aware module system. In: ACM SIGPLAN Notices, vol. 47, pp. 773–792. ACM (2012)

12. Kim, J., Kang, S., Lee, J.: A comparison of software product line traceability approaches from end-to-end traceability perspectives. Int. J. Software Eng. Knowl. Eng. **24**(04), 677–714 (2014)
13. Pohl, K., Böckle, G., van der Linden, F.J.: Software Product Line Engineering: Foundations, Principles and Techniques. Springer Science & Business Media, Heidelberg (2005)
14. Schmid, K., John, I.: A customizable approach to full lifecycle variability management. Sci. Comput. Program. **53**(3), 259–284 (2004)

Verification and Refactoring for Reuse

Composition of Verification Assets for Software Product Lines of Cyber Physical Systems

Ethan T. McGee[1]($\boxtimes$), Roselane S. Silva[2], and John D. McGregor[1]

[1] School of Computing, Clemson University, Clemson, SC, USA
{etmcgee,johnmc}@clemson.edu
[2] Department of Computer Science, Federal University of Bahia (UFBA),
Salvador, BA 40170-110, Brazil
rosesilva@dcc.ufba.br

Abstract. The emerging Internet of Things (IoT) has facilitated an explosion of everyday items now augmented with networking and computational features. Some of these devices are developed using a Software Product Line (SPL) approach in which each device, or product, is instantiated with unique features while reusing a common core. The need to rapidly develop and deploy these systems in order to meet customer demand and reach niche markets first requires shortened development schedules. However, many of these systems perform roles requiring thorough verification, for example, securing homes. In these systems, the detection and correction of errors early in the development life cycle is essential to the success of such projects, with particular emphasis on the requirements and design phases where approximately 70% of faults are introduced. Tools such as the Architecture Analysis & Design Language (AADL) and its verification utilities aid in the development of an assured design for embedded systems. However, while AADL has excellent support for the specification of SPLs, current verification utilities for AADL do not fully support SPLs, particularly SPL models utilizing composition. We introduce an extended version of AGREE, a verification utility for AADL, with support for compositional verification of SPLs.

Keywords: Verification · AADL · AGREE

1 Introduction

Cyber-Physical Systems (CPS) are physical systems that are monitored, controlled, integrated and coordinated by a software layer. These systems bridge the gap between the discrete and continuous worlds [7] and are used in multiple domains: automotive, medicinal and aerospace among others. They also form the backbone of the emerging Internet of Things (IoT). Due to a need of being first to market, some manufacturers of IoT CPS have adopted a Software Product Line (SPL) strategy allowing them to reuse core functionality among products while tailoring the features of each product to the device's intended use. First to market also necessitates shortened development cycles imposing the need for

© Springer International Publishing AG 2017
G. Botterweck and C. Werner (Eds.): ICSR 2017, LNCS 10221, pp. 123–138, 2017.
DOI: 10.1007/978-3-319-56856-0_9

faults to be discovered quickly. Research has shown that approximately 70% of all faults originate in the requirements and design phases of the Software Development Life Cycle; the majority, 80%, of these errors are not caught until later in the development life cycle [2]. The Architecture Analysis & Design Language (AADL), designed for modeling embedded systems, also has shown good success in modeling the intricacies of SPLs [1]. AADL has a strong set of verification tools that allow system designs to be tested for defects, thus allowing more defects to be caught early. However, none of the verification tools for AADL currently available fully support the verification of SPLs.

AADL supports compositional construction of design components, allowing it to natively represent the design of SPLs using design operators, such as substitution, to satisfy the variation needs of the implementation hierarchy within a component. AADL also provides variation mechanisms that support the incremental definition of component variants. The language provides facilities allowing one component to be defined by *extending* another component and permitting the inherited types to be *refined* into more contextually appropriate types, demonstrated with a model in Figs. 1 and 2. This allows the designer to specify, for example, a functional interface which each product of the SPL will implement and have each product inherit the interface rather than re-specify it for each product individually. AADL's primary behavioral verification mechanism, the Assume Guarantee REasoning Environment (AGREE), does not natively support component extension requiring more cumbersome verification conditions for verifying designs incorporating extension than should be necessary. If AGREE fully supported AADL's inheritance mechanisms it could be used to verify complex SPL designs more naturally, and it would enable the reuse of verification assets in SPLs just as AADL interfaces can be reused.

In this paper, we present an extension to the AGREE language that provides inheritance support. This is done via two accomplishments:

- detecting the AADL *extends* keyword (how AADL natively indicates inheritance) and overriding the behavior so that AGREE can utilize the connection, and
- introducing abstraction into the AGREE annex allowing children to override functionality inherited from their parent(s).

The remainder of this paper is structured as follows. In Sect. 2 we provide the background necessary for understanding the remainder of this work. In Sect. 3, we present the method used in modifying AGREE, and we present an extended example in Sect. 4. Finally, related work is over-viewed in Sect. 5.

2   Background

2.1   AADL

AADL is a language for the architectural modeling of embedded software [12]. It is a standard of the Society of Automotive Engineers (SAE) [13] and incorporates many features for the representation of both hardware (i.e. processors, memory, buses) and software (i.e. data, thread, subprograms). AADL supports a model-based architecture design through fine-grained modularity and separation of concerns. It's syntax also includes capabilities for querying the architectural model facilitating verification and validation of the models.

Our extension to AGREE utilizes the extensibility feature of the language. This is represented by the *extends* keyword and is how AADL designates inheritance. An extender receives all of the features, sub-components and connections of the component it extends. The extender is also permitted to *refine* components inherited from the parent. An AADL snippet using *extends* and *refines* is shown in Figs. 1 and 2. However, unlike features, properties and other native AADL elements which can be extended and refined, annexes are not inherited by extenders.

```
system parent
  features
    input: in data port;
    output: out data port;
  annex agree {**
    assume "input greater than 2":
      input > 2;
    guarantee "output input * 2":
      output = input * 2;
  **};
end parent;
```

Fig. 1. AADL parent example

```
system child extends parent
  --inherited from parent
  --features
    --output: out data port;
    input: refined to in data port
      Base_Types::Integer;
  annex agree {**
    assume "input greater than 2":
      input > 2;
    guarantee "output input * 2":
      output = input * 2;
  **};
end child;
```

Fig. 2. AADL child *extends* example

2.2 AGREE

AGREE is a compositional verification tool for AADL based on the widely-used assume-guarantee contract verification method [18]. Designers state their assumptions about input and specify guarantees concerning output provided the assumptions are met. Designers also specify the behavior of a system to ensure that the system can fulfill its guarantees. Analysis work in AGREE is performed by a Satisfiability-Modulo Theorem (SMT) prover that checks the behavior model for contradictions that would prevent the system from fulfilling its guarantees. Any found contradictions are then presented to the user as a case against the system's correctness.

AGREE is an AADL annex that encapsulates the definitions of contracts and specifications. A sample of AGREE's syntax, an assume-guarantee contract, is shown in Fig. 1. Note that AGREE splits the assume-guarantee contracts from their behavior specification. The assume-guarantee contract is placed in the functional interface along with the input / output specifications, and the behavior specification is placed in the implementation. In this way, the multiple implementations common in an SPL can use the same assumptions and guarantees while each has its own behavior specification.

2.3   Software Product Lines

A Software Product Line (SPL) is a set of software-intensive systems sharing a common, managed set of features that satisfy the specific needs of a particular market segment / mission and are developed from a common set of core assets in a prescribed way [22]. SPLs have achieved remarkable benefits including productivity gains, increased agility, increased product quality and mass customization [8].

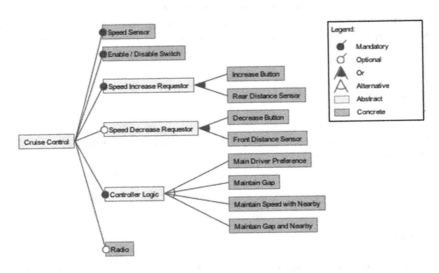

Fig. 3. SPL feature model

SPLs are of particular importance to the IoT, particularly for their cost / time savings and productivity gains. They enable IoT companies to maintain a common core of features which can be reused across several products through customization of the product instantiation. This reuse permits shortened development schedules and also allows companies to maintain a common set of applications, each targeted to a specific audience.

Figure 3 represents an example SPL feature model, a diagram of the configurations each product in the product line can choose. Some features of the cruise control are required, for example, the sensor which determines the current speed of the vehicle, a method of requesting the vehicle accelerate and a method of enabling / disabling the cruise control system. Other features, like the radio to facilitate communication between vehicles, are optional. Each product will make a selection of which features to include and, for the features, which have multiple variations, which variations to use.

3   Method

AGREE is packaged as a plug-in for the Open Source AADL Tool Environment (OSATE) development workbench, which is built on top of Eclipse [21]. AGREE adds several features to OSATE. The first addition is a right-click context menu for the model outline viewer, shown in Fig. 5. This context menu exposes the verification options supported by AGREE and allows the user to select which component(s) he wishes to verify. The second addition is that of an annex which exposes the AGREE language, its parser, and its semantic analyzer as well as the interface to the prover. An overview of the work-flow of the plug-in can be seen in Fig. 4.

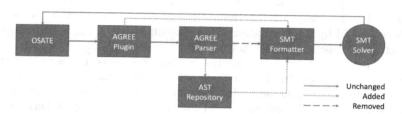

Fig. 4. Workflow for AGREE

The user accesses the context menu for a component and selects a verification task. The architectural description of the component, the AGREE annex contents and any sub-components are then provided to the plug-in. The AGREE contract statements are extracted from the component and parsed into an Abstract Syntax Tree (AST). The AST is provided to a formatter which transforms the AST into the syntax expected by the Satisfiability-Modulo Theorem (SMT) prover. The results of the SMT prover's execution are provided back to OSATE in a displayable format which OSATE renders. A view of the rendered results can be seen in Fig. 5. Note that OSATE displays successfully verified conditions of a component with green checks, and errors are displayed with a red X. Users can right-click the invalidated conditions for more detail.

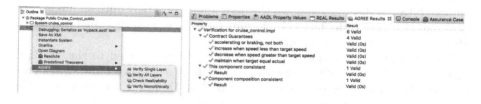

Fig. 5. Context menu & AGREE console

AGREE can be used for both architectural design and verification. When used for design, AGREE contracts are specified at a broad level first, then as the architecture matures, they become increasingly refined. Throughout this paper, we primarily focus on AGREE's verification functionality. Note, however, that our work is applicable to the design functionalities of AGREE as well.

Our extension to AGREE includes modifications to the architecture of the plugin facilitating inheritance support [1]. We also introduce new statements to the language which facilitate inheritance while also providing the ability to disable it for backwards compatibility. We first cover the modifications made to the architecture of the plugin.

In order to facilitate inheritance, we modified the parser of AGREE so that it no longer directly communicated ASTs to the SMT Formatter. We also added a repository which serves two purposes. It first functions as a temporary bank which holds all ASTs of the architectural model. Secondly, it functions as a composer that is capable of stitching together parent and child ASTs into a single, unified AST. The composer functionality is invoked only when a component's AST is requested by the Formatter. These modifications along with the original architecture are visualized in Fig. 4.

From the perspective of the composer, there are three types of statements that an annex can contain. The first are original, or normal, statements. These are statements that are introduced in the current specification and do not exist at any higher level of the inheritance hierarchy. The second are inherited statements, statements that are introduced at a higher level of the inheritance hierarchy which are copied down into the behavior of the child. And finally, override statements are statements which amend the behavior of inherited statements.

When an AST is requested from the Formatter, the inheritance hierarchy of the requested component is gathered, and then a composed AST is generated starting at the highest level of the hierarchy. As the composer moves down each level of the hierarchy, it invokes a merging formula

$$C = (I + O) + N$$

where C is the composed behavior of the current level and all higher levels. I represents inherited behavior, N represents normal behavior and O is the override behavior. As the order of statements in the AGREE annex is important, inherited behavior is always included first, taking care to account for any overrides. Finally, new behavior introduced in the current level is appended. The composed AST is then passed down the inheritance hierarchy until all levels have been evaluated. Once the hierarchy is completely traversed, the final composed behavior is returned to the Formatter.

We now cover the modified / additional statements added to the AGREE language in order to facilitate inheritance. A short overview of the statements that have been added or modified is presented in Table 1. Each statement will be discussed and an example of its use provided.

Guarantee / Assume Statements. The *guarantee* and *assume* statements of the AGREE language are analogous to the pre-condition / post-condition concepts

---

[1] We will refer to the AGREE language provided in the standard OSATE distribution as "traditional" and our version as "extended".

Table 1. AGREE syntax overview

Keyword	Description
assume	declare that the system expects input to conform to the following statement
do not inherit	explicitly disable inheritance
eq	declare a concrete variable or override an abstract variable
eq abstract	declare an abstract variable
guarantee	declare that output of the system will conform to the following statement
inherit	explicitly state that inheritance from a parent occurs

of other verification tools. With traditional AGREE, the assumptions and guarantees of parent components are not inherited by their children despite the fact that many times the children will use the same inputs, outputs, assumptions and guarantees as their parents. Our extended version of AGREE allows for such inheritance. We also recognize that it is sometimes necessary to tweak the assumptions or guarantees of your parent, particularly if the child introduces new inputs or outputs that the parent does not have.

An example of AGREE's assume and guarantees are shown in Figs. 6 and 7. Also shown in these figures is a demonstration of how our extended version of AGREE permits verification assets to be reused across different components of the model hierarchy as well as how assumptions and guarantees can be overridden by children if necessary. The parent component, introduced in Fig. 6 has two features, a single input and output, and the AGREE annex assumes that the input will be greater than or equal to 0 while guaranteeing that the output will be greater than or equal to 1. The behavior of the parent is simply to take the input value and set the output to the input plus 1. The child, shown in Fig. 7, adds an additional complication by adding a second output. Note that in Fig. 7 all inherited pieces are shown using comments (denoted by a double dash in AGREE and AADL). The guarantees of the child have to be modified or amended to account for this extra output. The override is driven by the descriptor string, or, children who have an assumption or guarantee with a descriptor that matches a parent assumption / guarantee's descriptor will override the parent's matching descriptor.

Eq / Eq Abstract Statements. In traditional AGREE, the *eq* statement allows for the declaration of a single variable. In introducing inheritance, we modified the *eq* statement to either introduce a new variable or to override an existing variable if the variable in the child has the same name as a variable in the parent. We also introduced an *eq abstract* statement that provides a way to define a variable without providing an implementation for that variable. Abstract variables in AGREE are much like abstract variables in Java or C++. They can

```
                                    system child extends parent
                                      features
                                        --ip: in data port Base_Types::Integer;
                                        --op: out data port Base_Types::Integer;
system parent                           op2: out data port Base_Types::Integer;
  features                              annex agree {**
    ip: in data port Base_Types::Integer;   --assume "input req": ip >= 0;
    op: out data port Base_Types::Integer;  guarantee "output req": op >= 1
    annex agree {**                           and op2 >= 1;
      assume "input req": ip >= 0;        **};
      guarantee "output req": op >= 1;  end child;
    **};
end parent;                           system implementation child.impl
                                          extends parent.impl
system implementation parent.impl       annex agree {**
  annex agree {**                          --assert op = ip + 1;
    assert op = ip + 1;                    assert op2 = ip + 1;
  **};                                  **};
end parent.impl;                      end child.impl;
```

Fig. 6. AADL G / A example   **Fig. 7.** AADL child G / A example

be used in calculations and statements just like any other variable but their implementation is left for children, or extenders, to provide. We also introduce the concept of an abstract implementation, an implementation specification that contains an AGREE annex which introduces or inherits an abstract variable. In order for an implementation specification to be non-abstract, or concrete, it must override and provide an implementation for all inherited abstract variables without introducing any new abstract variables.

An example of eq and eq abstract statements and how they are used in inheritance is shown in Figs. 8 and 9. Once again comment lines (those starting with a double dash) represent components that have been inherited. The parent figure, shown in Fig. 8, has one output, a string representing the type. In the parent figure, the type produced by the component is guaranteed to be null. This is reflected in the parent's implementation as *myType* has been declared abstract and not provided with an implementation. The child figure, shown in Fig. 9, overrides the parent's guarantee and asserts that the component will declare its type as "child". The child, however, does not have a full implementation, only a provision of a definition for the inherited abstract variable. The assert that ties the abstract variable to the output is inherited and does not require respecification.

Inherit / Do Not Inherit Statements. The *inherit* and *do not inherit* statements are unique to our extended implementation of AGREE. The *do not inherit* statement allows inheritance to be explicitly disabled allowing the traditional behavior of the plug-in to be used. This statement was introduced to provide a means of enabling backwards compatibility. When encountered, the composer

```
system parent
  features
    type: out data port Base_Types::String;
    annex agree {**
    guarantee "output req": type = null;
    **};
end parent;


system implementation parent.impl
  annex agree {**
    eq abstract myType: string;
    assert type = myType;
  **};
end parent.impl;
```

Fig. 8. AADL Eq example

```
system child extends parent
  --features
    --type: out data port Base_Types::String;
    annex agree {**
    guarantee "output req": type = "child";
    **};
end child;


system implementation child.impl
  extends parent.impl
  annex agree {**
    eq myType: string = "child";
    --assert type = myType;
  **};
end child.impl;
```

Fig. 9. AADL child Eq example

of the repository component halts and the current results are returned without including any statements from parent annexes. The *inherit* statement is similar to the *do not inherit* statement in that it allows a developer to explicitly state that inheritance does occur. The statement has no effect on the composer, however, it does allow developers to specify which hierarchies use inheritance and which hierarchies do not if a mixed model is being utilized.

Finally, we provide an example where inheritance is controlled using the *inherit* and *do not inherit* statements. This example is shown in Figs. 10 and 11 and can be seen in the implementation's AGREE annexes. Note that the child's annex does not inherit the assert of the parent due to the child specifying that inheritance should not be used. Note, however, that the *do not inherit* statement does not affect extends. The child will still inherit the features of the parent even though the AGREE annex will not inherit any attributes of the parent.

A video providing more detail and an example can be found online at https:// goo.gl/VK6NKe. The source of the implementation is available at https://goo. gl/TG9A4r, and an Eclipse / OSATE compatible update site is provided at https://goo.gl/QZhSrv.

4   Example

We now provide an example of a SPL verified using our extended version of AGREE. First, an overview of the architecture and excerpts of AADL are provided for discussion. Also shown are examples of AGREE using the features introduced in our extended version. Second, we demonstrate that the extended version of AGREE is capable of working with models that use several layers of inheritance.

```
system parent
  features
    ip: in data port Base_Types::Integer;
    op: out data port Base_Types::Integer;
  annex agree {**
    assume "input req": ip >= 0;
    guarantee "output req": op >= 1;
  **};
end parent;

system implementation parent.impl
  annex agree {**
    assert op = ip + 1;
  **};
end parent.impl;
```

Fig. 10. AADL inherit example

```
system child extends parent
  features
    --ip: in data port Base_Types::Integer;
    --op: out data port Base_Types::Integer;
    op2: out data port Base_Types::Integer;
  annex agree {**
    do not inherit;
    assume "input req": ip < 1;
    guarantee "output req": op <= 0
      and op2 <= 0;
  **};
end child;

system implementation child.impl
  extends parent.impl
  annex agree {**
    do not inherit;
    assert op = ip - 1;
    assert op2 = ip - 1;
  **};
end child.impl;
```

Fig. 11. AADL child inherit example

4.1   Architecture Overview

The example SCSPL architecture, whose product hierarchy is diagrammed in Fig. 12 and whose feature model is shown in Fig. 3, has three levels. The top-most level is a collection of core assets shared by each of the different types of cruise controls, or products. The middle level includes a standard cruise control and an adaptive cruise control. The standard cruise control is the type common in many vehicles, particularly older vehicles. It uses the "Maintain Driver Preference" variant for the controller logic feature and does not have a radio or speed decrease detector, and its increase requestor feature variant is simply a button. It allows a user to manually set a speed for the car to maintain, and sensors in the engine determine how the throttle needs to be modified in order for the requested speed to be achieved. The adaptive cruise control, found in some vehicles, is the same as the standard cruise control except that it has extra sensors on the front of the vehicle that also feed into the throttle actuator as well as the braking system. If the cruise control is causing the vehicle to approach another vehicle too rapidly, the adaptive cruise control can use the brake actuators to match the speed of the vehicle in front. This product uses the "Rear Distance Sensor" variant and a button for the increase speed requestor feature and the "Front Distance Sensor" and a button for the decrease speed requestor feature. The "Maintain Gap" variant is chosen for the controller feature. Finally, the bottom of the hierarchy contains a collaborative-adaptive cruise control. This cruise control, in addition to front sensors, includes networking capabilities that allow vehicles to communicate amongst one another to determine the safest

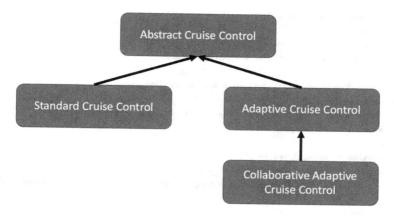

Fig. 12. Example SPL architecture

speed for all vehicles to be traveling considering the location and lane of the vehicle, so the optional radio feature is selected. This cruise control uses the "Maintain Gap and Nearby" variant for the controller logic feature. In addition to other vehicles, collaborative-adaptive cruise controls could communicate with Traffic Management Centers or roadside infrastructure, however, this is outside the scope of this architecture.

4.2   Verifying Multi-layered Architectures

We will now introduce several models which represent parts of the cruise control architecture. These models will be used to demonstrate, using a more extensive example, how the extended version of AGREE facilitates reuse within models utilizing the inheritance features of AGREE.

The first model used is the model of the abstract cruise control, shown in Fig. 13. This represents all of the shared features found in each cruise control present in the SPL of cruise controls. There are 3 inputs and 1 output. The inputs represent whether or not the cruise control is turned on (*enabled*), what the target speed of the cruise control should be (*targetSpeed*) and what the current speed of the vehicle is (*actualSpeed*). Note that many cruise controls will not operate below a minimum speed threshold, and for our purposes, we have set this threshold at 30 miles per hour.

The single output represents the throttle setting for the vehicle. A method of decreasing the speed is not included in the shared model as this is not a shared trait of the cruise controls in our product line. For example, the standard cruise control is not connected to the braking system of the vehicle. It can moderate the speed by letting off of the throttle, allowing the vehicle to slow down, but it cannot stop the vehicle; this task is left up to the driver. The adaptive cruise control, however, is connected to the braking system of the vehicle and it can issue a command to the braking system over the vehicle bus slowing the vehicle.

```
system abstract_cruise_control
  features
    enabled: in data port Base_Types::Boolean;
    targetSpeed: in data port Base_Types::Integer;
    actualSpeed: in data port Base_Types::Integer;
    increaseSpeed: out event data port Base_Types::Boolean;
  annex agree {**
    assume "target speed is greater than lower threshold when enabled":
      enabled => targetSpeed >= 30;
    assume "actual speed is greater than lower threshold when enabled":
      enabled => actualSpeed >= 30;
    guarantee "increase speed only when enabled":
      not increaseSpeed or (enabled and targetSpeed < actualSpeed and increaseSpeed);
  **};
end abstract_cruise_control;

system implementation abstract_cruise_control.impl
  annex agree {**
    eq abstract shouldIncreaseSpeed : bool;
    assert increaseSpeed = shouldIncreaseSpeed;
  **};
end abstract_cruise_control.impl;
```

Fig. 13. Shared core asset model

The AGREE annex of Fig. 13 focuses on the verification of a single property, assuring that the increase speed event fires only when the cruise control system is enabled and the target speed is less than the actual speed. In all other instances, the increase speed event should be disabled. The controls around whether or not the speed should be increased will depend largely on the components used by the instantiated product of the product line, so an abstract variable *shouldIncreaseSpeed* is introduced in the abstract cruise control system's implementation that children will override based on their requirements.

The second model provided is a representation of the adaptive cruise control. Recall that the adaptive cruise control is connected to various other sensors on the vehicle that allow it to maintain both speed and, in the presence of another vehicle, a gap between the vehicles.

The adaptive model is shown in Fig. 14. Note that 3 additional inputs are provided as well as 1 additional output. The additional output represents the connection to the braking system of the vehicle and can be used to slow the vehicle down when necessary. The additional inputs represent the upper limit of the gap between the vehicle and the vehicle in front (*upperGapLimit*) as well as the lower limit on that gap (*lowerGapLimit*). The final input is the current measured gap distance (*gap*).

Notice that the adaptive model has many more assumptions and guarantees than the shared model, including guarantees from the shared model that are overridden. The implementation is also much more detailed, and it provides an implementation for the abstract variable of the shared model (*shouldIncreaseSpeed*). The reason for the extra complexity, of course, is due to the need to factor a gap

```
system adaptive_cruise_control extends abstract_cruise_control
  features
    decreaseSpeed: out event data port Base_Types::Boolean;
    upperGapLimit: in data port Base_Types::Integer;
    lowerGapLimit: in data port Base_Types::Integer;
    gap: in data port Base_Types::Integer;
    annex agree {**
      guarantee "decrease when speed greater than target speed":
        enabled and actualSpeed > targetSpeed => decreaseSpeed;
      assume "upper gap limit is non-negative and non-zero": upperGapLimit > 0;
      assume "lower gap limit is non-negative and non-zero": lowerGapLimit > 0;
      assume "gap is non-negative and non-zero": gap > 0 ;
      assume "gap is above lower limit": lowerGapLimit <= gap;
      guarantee "increase speed when gap reaches lower limit":
        enabled and gap = upperGapLimit => increaseSpeed;
      guarantee "decrease speed when gap reaches lower limit":
        enabled and gap = lowerGapLimit => decreaseSpeed;
      --override
      guarantee "maintain when target equal actual":
        enabled and actualSpeed = targetSpeed and
        lowerGapLimit < gap and gap < upperGapLimit => not increaseSpeed;
    **};
end adaptive_cruise_control;


system implementation adaptive_cruise_control.impl extends abstract_cruise_control.impl
  annex agree {**
    eq shouldIncreaseSpeed: bool =
      if enabled and (actualSpeed < targetSpeed or gap = upperGapLimit) then
        true
      else
        false;
    eq shouldDecreaseSpeed: bool =
      if enabled and (actualSpeed > targetSpeed or gap = lowerGapLimit) then
        true
      else
        false;
    assert decreaseSpeed = shouldDecreaseSpeed;
  **};
end adaptive_cruise_control.impl;
```

Fig. 14. Adaptive cruise control model

calculation into whether or not the increase speed event should be fired as well as constraints on the decrease speed event. However, notice that, other than the over-ridden guarantee and abstract, none of the parent's restrictions or implementation details need to be copied down into the child. This allows that only verification assets unique to the adaptive cruise control are required to be attached to the adaptive cruise control. This reuse increases the maintainability of the model and reduces the workload / cognitive load on those developing the model.

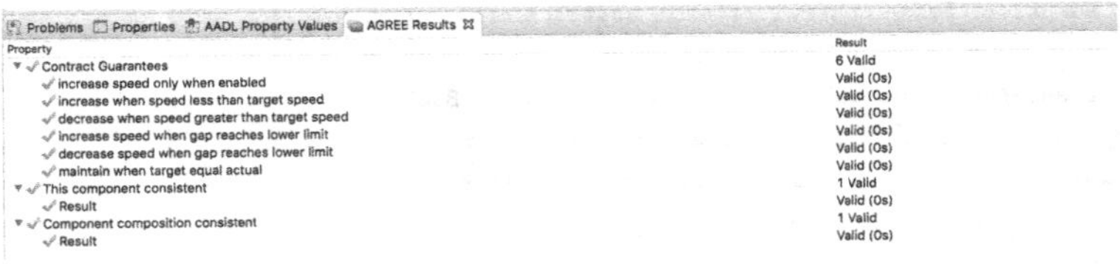

Fig. 15. Adaptive cruise control verification results

Finally, we provide the results of verifying the adaptive cruise control using the extended AGREE implementation in Fig. 15. Note in the figure that the assumptions / guarantees of both models are present despite the assumptions / guarantees of the parent not being specified in the child. This demonstrates that our inheritance mechanism works as expected, and the results of the composition can be validated by a SMT prover.

5   Related Work

Compositionally composed assume-guarantee verification is a popular verification technique, and it has been used successfully in many other ecosystems outside of AADL. Some examples of this are [15,16]. Our work differs from these groups in where verification is applied to the system. We apply compositional verification to the architecture during the design phase of the development life cycle, while these projects apply verification technique later.

Our work is most similar to the work performed by the following groups, particularly [18,26], both of which used AADL. Additional architecture-based techniques exist, such as [14,17,20]. Our work differs from these groups in that we are explicitly focused on allowing the verification assets to be reused in the same manner as SPL assets, exploiting the inheritance features of the AADL language.

6   Conclusion

We have introduced an extension to the AGREE language allowing it to support compositional verification of SPL models that utilize inheritance. Our extended version of AGREE facilitates the re-use of verification assets across multiple levels of inheritance hierarchies present in SPL. It also allows verification assets to incorporate abstraction and refinement into their definitions further simplifying the verification assets to be shared and ensuring they are more maintainable. In future work, we plan to incorporate abstraction in the other statements of traditional AGREE. We also plan to further validate our claims of verification asset reusability by utilizing the extended AGREE module to analyze more complex models, particularly dynamic SPL. The extended version of AGREE will be used to determine the correctness of such models and their appropriateness to an organization's goals.

Acknowledgements. The work of the authors was funded by the National Science Foundation (NSF) grant # 2008912.

References

1. Gonzalez-Huerta, J., Abrahão, S.M., Insfrán, E., Lewis, B.: Automatic derivation of AADL product architectures in software product line development. In: MODELS (2014)
2. Feiler, P., Goodenough, J., Gurfinkel, A., Weinstock, C., Wrage, L.: Four pillars for improving the quality of safety-critical software-reliant systems. DTIC Document (2013)
3. Klein, A., Goodenough, J., McGregor, J., Weinstock, C.: Increasing confidence by strengthening an inference in a single argument leg: An alternative to multi-legged arguments. In: Proceedings of the 44th Annual IEEE/IFIP International Conference on Dependable Systems and Networks (2014)
4. McGee, E.T., McGregor, J.D.: Composition of proof-carrying architectures for cyber-physical systems. In: Proceedings of the 19th International Conference on Software Product Line, pp. 419–426 (2015)
5. Wheeler, D.: http://www.openproofs.org/wiki/Main_Page.OpenProofs (2010)
6. McGee, E.: http://dx.doi.org/10.5281/zenodo.33234 (2015)
7. Rajkumar, R.R., Lee, I., Sha, L., Stankovic, J.: Cyber-physical systems: The next computing revolution. In: Proceedings of the 47th Design Automation Conference, pp. 731–736 (2010)
8. Clements, P., McGregor, J.: Better, faster, cheaper: Pick any three. Bus. Horiz. **55**, 201–208 (2012)
9. Bishop, P., Bloomfield, R., Guerra, S.: The future of goal-based assurance cases. In: Proceedings of the Workshop on Assurance Cases, pp. 390–395 (2004)
10. Gacek, A., Backes, J., Whalen, M., Cofer, D.: AGREE User's Guide (2015). https://github.com/smaccm/smaccm/blob/master/documentation/agree/AGREE%20Users%20Guide.pdf
11. Feiler, P.H., Hansson, J., Niz, D.D., Wrage, L.: System architecture virtual integration: An industrial case study (2009)
12. Feiler, P.H., Gluch, D.P., Hudak, J.J.: The architecture analysis & design language (AADL): An introduction (2006)
13. Feiler, H.P., Lewis, B., Vestal, S.: The SAE architecture analysis and design language (AADL) standard. In: IEEE RTAS Workshop (2003)
14. Goodloe, A.E., Muñoz, C.A.: Compositional verification of a communication protocol for a remotely operated aircraft. Sci. Comput. Program. **78**, 813–827 (2013)
15. Fong, P.W.L., Cameron, R.D.: Proof linking: Modular verification of mobile programs in the presence of lazy, dynamic linking. ACM Trans. Softw. Eng. Methodol. **9**, 379–409 (2000)
16. Chaki, S., Clarke, E.M., Groce, A., Jha, S., Veith, H.: Modular verification of software components in C. IEEE Trans. Softw. Eng. **30**, 368–402 (2004)
17. Cofer, D., Gacek, A., Miller, S., Whalen, M.W., LaValley, B., Sha, L.: Compositional verification of architectural models. In: NASA Formal Methods, pp. 126–140 (2012)
18. Murugesan, A., Whalen, M.W., Rayadurgam, S., Heimdahl, M.P.: Compositional verification of a medical device system. ACM SIGAda Ada Lett. **33**, 51–64 (2013)

19. White, J., Clarke, S., Groba, C., Dougherty, B., Thompson, C., Schmidt, D.C.: R&D challenges and solutions for mobile cyber-physical applications and supporting internet services. J. Internet Serv. Appl. **1**, 45–56 (2010)
20. Hsiung, P., Chen, Y., Lin, Y.: Model checking safety-critical systems using safecharts. IEEE Trans. Comput. **56**, 692–705 (2007)
21. Delange, J.: AADL Tools: Leveraging the Ecosystem. SEI Insights (2016)
22. Clements, P., Northrop, L.: Software Product Lines: Practices and Patterns. Addison-Wesley Longman Publishing Co, Inc., Boston (2002)
23. Nair, S., Vara, J.L., Sabetzadeh, M., Briand, L.: An extended systematic literature review on provision of evidence for safety certification. Inf. Softw. Technol. **56**(7), 689–717 (2014)
24. Braga, R.T.V., Junior, O.T., Castelo Branco, K.R., De Oliveira Neris, L., Lee, J.: Adapting a software product line engineering process for certifying safety critical embedded systems. In: Ortmeier, F., Daniel, P. (eds.) SAFECOMP 2012. LNCS, vol. 7612, pp. 352–363. Springer, Heidelberg (2012). doi:10.1007/978-3-642-33678-2_30
25. Feiler, P., Gluch, D.P.: Model-Based Engineering with AADL: An Introduction to the SAE Architecture Analysis & Design Language. Addison-Wesley, Boston (2012)
26. Yushtein, Y., Bozzano, M., Cimatti, A., Katoen, J., Nguyen, V., Noll, T., Olive, X., Roveri, M.: System-software co-engineering: Dependability and safety perspective. In: 2011 IEEE Fourth International Conference on Space Mission Challenges for Information Technology, pp. 18–25 (2011)
27. Agosta, G., Barenghi, A., Brandolese, C., Fornaciari, W., Pelosi, G., Delucchi, S., Massa, M., Mongelli, M., Ferrari, E., Napoletani, L., et al.: V2I Cooperation for traffic management with SafeCop. In: 2016 Euromicro Conference on Digital System Design, pp. 621–627 (2016)

Engineering and Employing Reusable Software Components for Modular Verification

Daniel Welch[(✉)] and Murali Sitaraman

School of Computing, Clemson University, Clemson, SC 29631, USA
{dtwelch,msitara}@clemson.edu

Abstract. The aim of this paper is to illustrate the central role of reusable software components in developing high assurance software systems and a practical framework and environment for building such systems. The paper presents in detail elements of an actual implementation of a component-based system wherein all components are engineered for reuse and are equipped with interface contracts formalized via mathematical models so that they are amenable to automated verification. The components in the system themselves are built reusing other components, and for scalability, can be verified in a modular fashion one component at a time, using only the interface contracts of reused components. While building such components is necessarily expensive, reuse has the power to amortize the costs. Specification, research, development, verification, and reuse of components in this paper have been performed in the context of an experimental, desktop-based IDE we have built.

1 Introduction

While the need for well-engineered component-based software in improving software productivity and quality is widely acknowledged, the benefits are significantly enhanced if the engineering involves components with formal specification and verification. The year software reuse became the topic of a major international conference at Rio, Brazil in 1994, in an IEEE Software special issue edited by Frakes [5], a futuristic component-based system built from multiple generic, formally specified concepts is envisioned [20]. Twenty years later, this paper presents a practical realization of that reuse vision and the accompanying component-based system. The reusable concepts are described precisely using mathematical models which enhance generality and applicability, facilitate alternative component implementations with varying performance behaviors, and last but not least, serve as the basis for modular formal analysis and reasoning that can lead to automatically verifiable component-based software systems.

Developing verified software components is an expensive activity because it entails investment in formal specification and code annotations, such as invariants. But there is no alternative for achieving high quality and the ideal of one time cost of development being amortized through a lifetime of uses. The specific system illustrated in this paper arises from a graph algorithm domain where typical reuse involves source code and algorithm modification for context.

© Springer International Publishing AG 2017
G. Botterweck and C. Werner (Eds.): ICSR 2017, LNCS 10221, pp. 139–154, 2017.
DOI: 10.1007/978-3-319-56856-0_10

So componentization is necessary and the ideas are domain-independent. In principle, the behavior of any reusable concept can and should be captured formally through mathematical models so that implementation(s) can be verified.

The artifacts presented in this paper are written in RESOLVE [16]—an integrated programming and specification language designed for building verifiable, reusable components. The programming language is similar in spirit to object-oriented languages, such as C++ and Java. While the ideas in this paper can be expressed to an extent in other modeling and programming language-dependent (such as JML [10]) or independent formalisms [1], one of the primary reasons we choose to employ RESOLVE is its support for modular specification that enforces a strict separation between mathematical contracts and code and modular verification. This makes it possible to produce highly reusable concepts specified exclusively in terms of purely mathematical models that are not only devoid of implementation bias, but also effectively hide *which* structures are used in underlying computations and *when* such computations occur. Thus, each reusable concept described is shown to have a host of implementation possibilities.[1] The language and its specifications are extensible and generalizable, as it allows users to create and employ new mathematical theories in their specifications.

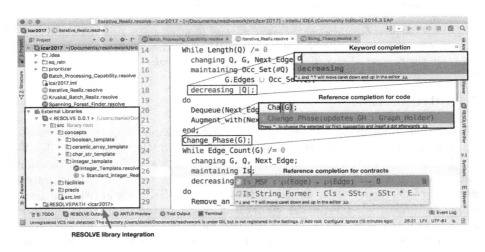

Fig. 1. A desktop-based IDE with support for RESOLVE.

More than the modular and extensible nature of its specification language, the RESOLVE compiler itself is host to a number of amenities, including an integrated proof obligation generator[2], an experimental, minimalist automated

---

[1] Though not a focus of this paper, the conceptual models presented can be extended to specify non-functional performance behaviors of alternative component implementations.

[2] Henceforth referred to as a Verification Condition (VC) generator.

prover, and a code generator which, given verified client code, produces correct-by-construction Java for execution [18].

The language also enjoys the support of a number of development tools including a web-based IDE [2] that has been widely used in software engineering and reuse education, and a more fully featured, experimental desktop based environment that integrates support for RESOLVE into commercial and open source JetBrains IDEs [7]. The examples in this particular paper were developed using the latter, desktop based IDE. Figure 1 highlights some of the advantages in using such an environment, which range from support for input of non-ASCII notations (which are utilized extensively throughout the examples in this paper), to responsive reference completion for contracts, code, and keywords. The environment is also fully integrated with RESOLVE, including its library of reusable core components.

2   A High Level Overview of the Example

To illustrate the notions of engineering reusable concepts and employing them in component-based implementations, we use a well-known optimization problem from the domain of graph algorithms:

– Finding a minimum spanning tree in a (connected), edge-weighted graph.[3]

Rather than designing a concept around one specific algorithm for solving this problem, we instead consider how this problem can be generalized to yield a reusable concept that is:

– Generalized so that optimization is based on some general function of edge information.
– Modeled as a two-phase machine that allows for the incremental delivery of edges of interest, and extraction of only a subset of minimum spanning edges (including, of course, the entire set).
– Designed so that it is suitable even when the input graph is not connected (in which case the solution is said to be a *minimum spanning forest*).

The generalization of weighting based on edge information allows possibilities such as, for example, traffic times in a graph of streets to be affected by a variety of factors, such as geography or weather conditions—rather than just distances. The notion of *incremental construction* is motivated by efficiency, generality, and reuse concerns. Indeed, there are many conceivable applications in which clients of such an interface might not wish (or need) to process/obtain all edges of the resulting spanning forest, such as when a fixed total threshold bound can be met. Finally, the importance and utility of such a concept being able to scale to the problem of unconnected networks, thus producing minimum spanning forests (MSFs) as solutions is obvious. We term the concept designed to take these

---

[3] Informally, a minimum spanning tree is defined to be a subset of a graph's weighted-edges such that all vertices are connected with minimum total weight.

considerations into account a `Spanning_Forest_Finder` (or, SFF for short) and discuss it, and a range of possible component-based implementations in greater detail in Sect. 4.

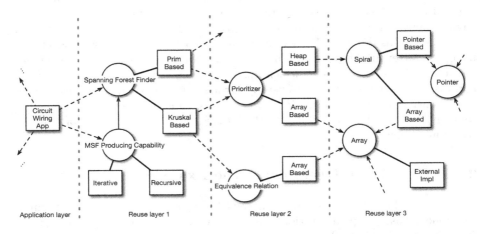

Fig. 2. A design-time diagram sampling a hypothetical client application built on top of layers of reusable concepts and realizations.

A design time diagram illustrating the relationships between the application and various reusable concepts and realizations involved in the proposed software system are illustrated in Fig. 2. In this figure, circles represent concept interfaces and square boxes represent realizations. The thick solid lines connecting a realization to a concept denote an 'implements' relationship, while directed, dashed arrows emanating from realizations to other concepts indicate a 'uses' (or 'relies-on') relationship.

Note that all realizations in Fig. 2 rely solely on concept interfaces, a fact that allows formal reasoning to be performed in a modular fashion: that is, strictly on the basis of other concepts and their respective mathematical models and contracts. For example, in the first layer of the software system, the Kruskal-based realization of the SFF concept relies only on two additional, reusable concepts: one capturing the idea of connectivity, and the other capturing the idea of prioritization. Though these can of course be implemented in a variety of functionally interchangeable ways, client code will ultimately be calling the operations described in the interface contract, thus keeping reasoning modular and in terms of suitably high level, abstract contracts.

The focus of this paper is on concepts inhabiting the first two layers of the proposed system. The third layer, which introduces a mathematical abstraction for modeling arrays, as well as a spiral-like abstraction useful in the representation k-ary heaps, falls outside the scope of this particular paper.

3 Motivating a System of Tiered Reuse: A Spanning Forest Client Application

To motivate the system described, and the extensibility mechanisms our reusable solution affords, consider a small sample design problem in which the goal is to design a portion of a circuit wiring/layout application. Circuit wirings consist of a set of terminals and wires of varying lengths. The goal is to implement an option for the app that connects all the terminals with minimal wiring.[4] The incremental interface of the SFF concept by default allows clients to iteratively insert each wire into the component, then iteratively retrieve some subset of wires that make up a minimal cost solution.

While the incremental interface of the SFF indeed allows one to implement such functionality natively via *primary methods* as described, it pays in some applications (e.g. when all edges are initially present) to support a means of computing the entire solution in bulk. We solve this in a reusable way—without modifying existing interfaces and/or realizations—in the proceeding subsection.

3.1 Enhancing the SFF Concept: A Reuse-Favoring Solution

The reusable solution to the problem of computing an entire MSF in bulk (as opposed to just a subset) involves *enhancing* the original SFF concept with a *secondary operation* that provides MSF_Producing_Capability[5]. The enhancement—shown in Fig. 3—introduces a single operation, Find_MSF, that takes a queue of edges and **updates** it such that it holds only the edges of a resulting MSF.[6]

The relationship between the client application, SFF concept, and the proposed enhancement is illustrated in Fig. 2, which uses a solid arrow to indicate an 'enhances' relationship between two interfaces.

One thing to note is that enhancements and their interchangeable realizations are completely independent of any one particular realization of the base concept. Enhancement implementations (template methods) therefore are written solely in terms of the primary (hook) operations made available through the concept being enhanced.

Abstract Specification. Specification of the operation employs pre- and post conditions, formalized via **requires** and **ensures** clauses (respectively) that are written exclusively in terms of abstract mathematical models. In this case, since a Queue is passed, a portion of the contracts are expressed using the queue's abstract model, which is a mathematical string.[7] The uses clause therefore

---

[4] For a simple variation in which the minimal wiring needed falls within a fixed total threshold bound, consult [20].

[5] In design pattern parlance, this solution is a *template method* that invokes primary, *hook* methods from the interface.

[6] While in general there may many potential MSFs for a given graph, we are interested in any one.

[7] A string can be thought of as a sequence of values, such as $\langle 5, 1, 2, 3, 1 \rangle$.

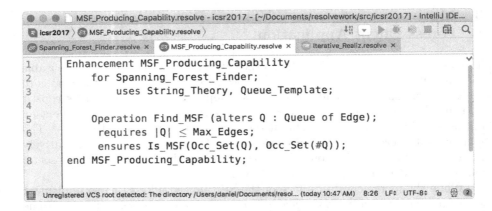

Fig. 3. A secondary (extension) operation to the SFF concept.

brings in a theory module (**String_Theory**), which gives specifiers access to string-specific definitions and notations such as string length $|\dots|$ and Occ_Set—which maps the contents of a string to a set. This is needed in order to apply the Is_MSF predicate, which expects two sets of edges G and H, and is true iff the edges in G represent a minimum spanning forest of those in H (such a predicate is locally defined in the SFF concept, which is the topic of Sect. 4).

Stated in English, the Find_MSF operation therefore **requires** that the length of the edge queue is within Max_Edges, a constant parameter to the SFF concept, and **ensures** that the set of edges for the outgoing value of the queue (Q) is a minimum spanning forest of the incoming value of the queue's (#Qs) edges.

The contracts also include *specification parameter modes* which describe how each parameter is affected by the operation. For example, a parameter with a mode of **updates** specifies that its value will be affected in the manner specified in the ensures clause. Additional parameter modes include **evaluates** (an expression is expected), **replaces** (the incoming value is irrelevant, but the outgoing value is relevant), and **alters** (a meaningful incoming value that assumes an arbitrary outgoing value).

An Iterative Realization. The realization of MSF_Producing_Capability, shown in Fig. 4, is carried out much in the same way a client would in the context of the original wiring application—namely by reusing/relying-on the primary hook operations provided by the concept. The procedure works as follows: first, edges from Q are iteratively dequeued and inserted into a local graph machine G (via the Augment_with operation). The graph is then switched into edge extraction phase (via the Change_Phase operation), at which point the resulting MSF edges are iteratively removed from G and re-enqueued, thus updating Q (as stated by the **updates** parameter mode).

As Fig. 4 illustrates, the behavior of each loop is explicitly captured through the use of several formal annotations including a **maintaining** clause to specify a

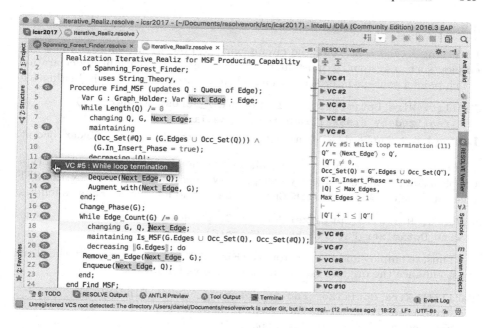

Fig. 4. MSF_Producing_Capability enhancing the original, SFF concept.

loop invariant that must be true at the beginning and end of each iteration, a list of variables that are **changing** within the body, and a **decreasing** clause used to specify a progress metric for the loop—which is needed to prove termination. These assertions (like the pre- and post conditions already mentioned) are also expressed in terms of abstract models.

In this case, the **maintaining** clause for the first loop (lines 8–10) simply relate the set of edges underlying the incoming value of the queue to the collection of edges already in the graph G and those that remain to be added (and also asserts that the graph remains in insertion phase). The **maintaining** clause for the second loop (line 19) on the other hand asserts that for each iteration, the set of edges inhabiting the outgoing queue is a minimum spanning forest of those in the incoming queue. Additionally, note that since the second loop is removing edges from a graph, as opposed to a queue, we employ the set cardinality operator $\| \dots \|$ to express the fact that G's edge-set is decreasing in size each iteration.

And while there are indeed ongoing efforts to infer loop invariants automatically, we note that many automated tools [9] still require users to manually supply such invariants and other assertions. Readers interested in a more thorough discussion of loop invariants, their design, and the feedback provided by the tool, are encouraged to refer to [15].

3.2   Client Application Context

Returning to the context of the circuit wiring application, before a client can employ such a system, it must first be instantiated via a facility[8] declaration which pairs a concept interface with a realization, as shown below in Listing 1.1.

```
Facility Wire_Optimizer_Fac is Spanning_Forest_Finder(...)
    realized by Kruskal_Incremental_Realiz(...).
```
Listing 1.1. A simplified facility instantiation of the Spanning_Forest_Finder concept.

Once instantiated, such a facility allows the client to declare variables of type Graph_Holder and subsequently call primary operations exported by the SFF concept—such as Augment_with, Change_Phase, and Remove_an_Edge as follows:

```
Var G, H : Wire_Optimizer_Fac :: Graph_Holder;
Wire_Optimizer_Fac :: Change_Phase(G); ...
```

Thus, to employ and benefit from the Find_MSF operation designed, the client must enhance the original facility instantiation as follows:

```
Facility Wire_Optimizer_Fac is Spanning_Forest_Finder(..)
    realized by Kruskal_Incremental_Realiz(..)
  enhanced by MSF_Producing_Capability
    realized by Iterative_Realiz;
```
Listing 1.2. A simplified, singly enhanced facility instantiation.

Such a mechanism for layering functionality generalizes to an arbitrary number of enhancements and hence permits clients to create, reuse, and layer as much functionality as needed onto data abstractions, without the need to change core interfaces or understand specific realizations of the core concept.

4   Reuse Layer 1: A Formal Concept for Finding MSFs

This section describes the Spanning_Forest_Finder concept that inhabits the first reusable layer of the system enhanced in the previous section. We emphasize both the abstract modeling and contracts of such a concept, discuss the organization of its primary operations and outline the elements of a sample, incremental, Kruskal-based implementation.

4.1   Mathematical Modeling

In constructing our abstract, mathematical model of the graph, we use the usual formalization of an Edge as the cartesian product of natural numbers and a generic label: (u : $\mathbb{N}$, v : $\mathbb{N}$, Lab : Edge_Info). The natural numbers u and v simply represent tags for the vertices bookending the edge, while the weight

---

[8] One can safely consider 'facility' as a synonym for 'factory' in design pattern terminology.

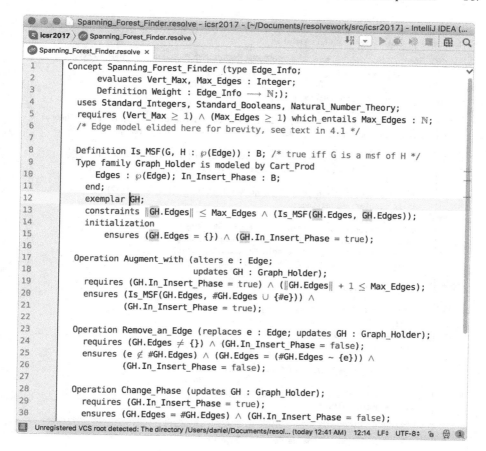

```
1   Concept Spanning_Forest_Finder (type Edge_Info;
2        evaluates Vert_Max, Max_Edges : Integer;
3        Definition Weight : Edge_Info ⟶ ℕ;);
4   uses Standard_Integers, Standard_Booleans, Natural_Number_Theory;
5   requires (Vert_Max ≥ 1) ∧ (Max_Edges ≥ 1) which_entails Max_Edges : ℕ;
6   /* Edge model elided here for brevity, see text in 4.1 */
7
8   Definition Is_MSF(G, H : ℘(Edge)) : B; /* true iff G is a msf of H */
9   Type family Graph_Holder is modeled by Cart_Prod
10       Edges : ℘(Edge); In_Insert_Phase : B;
11      end;
12      exemplar GH;
13      constraints ‖GH.Edges‖ ≤ Max_Edges ∧ (Is_MSF(GH.Edges, GH.Edges));
14      initialization
15          ensures (GH.Edges = {}) ∧ (GH.In_Insert_Phase = true);
16
17  Operation Augment_with (alters e : Edge;
18                          updates GH : Graph_Holder);
19      requires (GH.In_Insert_Phase = true) ∧ (‖GH.Edges‖ + 1 ≤ Max_Edges);
20      ensures (Is_MSF(GH.Edges, #GH.Edges ∪ {#e})) ∧
21              (GH.In_Insert_Phase = true);
22
23  Operation Remove_an_Edge (replaces e : Edge; updates GH : Graph_Holder);
24      requires (GH.Edges ≠ {}) ∧ (GH.In_Insert_Phase = false);
25      ensures (e ∉ #GH.Edges) ∧ (GH.Edges = (#GH.Edges ~ {e})) ∧
26              (GH.In_Insert_Phase = false);
27
28  Operation Change_Phase (updates GH : Graph_Holder);
29      requires (GH.In_Insert_Phase = true);
30      ensures (GH.Edges = #GH.Edges) ∧ (GH.In_Insert_Phase = false);
```

Fig. 5. A concept interface for the minimum spanning forest.

used in optimization is based on `Edge_Info`, and is some application-dependent function of `Weight`—which is supplied as a parameter to the concept by a user at the time of instantiation.

The model for the graph itself, shown in Fig. 5, is introduced via the `type family` clause which consists of an edge-set (formulated as a member of $\mathcal{P}(\texttt{Edge})$) and a boolean flag `In_Insert_Phase` to indicate the phase the graph machine is currently operating under: edge insertion or extraction phase.

The `exemplar` provides specifiers a handle for referring to the model, and is used below in the `constraints` (i.e., conceptual invariants) to assert that a graph's edge-set is bounded by `Max_Edges`, and that it can only contain edges in a MSF of the input graph—expressed with the help of a locally defined predicate, `Is_MSF`. Of course, this is just an abstraction: that such a component implementation can indeed compute a MSF incrementally as and when edges are extracted—and that implementation requires an abstraction relation for

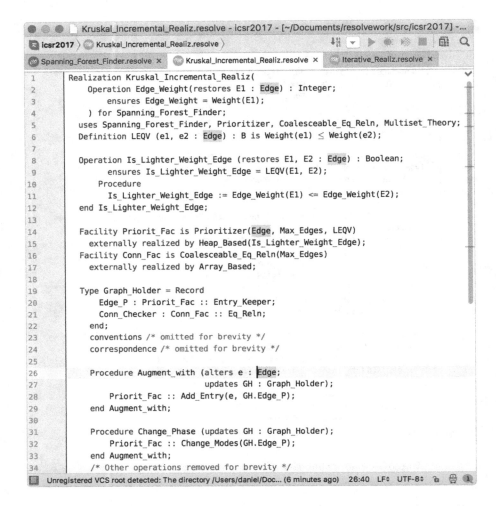

Fig. 6. An incremental Kruskal-based realization of the SFF concept (excerpt).

verification—is the topic of [17]. Finally, the `initialization ensures` clause that immediately follows specifies the abstract state the model must be in when variables or parameters of type `Graph_Holder` are initialized: namely, that the set of edges is the empty-set and the machine must be accepting new edges.

As outlined in [20], to provide functional and performance flexibility for clients, the SFF concept has multiple "small effect" (incremental) primary operations instead of a singular large effect operation such as `Find_MSF`—which, as demonstrated in Sect. 3.1, can be implemented instead as a secondary operation by reusing the primary operations.

Example: An Incremental Realization. To illustrate these points, Fig. 6 shows a portion of one possible realization of the SFF. Since the realization shown is based upon Kruskal's greedy algorithm, it hinges on the ability to (1) order edges with a weighting function based on edge information and (2) test whether adding an edge to the under-construction forest produces a cycle. To accomplish these tasks, two reusable concepts from the second layer (which are discussed in Sect. 5) are instantiated via facilities and used in the Record-based representation of the Graph_Holder type which consists of two fields: one for holding and ordering the edges currently inserted into the graph (Edge_P) and another for checking edge connectivity (Conn_Checker).

The presentation of the realization omits details of internal annotations needed for verification. Specifically, a conventions clause that captures a *representation invariant*: That no vertices in Conn_Checker are related when in the accepting phase; and a correspondence clause that captures an *abstraction relation*: That the conceptual set of edges is an MSF of the (multi)-set of edges in the prioritizer when in the accepting phase and that the conceptual set of edges is an MSF of the (multi)-set of edges, excluding those edges that connect vertices already connected by Conn_Checker when not in the accepting phase. The correspondence clause in this case would also tie the conceptual accepting flag from the SFF concept to a similar flag within the model of the prioritizer.

The realization shown is an efficient one: Each time a user calls Augment_with to add a new edge to the graph, it is added to the prioritizer while Change_Phase effectively does nothing, except prepare the prioritizer for edge removal (see next section). It is in Remove_an_Edge (elided) where a bulk of the work takes place, as it essentially carries out a "single" step of Kruskal's algorithm—though this is unbeknownst to the caller.

5 Reuse Layer 2: Additional Models for Prioritization and Connectivity Checking

5.1 A Concept for Prioritizing

Figure 7 shows a concept for prioritizing generic Entrys. Like the SFF, the prioritizer is parameterized by a generic Entry type, a constant parameter Max_Capacity that holds the maximum number of allowable elements, and a binary preordering relation $\preccurlyeq$ that provides a means of ordering the generic elements that make up the abstract state of the concept. As a precondition, the concept requires this relation to be a total preordering (i.e., total and transitive), and is expressed via the higher-order predicate Is_Total_Preordering.

Mathematical Modeling. Like the SFF concept, the organization of the prioritizer also conforms to the aforementioned machine oriented design principle, which lends it similar advantages both in terms of understandability and reuse, as well as implementation and performance flexibility.

```
        Prioritizer.resolve - icsr2017 - [~/Documents/resolvework/src/icsr2017] - IntelliJ IDEA (Community E...
   icsr2017 ⟩ prioritizer ⟩ Prioritizer.resolve ⟩
   Coalesceable_Eq_Reln.resolve ×        Prioritizer.resolve ×
1      Concept Prioritizer (type Entry; evaluates Max_Capacity : Integer;
2              Definition (x : Entry) ≼ (y : Entry) : B;);
3          uses Standard_Integers, Natural_Number_Theory,
4              Multiset_Theory, Binary_Universalizer_Theory,
5              Ordering_Theory;
6          requires Is_Total_Preordering(≼) ∧ (Max_Capacity > 0)
7              which_entails Max_Capacity : ℕ;
8
9      Type family Entry_Keeper is modeled by Cart_Prod
10         Entry_Tally : FMSet(Entry);
11         Is_Accepting : B;
12      end;
13      exemplar K;
14      constraints ‖K.Entry_Tally‖ ≤ Max_Capacity;
15      initialization
16          ensures (K.Is_Accepting = true) ∧ (K.Entry_Tally = Φ);
17
18      Operation Add_Entry (alters x : Entry; updates P : Entry_Keeper);
19          requires (‖P.Entry_Tally‖ < Max_Capacity) ∧ (P.Is_Accepting = true);
20          ensures (P.Is_Accepting = true) ∧
21              (P.Entry_Tally = (#P.Entry_Tally ⊎ \#x/ ));
22
23      Operation Remove_a_Smallest_Entry (replaces e : Entry;
24                                         updates P : Entry_Keeper);
25          requires ¬(P.Is_Accepting) ∧ (‖P.Entry_Tally‖ > 0);
26          ensures (#P.Entry_Tally⌈e⌉ > 0) ∧ (P.Is_Accepting = false) ∧
27          (Is_Universally_Related(≼, {e}, Undrln_Set(#P.Entry_Tally)));
28
29      Operation Change_Modes (updates P : Entry_Keeper);
30          ensures (P.Is_Accepting = ¬(#P.Is_Accepting));
   Unregistered VCS root detected: The directory /Users/daniel/Documents/res... (today 10:47 AM)  6:33  LF⇔  UTF-8⇔
```

Fig. 7. A concept interface for prioritizing generic Entrys.

Operating at the core of the prioritizer's mathematical model is a finite multi-set (FMSet)[9], with relevant notations defined in the imported Multiset_Theory. While the contracts for the most part are made straightforward through the usage of Multiset_Theory, one worthy of mention is the ensures clause of Remove_a_Smallest_Entry, which uses a higher order predicate Is_Universally_Related, to state that every element in {e} is related to every element in the incoming multiset's (underlying) set[10] via the ≼ predicate.

---

[9] A multiset is an unordered collection of elements that may contain duplicates, such as $\lfloor 1, 1, 3, 5, 3, 1 \rfloor$. Multiset union is ⊎ and $\lceil \ldots \rceil$ 'tallies' the number of times an element appears in a given multiset.

[10] Like Occ_Set for strings, Underln_Set maps elements of a multiset to regular set. For example: $\text{Underln\_Set}(\lfloor 1, 1, 3, 3, 3, 2 \rfloor) = \{1, 3, 2\}$.

5.2 A Concept for Maintaining Equivalence Relations

The final concept we present is one concerned with capturing arbitrary object equivalences. A general, formal concept for forming and maintaining such equivalence relations is shown in Fig. 8.

To ensure that instances of equivalence relation type conform with the mathematical modeling, the concept makes use of several reusable, higher-order predicates from Basic_Binary_Relation_Properties. In particular, the constraints asserts that the model is indeed reflexive $(\forall x, f(x,x))$, symmetric $(\forall x \forall y, f(x,y) \implies f(y,x))$, and transitive $(\forall x \forall y \forall z, f(x,y) \wedge f(y,z) \implies f(x,z))$. The initialization clause ensures that all indices are initially disjoint (in other words, each element initially inhabits its own equivalence class). The set of primary operations for such a concept provide what

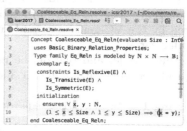

Fig. 8. A concept for maintaining equivalence relations.

one would expect: that is, the ability to form, test, and clear equivalencies. Once again, irrespective of the formal contract for the concept laid out above, clients are free to implement such a concept in any number of efficient ways including (but not limited to) approaches utilizing the well-known 'union by rank' and 'path compression' optimizations [3].

6   The Verification Process

In a prior work [16] the idea of verification conditions (VCs) that describe both what is necessary and sufficient to prove in order to establish functional correctness of a given component is discussed. Sound VC generation is a non-trivial process in general [6], and for the system we employ (RESOLVE), generated VCs can be read as sequents of the form: $\{A_1, \ldots, A_n\} \vdash C$ where each comma-separated A_i $(1 \leqslant i \leqslant n)$ represents a given and C is the goal that must be proven. VCs arise from a variety of different places in code including: establishing the preconditions of called operations, postconditions of operation's being proved, or progress metrics for establishing termination of iteration or recursion.

Figure 4 illustrates how the IDE displays generated VCs. Lines that raise one or more proof obligations are marked by an orange 'vc' button in gutter, which, upon being selected, brings up a context menu that navigates the user to the right hand side verifier panel which allows them to view any or all VCs and (optionally) export a summary.[11]

---

[11] In the future, we also aim to offer researchers the ability to view and export VC derivation details for specified blocks of code—this feature is forthcoming.

Enhancement Realization. Verification of the iterative realization of the MSF_Producing_Capability shown in Fig. 4 produces 17 VCs, many of which arise from the loops—which entail establishing a base case and inductive hypothesis (for their respective **maintaining** clauses), along with establishing preconditions for the various calls to spanning forest and queue operations scattered throughout. The variables proceeded by primes are intermediate variables conjured by the VC-generator, and are used to reflect the changing state of a particular variable.

One simple, and one of the more complicated examples of these VCs are reproduced below in Listings 1.3 and 1.4, respectively.

Listing 1.3. Augment_with requires.

$|Q''| \neq 0$,
$\mathrm{Occ\_Set}(Q) = G''.\mathrm{Edges} \cup \mathrm{Occ\_Set}(Q'')$,
$G''.\mathrm{In\_Insert\_Phase} = \mathrm{true}$,
$|Q| \leqslant \mathrm{Max\_Edges}$,
$\mathrm{Max\_Edges} \geqslant 1$
$\vdash$
$\|G''.\mathrm{Edges}\| + 1 \leqslant \mathrm{Max\_Edges}$

Listing 1.4. Second loop inductive hypo.

$\mathrm{Next\_Edge}' \notin G'.\mathrm{Edges}$,
$\|G'.\mathrm{Edges}\| \neq 0$, $|Q''| = 0$,
$\mathrm{Is\_MSF}(G'.\mathrm{Edges} \cup \mathrm{Occ\_Set}(Q'), \mathrm{Occ\_Set}(Q))$,
$\mathrm{Occ\_Set}(Q) = G'''.\mathrm{Edges} \cup \mathrm{Occ\_Set}(Q'')$,
$|Q| \leqslant \mathrm{Max\_Edges}$, $\mathrm{Max\_Edges} \geqslant 1$,
$\vdash$
$\mathrm{Is\_MSF}(G'.\mathrm{Edges} \sim \{\mathrm{Next\_Edge}'\} \cup$
$\quad \mathrm{Occ\_Set}(Q' \circ \langle e \rangle), \mathrm{Occ\_Set}(Q))$

SFF Concept Realization. The preliminary, incremental realization of the SFF concept sketched in Fig. 6, generates upwards of 40 VCs. Unlike those generated for the previous example, VCs that arise in practice from concept realizations typically come from more diverse sources such as establishing that correspondences hold for various type representations (such as **Edge** and **Graph_Holder**), and establishing module level preconditions from facility instantiations (such as **Priorit_Fac** and **Conn_Fac**).

Two representative VCs, including one involving multisets (right) are reproduced below in Listings 1.5 and 1.6.

Listing 1.5. Add_Entry requires.

$\mathrm{Is\_MSF}(\mathrm{conc.GH.Edges},$
$\quad \mathrm{Undrln\_Set}(\mathrm{GH.Edge\_P.Entry\_Tally}))$,
$\|\mathrm{conc.GH.Edges}\| + 1 \leqslant \mathrm{Max\_Edges}$,
$\dots$,
$\mathrm{Max\_Edges} \geqslant 1, \mathrm{Max\_Edges} > 0$
$\vdash$
$\|\mathrm{GH.Edge\_P.Entry\_Tally}\| < \mathrm{Max\_Edges}$

Listing 1.6. Augment_with ensures.

$\mathrm{Is\_MSF}(\mathrm{conc.GH.Edges},$
$\quad \mathrm{Undrln\_Set}(\mathrm{GH.Edge\_P.Entry\_Tally} \uplus \lfloor e \rfloor))$,
$\|\mathrm{conc.GH.Edges}\| + 1 \leqslant \mathrm{Max\_Edges}$,
$\mathrm{Max\_Edges} \geqslant 1$,
$\mathrm{Max\_Edges} > 0$
$\vdash$
$\mathrm{Is\_MSF}(\mathrm{conc.GH.Edges}, \mathrm{conc.GH.Edges} \cup \{e\})$

Discussion. While the VCs generated from the present components have not yet been verified automatically, we have made significant progress in automated verification of VCs for typical components [2,8], including those developed in undergraduate software engineering classes. Thus, while the VCs presented here—which span multiple theories—are straightforward enough to dispatch by hand, many continue to pose a significant challenge to current decision procedures and automated provers.

7 Related Work and Conclusions

While the role of modeling in specifying safety and behavioral properties for reusable component-based software systems has become increasingly more prevalent and widely practiced [13, 14], the verification community has focused on and achieved impressive feats (e.g. [12]) over the years through one-time manual efforts (typically using proof assistants). However, the detailed constructions, complexity, and nontrivial libraries that typically enable these impressive achievements continue to present new and pressing reuse challenges [19].

On the other hand, efforts that have considered components, such as Dafny [11], RESOLVE, Why3 [4], and others have achieved notable successes in specifying and verifying automatically a variety of individual components such as lists, sequences, queues, and trees—but have not ventured far beyond these boundaries by attempting abstract specification and modular verification of larger, layered reusable component assemblies of the sort presented in this paper.

The contribution of this paper is in presenting a practical implementation of a verifiable, comprehensive component-based software system involving multiple formally specified reusable components. Furthermore, the system has been developed with an IDE built for reuse-based software engineering. While we have automatically verified a number of component implementations, automated verification of the components presented in this paper remains an immediate future direction. As such, the theories and concepts will no doubt need to undergo further formalization and development to ultimately facilitate automation. While significant, the system presented in this paper is still much smaller than typical practical systems thus, studies that involve further scaling up to even bigger systems is another important direction for future work.

Acknowledgments. This research is funded in part by NSF grants CCF-0811748, CCF-1161916, and DUE-1022941.

References

1. Abrial, J.R.: Modeling in Event-B: System and Software Engineering, 1st edn. Cambridge University Press, New York (2010)
2. Cook, C.T., Harton, H., Smith, H., Sitaraman, M.: Specification engineering and modular verification using a web-integrated verifying compiler. In: 2012 34th International Conference on Software Engineering (ICSE), pp. 1379–1382, June 2012
3. Cormen, T.H., Stein, C., Rivest, R.L., Leiserson, C.E.: Introduction to Algorithms, 2nd edn. McGraw-Hill Higher Education, New York (2001)
4. Filliâtre, J.-C., Paskevich, A.: Why3 — Where programs meet provers. In: Felleisen, M., Gardner, P. (eds.) ESOP 2013. LNCS, vol. 7792, pp. 125–128. Springer, Heidelberg (2013). doi:10.1007/978-3-642-37036-6_8

5. Frakes, W.B., Isoda, S.: Success factors of systematic reuse. IEEE Softw. **11**(5), 14–19 (1994)
6. Harton, H.: Mechanical and modular verification condition generation for object-based software. Ph.D. thesis, Clemson University (2011)
7. JetBrains: IDEs. Software product line. https://www.jetbrains.com/
8. Kirschenbaum, J., Adcock, B., Bronish, D., Smith, H., Harton, H., Sitaraman, M., Weide, B.W.: Verifying component-based software: deep mathematics or simple bookkeeping? In: Edwards, S.H., Kulczycki, G. (eds.) ICSR 2009. LNCS, vol. 5791, pp. 31–40. Springer, Heidelberg (2009). doi:10.1007/978-3-642-04211-9_4
9. Klebanov, V., et al.: The 1st verified software competition: experience report. In: Butler, M., Schulte, W. (eds.) FM 2011. LNCS, vol. 6664, pp. 154–168. Springer, Heidelberg (2011). doi:10.1007/978-3-642-21437-0_14
10. Leavens, G.: JML: expressive contracts, specification inheritance, and behavioral subtyping. In: Proceedings of the Principles and Practices of Programming on the Java Platform, PPPJ 2015, p. 1. ACM, New York (2015)
11. Leino, K.R.M.: Dafny: an automatic program verifier for functional correctness. In: Clarke, E.M., Voronkov, A. (eds.) LPAR 2010. LNCS (LNAI), vol. 6355, pp. 348–370. Springer, Heidelberg (2010). doi:10.1007/978-3-642-17511-4_20
12. Leroy, X.: Formal verification of a realistic compiler. Commun. ACM **52**(7), 107–115 (2009)
13. Li, J., Sun, X., Xie, F., Song, X.: Component-based abstraction and refinement. In: Mei, H. (ed.) ICSR 2008. LNCS, vol. 5030, pp. 39–51. Springer, Heidelberg (2008). doi:10.1007/978-3-540-68073-4_4
14. Penzenstadler, B., Koss, D.: High confidence subsystem modelling for reuse. In: Mei, H. (ed.) ICSR 2008. LNCS, vol. 5030, pp. 52–63. Springer, Heidelberg (2008). doi:10.1007/978-3-540-68073-4_5
15. Priester, C., Sun, Y.S., Sitaraman, M.: Tool-assisted loop invariant development and analysis. In: 2016 IEEE 29th International Conference on Software Engineering Education and Training (CSEET), pp. 66–70, April 2016
16. Sitaraman, M., Adcock, B.M., Avigad, J., Bronish, D., Bucci, P., Frazier, D., Friedman, H.M., Harton, H.K., Heym, W.D., Kirschenbaum, J., Krone, J., Smith, H., Weide, B.W.: Building a push-button RESOLVE verifier: progress and challenges. Formal Aspects Comput. **23**(5), 607–626 (2011)
17. Sitaraman, M., Weide, B.W., Ogden, W.F.: On the practical need for abstraction relations to verify abstract data type representations. IEEE Trans. Softw. Eng. **23**(3), 157–170 (1997)
18. Smith, H., Harton, H., Frazier, D., Mohan, R., Sitaraman, M.: Generating verified Java components through RESOLVE. In: Edwards, S.H., Kulczycki, G. (eds.) ICSR 2009. LNCS, vol. 5791, pp. 11–20. Springer, Heidelberg (2009). doi:10.1007/978-3-642-04211-9_2
19. Tankink, C., Kaliszyk, C., Urban, J., Geuvers, H.: Formal mathematics on display: a wiki for Flyspeck. In: Carette, J., Aspinall, D., Lange, C., Sojka, P., Windsteiger, W. (eds.) CICM 2013. LNCS (LNAI), vol. 7961, pp. 152–167. Springer, Heidelberg (2013). doi:10.1007/978-3-642-39320-4_10
20. Weide, B.W., Ogden, W.F., Sitaraman, M.: Recasting algorithms to encourage reuse. IEEE Softw. **11**(5), 80–88 (1994)

Refactoring Legacy JavaScript Code to Use Classes: The Good, The Bad and The Ugly

Leonardo Humberto Silva[1]([✉]) [iD], Marco Tulio Valente[2] [iD],
and Alexandre Bergel[3] [iD]

[1] Federal Institute of Northern Minas Gerais, Salinas, Brazil
leonardo.silva@ifnmg.edu.br
[2] Federal University of Minas Gerais, Belo Horizonte, Brazil
mtov@dcc.ufmg.br
[3] PLEIAD Lab, DCC, University of Chile, Santiago, Chile
abergel@dcc.uchile.cl

Abstract. JavaScript systems are becoming increasingly complex and large. To tackle the challenges involved in implementing these systems, the language is evolving to include several constructions for programming-in-the-large. For example, although the language is prototype-based, the latest JavaScript standard, named ECMAScript 6 (ES6), provides native support for implementing classes. Even though most modern web browsers support ES6, only a very few applications use the class syntax. In this paper, we analyze the process of migrating structures that emulate classes in legacy JavaScript code to adopt the new syntax for classes introduced by ES6. We apply a set of migration rules on eight legacy JavaScript systems. In our study, we document: (a) cases that are straightforward to migrate (the good parts); (b) cases that require manual and ad-hoc migration (the bad parts); and (c) cases that cannot be migrated due to limitations and restrictions of ES6 (the ugly parts). Six out of eight systems (75%) contain instances of bad and/or ugly cases. We also collect the perceptions of JavaScript developers about migrating their code to use the new syntax for classes.

Keywords: JavaScript · Refactoring · ECMAScript 6

1 Introduction

JavaScript is the most dominant web programming language. It was initially designed in the mid-1990s to extend web pages with small executable code. Since then, its popularity and relevance only grew [1–3]. Among the top 2,500 most popular systems on GitHub, according to their number of stars, 34.2% are implemented in JavaScript [4]. To mention another example, in the last year, JavaScript repositories had twice as many pull requests (PRs) than the second language, representing an increase of 97% over the previous year.[1] The language

---

[1] https://octoverse.github.com/.

© Springer International Publishing AG 2017
G. Botterweck and C. Werner (Eds.): ICSR 2017, LNCS 10221, pp. 155–171, 2017.
DOI: 10.1007/978-3-319-56856-0_11

can be used to implement both client and server-side applications. Moreover, JavaScript code can also be encapsulated as libraries and referred to by web pages. These characteristics make JavaScript suitable for implementing complex, single-page web systems, including mail clients, frameworks, mobile applications, and IDEs, which can reach hundreds of thousands of lines of code.

JavaScript is an imperative and object-oriented language centered on prototypes [5,6]. Recently, the release of the new standard version of the language, named ECMAScript 6 (or just ES6, as used throughout this paper), represented a significant update to the language. Among the new features, particularly important is the syntactical support for classes [7]. With ES6, it is possible to implement classes using a syntax very similar to the one of mainstream class-based object-oriented languages, such as Java and C++. However, although most modern browsers already support ES6, there is a large codebase of legacy JavaScript source code, i.e., code implemented in versions prior to the ES6 standard. Even in this code, it is common to find structures that in practice are very similar to classes, being used to encapsulate data and code. Although not using appropriate syntax, developers frequently emulate class-like structures in legacy JavaScript applications to easily reuse code and abstract functionalities into specialized objects. In a previous study, we show that structures emulating classes are present in 74% of the studied systems [8]. We also implemented a tool, JSClassFinder [9], to detect classes in legacy JavaScript code. Moreover, a recent empirical study shows that JavaScript developers are not fully aware of changes introduced in ES6, and very few are currently using object-oriented features, such as the new class syntax [10].

In this paper, we investigate the feasibility of rejuvenating legacy JavaScript code and, therefore, to increase the chances of code reuse in the language. Specifically, we describe an experiment on migrating eight real-world JavaScript systems to use the native syntax for classes provided by ES6. We first use JSClassFinder to identify class like structures in the selected systems. Then we convert these classes to use the new syntax.

This paper makes the following contributions:

- We present a basic set of rules to migrate class-like structures from ES5 (prior version of JavaScript) to the new syntax for classes provided by ES6 (Sect. 3.1).
- We quantify the amount of code (churned and deleted) that can be automatically migrated by the proposed rules (the good parts, Sect. 4.1).
- We describe the limitations of the proposed rules, i.e., a set of cases where manual adjusts are required to migrate the code (the bad parts, Sect. 4.2).
- We describe the limitations of the new syntax for classes provided by ES6, i.e., the cases where it is not possible to migrate the code and, therefore, we should expose the prototype-based object system to ES6 maintainers (the ugly parts, Sect. 4.3).
- We document a set of reasons that can lead developers to postpone/reject the adoption of ES6 classes (Sect. 5). These reasons are based on the feedback received after submitting pull requests suggesting the migration to the new syntax.

2   Background

2.1   Class Emulation in Legacy JavaScript Code

Using functions is the most common strategy to emulate classes in legacy JavaScript systems. Particularly, any function can be used as a template for the creation of objects. When a function is used as a class constructor, the this variable is bound to the new object under construction. Variables linked to this define properties that emulate attributes and methods. If a property is an inner function, it represents a *method*; otherwise, it is an *attribute*. The operator new is used to instantiate class objects.

To illustrate the emulation of classes in legacy JavaScript code, we use a simple Queue class. Listing 1.1 presents the function that defines this class (lines 1–8), which includes one attribute (_elements) and three methods (isEmpty, push, and pop). The implementation of a specialized queue is found in lines 9–17. Stack is a subclass of Queue (line 15). Method push (line 17) is overwritten to insert elements at the first position of the queue.

```
1  // Class Queue
2  function Queue() { // Constructor function
3      this._elements = new LinkedList();
4      ...
5  }
6  Queue.prototype.isEmpty = function() {...}
7  Queue.prototype.push = function(e) {...}
8  Queue.prototype.pop = function() {...}
9  // Class Stack
10 function Stack() {
11     // Calling parent's class constructor
12     Queue.call(this);
13 }
14 // Inheritance link
15 Stack.prototype = new Queue();
16 // Overwritten method
17 Stack.prototype.push = function(e) {...}
```

Listing 1.1. *Class* emulation in legacy JavaScript code

The implementation in Listing 1.1 represents one possibility of class emulation in JavaScript. Some variations are possible, like implementing methods inside/outside class constructors and using anonymous/non-anonymous functions [8,11].

2.2   ECMAScript 6 Classes

ES6 includes syntactical support for classes. Listing 1.2 presents an implementation for classes Queue and Stack (Listing 1.1) in this latest JavaScript standard. As can be observed, the implementation follows the syntax provided by mainstream class-based languages. We see, for example, the usage of the keywords class (lines 1 and 11), constructor (lines 2 and 12), extends (line 11), and super (line 13). Although ES6 classes provide a much simpler and clearer syntax to define classes and deal with inheritance, it is a syntactical sugar over

JavaScript's existing prototype-based inheritance. In other words, the new syntax does not impact the semantics of the language, which remains prototype-based.[2]

```
1  class Queue {
2      constructor() {
3          this._elements = new LinkedList();
4          ...
5      }
6      // Methods
7      isEmpty() {...}
8      push(e) {...}
9      pop() {...}
10 }
11 class Stack extends Queue {
12     constructor() {
13         super();
14     }
15     // Overwritten method
16     push(e) {...}
17 }
```

Listing 1.2. Class declaration using ES6 syntax

3 Study Design

In this section, we describe our study to migrate a set of legacy JavaScript systems (implemented in ES5) to use the new syntax for classes proposed by ES6. First, we describe the rules followed to conduct this migration (Sect. 3.1). Then, we present the set of selected systems in our dataset (Sect. 3.2). The results are discussed in Sect. 4.

3.1 Migration Rules

Figure 1 presents three basic rules to migrate classes emulated in legacy JavaScript code to use the ES6 syntax. Each rule defines a transformation that, when applied to legacy code (program on the left), produces a new code in ES6 (program on the right). Starting with Rule #1, each rule should be applied multiple times, until a fixed point is reached. After that, the migration proceeds by applying the next rule. The process finishes after reaching the fixed point of the last rule.

For each rule, the left side is the result of "desugaring" this program to the legacy syntax. The right side of the rule is a template for an ES6 program using the new syntax. Since there is no standard way to define classes in ES5, we consider three different patterns of method implementation, including methods inside/outside class constructors and using prototypes [8,11]. Rule #1 defines the migration of a class C with three methods (m1, m2, and m3) to the new class syntax (which relies on the keywords class and constructor). Method m1 is implemented inside the body of the class constructor, m2 is bound to the prototype of C, and m3 is implemented outside the class constructor but it is not bound to the prototype.[3] Rule #2, which is applied after migrating all

---

[2] https://developer.mozilla.org/en/docs/Web/JavaScript/Reference/Classes.

[3] For the sake of legibility, Rule #1 assumes a class with only one method in each idiom. The generalization for multiple methods is straightforward.

Rule #1: Classes

ES5   ES6

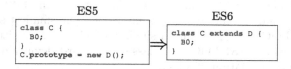

Rule#2: Subclasses

ES5
                    ES6

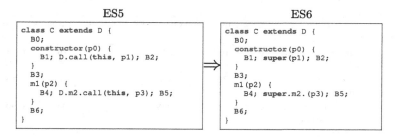

Rule #3: **super**() *calls*

ES5   ES6

Fig. 1. Migration rules (p_i is a formal parameter list and B_i is a block of statements)

constructor functions and methods, generates subclasses in the new syntax (by introducing the `extends` keyword). Finally, Rule #3 replaces calls to super class constructors and to super class methods by making use of the `super` keyword.

There are no rules for migrating fields, because they are declared with the same syntax both in ES5 and ES6 (see Listing 1.1, line 3; and Listing 1.2, line 3). Moreover, fields are most often declared in constructor functions or less frequently in methods. Therefore, when we migrate these elements to ES6, the field declarations performed in their code are also migrated.

3.2 Dataset

We select systems that emulate classes in legacy JavaScript code in order to migrate them to the new syntax. In a previous work [8], we conducted an empirical study on the use of classes with 50 popular JavaScript systems, before the release of ES6. In this paper, we select eight systems from the dataset used in this previous work. The selected systems have at minimum one and at maximum 100 classes, and 40 KLOC.

Table 1 presents the selected systems, including a brief description, checkout date, size (LOC), number of files, number of classes (NOC), number of methods (NOM), and class density (CD). CD is the ratio of functions in a program that are related to the emulation of classes (i.e., functions which act as methods or class constructors) [8]. JSClassFinder [9] was used to identify the classes emulated in legacy code and to compute the measures presented in Table 1. The selection includes well-known and widely used JavaScript systems, from different domains, covering frameworks (SOCKET.IO and GRUNT), graphic libraries (ISOMER), visualization engines (SLICK), data structures and algorithms (ALGORITHMS.JS), and a motion detector (PARALLAX). The largest system (PIXI.JS) has 23,952 LOC, 83 classes, and 134 files with .js extension. The smallest system (FASTCLICK) has 846 LOC, one class, and a single file. The average size is 4,681 LOC (standard deviation 7,881 LOC), 15 classes (standard deviation 28 classes) and 29 files (standard deviation 48 files).

Table 1. JavaScript systems ordered by the number of classes.

System	Description	Checkout date	LOC	Files	Classes	Methods	Class density
FASTCLICK	Library to remove click delays	01-Sep-16	846	1	1	16	0.74
GRUNT	JavaScript task runner	30-Aug-16	1,895	11	1	16	0.16
SLICK	Carousel visualization engine	24-Aug-16	2,905	1	1	94	0.90
PARALLAX	Motion detector for devices	31-Aug-16	1,018	3	2	56	0.95
SOCKET.IO	Realtime app framework	25-Aug-16	1,408	4	4	59	0.95
ISOMER	Isometric graphics library	02-Sep-16	990	9	7	35	0.79
ALGORITHMS.JS	Data structures & algorithms	21-Aug-16	4,437	70	20	101	0.54
PIXI.JS	Rendering engine	05-Sep-16	23,952	134	83	518	0.71

4   Migration Results

We followed the rules presented in Sect. 3 to migrate the systems in our dataset to ES6. We classify the migrated code in three groups:

- *The Good Parts.* Cases that are straightforward to migrate, without the need of further adjusts, by just following the migration rules defined in Sect. 3.1. As future work, we plan to develop a refactoring tool to handle these cases.
- *The Bad Parts.* Cases that require manual and ad-hoc migration. Essentially, these cases are associated with semantic conflicts between the structures used

to emulate classes in ES5 and the new constructs for implementing classes in ES6. For example, function declarations in ES5 are hoisted (i.e., they can be used before the point at which they are declared in the source code), whereas ES6 class declarations are not.

– *The Ugly Parts.* Cases that cannot be migrated due to limitations and restrictions of ES6 (e.g., lack of support to static fields). For this reason, in such cases we need to keep the legacy code unchanged, exposing the prototype mechanism of ES5 in the migrated code, which in our view results in "ugly code". As a result, developers are not shielded from manipulating prototypes.

In the following sections, we detail the migration results according to the proposed classification.

4.1   The Good Parts

As mentioned, the "good parts" are the ones handled by the rules presented in Sect. 3.1. To measure the amount of source code converted we use the following churn metrics [12]: (a) Churned LOC is the sum of the added and changed lines of code between the original and the migrated versions, (b) Deleted LOC is the number of lines of code deleted between the original and the migrated version, (c) Files churned is the number of source code files that churned. We also use a set of relative churn measures as follows: Churned LOC/Total LOC, Deleted LOC/Total LOC, Files churned/File count, and Churned LOC/Deleted LOC. This last measure quantifies new development. Churned and deleted LOC are computed by GitHub. Total LOC is computed on the migrated code.

Table 2 presents the measures for the proposed code churn metrics. PIXI.JS has the greatest absolute churned and deleted LOC, 8,879 and 8,805 lines of code, respectively. The smallest systems in terms of number of classes and methods are FASTCLICK and GRUNT. For this reason, they have the lowest values for absolute churned measures. Regarding the relative churn metrics, PARALLAX and SOCKET.IO are the systems with the greatest values for class density, 0.95 each, and they have the highest relative churned measures. PARALLAX has relative churned equals 0.76 and relative deleted equals 0.75. SOCKET.IO has relative churned equals 0.77 and relative deleted equals 0.75. Finally, the values of Churned/Deleted are approximately equal one in all systems, indicating that the impact in the size of the systems was minimum.

In summary, the relative measures to migrate to ES6 range from 0.16 to 0.77 for churned code, from 0.15 to 0.75 for deleted code, and from 0.21 to 1.11 for churned files. Essentially, these measures correlate with the class density.

4.2   The Bad Parts

As detailed in the beginning of this section, the "bad parts" are cases not handled by the proposed migration rules. To make the migration possible, they require manual adjustments in the source code. We found four types of "bad cases" in our experiment, which are described next.

Table 2. Churned metric measures

System	Absolute churn measures			Relative churn measures			Churned/deleted
	Churned	Deleted	Files	Churned	Deleted	Files	
FASTCLICK	635	630	1	0.75	0.74	1.00	1.01
GRUNT	296	291	1	0.16	0.15	0.09	1.02
SLICK	2,013	1,987	1	0.69	0.68	1.00	1.01
PARALLAX	772	764	2	0.76	0.75	0.67	1.01
SOCKET.IO	1,090	1,053	4	0.77	0.75	1.00	1.04
ISOMER	701	678	10	0.71	0.68	1.11	1.03
ALGORITHMS.JS	1,379	1,327	15	0.31	0.30	0.21	1.04
PIXI.JS	8,879	8,805	82	0.37	0.37	0.61	1.01

Accessing this *Before* super. To illustrate this case, Listing 1.3 shows the emulation of class `PriorityQueue` which inherits from `MinHeap`, in ALGO-RITHMS.JS. In this example, lines 7–8 call the super class constructor using a function as argument. This function makes direct references to this (line 8). However, in ES6, these references yield an error because super calls must proceed any reference to this. The rationale is to ensure that variables defined in a superclass are initialized before initializing variables of the current class. Other languages, such as Java, have the same policy regarding class constructors.

```
1  // Legacy code
2  function MinHeap(compareFn) {
3    this._comparator = compareFn;
4    ...
5  }
6  function PriorityQueue() {
7    MinHeap.call(this, function(a, b) {
8      return this.priority(a) < this.priority(b) ? -1 : 1;
9    });
10   ...
11 }
12 PriorityQueue.prototype = new MinHeap();
```

Listing 1.3. Passing this as argument to super class constructor

Listing 1.4 presents the solution adopted to migrate the code in Listing 1.3. First, we create a *setter* method to define the value of the _comparator property (lines 4–6). Then, in the constructor of `PriorityQueue` we first call super() (line 10) and then we call the created *setter* method (lines 11–14). In this way, we guarantee that super() is used before this.

```
1  // Migrated code
2  class MinHeap {
3    ...
4    setComparator(compareFn) {
5      this._comparator = compareFn;
6    }
7  }
8  class PriorityQueue extends MinHeap {
9    constructor() {
10     super();
11     this.setComparator(
12       (function(a, b) {
13         return this.priority(a) < this.priority(b) ? -1 : 1;
14       }).bind(this));
15     ...
16   }
17 }
```

Listing 1.4. By creating a setter method (lines 4–6) we guarantee that super is called before using this in the migrated code

We found three instances of classes accessing *this* before *super* in our study, two instances in ALGORITHMS.JS and one in PIXI.JS.

Calling Class Constructors Without new. This pattern is also known as "factory method" in the literature [13]. As an example, Listing 1.5 shows part of a Server class implementation in SOCKET.IO. The conditional statement (line 3) verifies if this is an instance of Server, returning a new Server otherwise (line 4). This implementation allows calling Server with or without creating an instance first. However, this class invocation without having an instance is not allowed in ES6.

```
1  // Legacy code
2  function Server(srv, opts){
3    if (!(this instanceof Server))
4      return new Server(srv, opts);
5  }
```

Listing 1.5. Constructor of class Server in system SOCKET.IO

Listing 1.6 shows the solution we adopted in this case. We first renamed class Server to _Server (line 2). Then we changed the function Server from the legacy code to return an instance of this new type (line 7). This solution does not have any impact in client systems.

```
1  // Migrated code
2  class _Server{
3    constructor(srv, opts) { ... }
4  }
5  function Server(srv, opts) {
6    if (!(this instanceof _Server))
7      return new _Server(srv, opts);
8  }
```

Listing 1.6. Workaround to allow calling Server with or without new

We found one case of calling a class constructor without *new* in SOCKET.IO.

Hoisting. In programming languages, hoisting denotes the possibility of referencing a variable anywhere in the code, even before its declaration. In ES5, legacy function declarations are hoisted, whereas ES6 class declarations are not.[4] As a result, in ES6 we first need to declare a class before making reference to it. As an example, Listing 1.7 shows the implementation of class Namespace in SOCKET.IO. Namespace is assigned to module.exports (line 2) before its constructor is declared (line 3). Therefore, in the migrated code we needed to change the order of these declarations.

```
1 // Legacy code
2 module.exports = Namespace;
3 function Namespace {...}  // constructor function
```

Listing 1.7. Function Namespace is referenced before its definition

Listing 1.8 shows another example of a hoisting problem, this time in PIXI.JS. In this case, a global variable receives an instance of the class DisplayObject (line 2) before the class definition (lines 3–6). However, in this case the variable _tempDisplayObjectParent is also used by the class DisplayObject (line 5). Furthermore, PIXI.JS uses a lint-like static checker, called ESLint[5], that prevents the use of variables before their definitions. For this reason, we cannot just reorder the statements to solve the problem, as in Listing 1.7.

```
1 // Legacy code
2 var _tempDisplayObjectParent = new DisplayObject();
3 DisplayObject.prototype.getBounds = function(..) {
4     ...
5     this.parent = _tempDisplayObjectParent;
6 }
```

Listing 1.8. Hoisting problem in PIXI.JS

Listing 1.9 shows the adopted solution in this case. First, we assigned null to _tempDisplayObjectParent (line 2), but keeping its definition before the implementation of class DisplayObject (line 4). Then we assign the original value, which makes reference to DisplayObject, after the class declaration.

```
1 // Migrated code
2 var _tempDisplayObjectParent = null;
3
4 class DisplayObject { ... }
5 _tempDisplayObjectParent = new DisplayObject();
```

Listing 1.9. Solution for hoisting problem in PIXI.JS

We found 88 instances of hoisting problems in our study, distributed over three instances in ALGORITHMS.JS, four instances in SOCKET.IO, one instance in GRUNT, and 80 instances in PIXI.JS.

---

[4] https://developer.mozilla.org/en/docs/Web/JavaScript/Reference/Classes.

[5] http://eslint.org/.

Alias for Method Names. Legacy JavaScript code can declare two or more methods pointing to the same function. This usually happens when developers want to rename a method without breaking the code of clients. The old name is kept for the sake of compatibility. Listing 1.10 shows an example of alias in SLICK. In this case, SLICK clients can use addSlide or slickAdd to perform the same task.

```
1  // Legacy code
2  Slick.prototype.addSlide =
3      Slick.prototype.slickAdd = function(markup, index, addBefore) { ... };
```

Listing 1.10. Two prototype properties sharing the same function

Since we do not have a specific syntax to declare method alias in ES6, the solution we adopted was to create two methods and to make one delegate the call to the other one that implements the feature, as presented in Listing 1.11. In this example, addSlide (line 6) just delegates any calls to slickAdd (line 4).

```
1  // Migrated code
2  class Slick {
3      ...
4      slickAdd(markup,index,addBefore) { ... }
5      // Method alias
6      addSlide(markup,index,addBefore) { return slickAdd(markup,index,addBefore);
            }
7  }
```

Listing 1.11. Adopted solution for method alias in SLICK

We found 39 instances of method alias in our study, distributed over 25 instances in SLICK (confined in one class), 8 instances in SOCKET.IO (spread over three classes), and 6 instances in PIXI.JS (spread over six classes).

4.3   The Ugly Parts

The "ugly parts" are the ones that make use of features not supported by ES6. To make the migration possible, these cases remain untouched in the legacy code.

Getters and Setters Only Known at Runtime (Meta-Programming). In the ES5 implementation supported by Mozilla, there are two features, __defineGetter__ and __defineSetter__, that allow binding an object's property to functions that work as *getters* and *setters*, respectively.[6] Listing 1.12 shows an example in SOCKET.IO. In this code, the first argument passed to __defineGetter__ (line 2) is the name of the property and the second one (line 3) is the function that will work as *getter* to this property.

```
1  // Legacy code
2  Socket.prototype.__defineGetter__('request',
3    function() { return this.conn.request; }
4  );
```

Listing 1.12. *Getter* definition in SOCKET.IO using __defineGetter__

---

[6] https://developer.mozilla.org/en-US/docs/Web/JavaScript/Guide.

ES6 provides specific syntax to implement *getters* and *setters* within the body of the class structure. Listing 1.13 presents the ES6 version of the example shown in Listing 1.12. Declarations of *setters* follow the same pattern.

```
1 // Migrated code
2 class Socket {
3   get request() { return this.conn.request; }
4   ...
5 }
```

Listing 1.13. *Getter* method in ES6

However, during the migration of a *getter* or *setter*, if the property's name is not known at compile time (e.g., if it is denoted by a variable), we cannot migrate it to ES6. Listing 1.14 shows an example from SOCKET.IO. In this case, a new *getter* is created for each string stored in an array called flags. Since the string values are only known at runtime, this implementation was left unchanged.

```
1 // Legacy code
2 flags.forEach(function(flag){
3   Socket.prototype.__defineGetter__(flag,
4     function(){ ... });
5 });
```

Listing 1.14. *Getter* methods only known in execution time

We found five instances of *getters* and *setters* defined for properties only known at runtime, all in SOCKET.IO.

Static Data Properties. In ES5, usually developers use prototypes to implement static properties, i.e., properties shared by all objects from a class. Listing 1.15 shows two examples of static properties, ww and orientationStatus, that are bound to the prototype of the class Parallax. By contrast, ES6 classes do not have specific syntax for static properties. Because of that, we adopted an "ugly" solution leaving code defining static properties unchanged in our migration.

```
1 // Prototype properties (legacy code)
2 Parallax.prototype.ww = null;
3 Parallax.prototype.orientationStatus = 0;
```

Listing 1.15. Static properties defined over the prototype in PARALLAX

We found 42 instances of *static properties*, 28 in PARALLAX and 14 in PIXI.JS.

Optional Features. Among the meta-programming functionalities supported by ES5, we found classes providing optional features by implementing them in separated modules [14]. Listing 1.16 shows a feature in PIXI.JS that is implemented in a module different than the one where the object's constructor function is defined. In this example, the class Container is defined in the module core, which is imported by using the function require (line 2). Therefore, getChildByName (line 4) is a feature that is only incorporated to the system's core when the module implemented in Listing 1.16 is used.

```
1 // Legacy code
2 var core = require('../core');
3
4 core.Container.prototype.getChildByName = function (name) { ... };
```

Listing 1.16. Method `getChildByName` is an optional feature in class `Container`

In our study, the mandatory features implemented in module `core` were properly migrated, but `core`'s optional features remained in the legacy code. Moving these features to `core` would make them mandatory in the system. We found six instances of classes with optional features in our study, all in PIXI.JS.

5   Feedback from Developers

After migrating the code and handling the bad parts, we take to the JavaScript developers the discussion about accepting the new version of their systems in ES6. For every system, we create a pull request (PR) with the migrated code, suggesting the adoption of ES6 classes. Table 3 details these pull requests presenting their ID on GitHub, the number of comments they triggered, the opening date, and their status on the date when the data was collected (October 12th, 2016).

Table 3. Created pull requests

System	ID	#Comments	Opening date	Status
FASTCLICK	#500	0	01-Sep-16	Open
GRUNT	#1549	2	31-Aug-16	Closed
SLICK	#2494	5	25-Aug-16	Open
PARALLAX	#159	1	01-Sep-16	Open
SOCKET.IO	#2661	4	29-Aug-16	Open
ISOMER	#87	3	05-Sep-16	Closed
ALGORITHMS.JS	#117	4	23-Aug-16	Open
PIXI.JS	#2936	14	09-Sep-16	Merged

Five PRs (62%) are still open. The PR for FASTCLICK has no comments. This repository seems to be sparsely maintained, since its last commit dates from April, 2016. The comments in the PRs for SLICK, SOCKET.IO, and PARALLAX suggest that they are still under evaluation by the developer's team. In the case of ALGORITHMS.JS, the developer is in favor of ES6 classes, although he believes that it is necessary to transpile the migrated code to ES5 for the sake of compatibility.[7] However, he does not want the project to depend on a transpiler, such as Babel[8], as stated in the following comment:

---

[7] A transpiler is a source-to-source compiler. Transpilers are used, for example, to convert back from ES6 to ES5, in order to guarantee compatibility with older browsers and runtime tools.

[8] https://babeljs.io/.

"I really like classes and I'm happy with your change. Even though most modern browsers support classes, it would be nice to transpile to ES5 to secure compatibility. And I'm not sure it would be good to add Babel as a dependency to this package. So for now I think we should keep this PR on hold for a little while..." *(Developer of system* ALGORITHMS.JS*)*

We have two closed PRs whose changes were not merged. The developer of GRUNT chose not to integrate the migrated code because the system has to keep compatibility with older versions of node.js, that do not support ES6 syntax, as stated in the following comment:

"We currently support node 0.10 that does not support this syntax. Once we are able to drop node 0.10 we might revisit this." *(Developer of system* GRUNT*)*

In the case of ISOMER, the developers decided to keep their code according to ES5, because they are not enthusiasts of the new class syntax in ES6:

"IMHO the class syntax is misleading, as JS "classes" are not actually classes. Using prototypal patterns seems like a simpler way to do inheritance." *(Developer of system* ISOMER*)*

The PR for system PIXI.JS was the largest one, with 82 churned files, and all the proposed changes were promptly accepted, as described in this comment:

"Awesome work! It is really great timing because we were planning on doing this very soon anyways." *(Developer of* PIXI.JS*)*

The developers also mentioned the need to use a transpiler to keep compatibility with other applications that do not support ES6 yet, and they chose to use Babel for transpiling, as stated in the following comments:

"Include the babel-preset-es2015 module in the package.json devDependencies."... *"Unfortunately, heavier dev dependencies are the cost right now for creating more maintainable code that's transpiled. Babel is pretty big and other tech like TypeScript, Coffeescript, Haxe, etc. have tradeoffs too."* *(Developer of* PIXI.JS*)*

Finally, PIXI.JS developers also discussed the adoption of other ES6 features, e.g., using arrow functions expressions and declaring variables with let and const, as stated in the following comment:

"I think it makes more sense for us to make a new Dev branch and start working on this conversion there (starting by merging this PR). I'd like to make additional passes on this for const/let usage, fat arrows instead of binds, statics and other ES6 features." *(Developer of* PIXI.JS*)*

6   Threats to Validity

External Validity. We studied eight open-source JavaScript systems. For this reason, our collection of "bad" and "ugly" cases might not represent all possible cases that require manual intervention or that cannot be migrated to the new syntax of ES6. If other systems are considered, this first catalogue of bad and ugly cases can increase.

Internal Validity. It is possible that we changed the semantics of the systems after the migration. However, we tackled this threat with two procedures. First, all systems in our dataset include a large number of tests. We assure that all tests also pass in the ES6 code. Second, we submitted our changes to the system's developers. They have not pointed any changes in the behavior of their code.

Construct Validity. The classes emulated in the legacy code were detected by JSClassFinder [8,9]. Therefore, it is possible that JSClassFinder wrongly identifies some structures as classes (false positives) or that it misses some classes in the legacy code (false negatives). However, the developers who analyzed our pull requests did not complain about such problems.

7   Related Work

In a previous work, we present a set of heuristics followed by an empirical study to analyze the prevalence of class-based structures in legacy JavaScript code [8]. The study was conducted on 50 popular JavaScript systems, all implemented according to ES5. The results indicated that class-based constructs are present in 74% of the studied systems. We also implemented a tool, JSClassFinder [9], to detect classes in legacy JavaScript code. We use this tool to statically identify class dependencies in legacy JavaScript systems [15] and also to identify the classes migrated to ES6 in this paper.

Hafiz et al. [10] present an empirical study to understand how different language features in JavaScript are used by developers. The authors conclude that: (a) developers are not fully aware about newly introduced JavaScript features; (b) developers continue to use deprecated features that are no longer recommended; (c) very few developers are currently using object-oriented features, such as the new class syntax. We believe this last finding corroborates the importance of our work to assist developers to start using ES6 classes.

Rostami et al. [16] propose a tool to detect constructor functions in legacy JavaScript systems. They first identify all object instantiations, even when there is no explicit object instantiation statement (*e.g.,* the keyword new), and then link each instance to its constructor function. Finally, the identified constructors represent the emulated classes and the functions that belong to these constructors (inner functions) represent the methods.

Gama et al. [11] identify five styles for implementing methods in JavaScript: inside/outside constructor functions using anonymous/non-anonymous functions and using prototypes. Their main goal is to implement an automated approach to normalize JavaScript code to a single consistent style. The migration algorithm used in this paper covers the five styles proposed by the authors. Additionally, we also migrate static methods, *getter* and *setters*, and inheritance relationships.

Feldthaus et al. [17] describe a methodology for implementing automated refactorings on a nearly complete subset of the JavaScript language. The authors specify and implement three refactorings: *rename property*, *extract module*, and *encapsulate property*. In summary, the proposed refactorings aim to transform

ES5 code in code that is more maintainable. However, they do not transform the code to the new JavaScript standard.

Previous works have also investigated the migration of legacy code, implemented in procedural languages, to object-oriented code, including the transformation of C functions to C++ function templates [18] and the adoption of class methods in PHP [19].

8   Final Remarks

In this paper, we report a study on replacing structures that emulate classes in legacy JavaScript code by native structures introduced by ES6, which can contribute to foster software reuse. We present a set of migration rules based on the most frequent use of class emulations in ES5. We then convert eight legacy JavaScript systems to use ES6 classes. In our study, we detail cases that are straightforward to migrate (the good parts), cases that require manual and ad-hoc migration (the bad parts), and cases that cannot be migrated due to limitations and restrictions of ES6 (the ugly parts). This study indicates that the migration rules are sound but incomplete, since most of the studied systems (75%) contain instances of bad and/or ugly cases. We also collect the perceptions of JavaScript developers about migrating their code to use the new syntax for classes. Our findings suggest that (a) proposals to automatically translate from ES5 to ES6 classes can be challenging and risky; (b) developers tend to move to ES6, but compatibility issues are making them postpone their decisions; (c) developer opinions diverge about the use of transpilers to keep compatibility with ES5; (d) there are demands for new class-related features in JavaScript, such as static fields, method deprecation, and partial classes.

As future work, we intend to enrich our research in two directions. First, we plan to extend our study migrating a larger set of JavaScript systems. In this way, we can identify other instances of bad and ugly cases. Second, we plan to implement a refactoring tool for a JavaScript IDE. This tool should be able to semi-automatically handle the good cases, and also alert developers about possible bad and ugly cases.

Acknowledgments. This research is supported by CNPq, CAPES and Fapemig.

References

1. Kienle, H.: It's about time to take JavaScript (more) seriously. IEEE Softw. **27**(3), 60–62 (2010)
2. Ocariza Jr., F.S., Pattabiraman, K., Zorn, B.: JavaScript errors in the wild: an empirical study. In: 22nd IEEE International Symposium on Software Reliability Engineering (ISSRE), pp. 100–109 (2011)
3. Nederlof, A., Mesbah, A., van Deursen, A.: Software engineering for the web: the state of the practice. In: 36th International Conference on Software Engineering (ICSE), pp. 4–13 (2014)

4. Borges, H., Hora, A., Valente, M.T.: Understanding the factors that impact the popularity of GitHub repositories. In: 32nd International Conference on Software Maintenance and Evolution (ICSME), pp. 1–10 (2016)

5. Borning, A.H.: Classes versus prototypes in object-oriented languages. In: ACM Fall Joint Computer Conference, pp. 36–40 (1986)

6. Guha, A., Saftoiu, C., Krishnamurthi, S.: The essence of JavaScript. In: D'Hondt, T. (ed.) ECOOP 2010. LNCS, vol. 6183, pp. 126–150. Springer, Heidelberg (2010). doi:10.1007/978-3-642-14107-2_7

7. European Association for Standardizing Information and Communication Systems (ECMA). ECMAScript Language Specification, 6th edn. (2015)

8. Silva, L.H., Ramos, M., Valente, M.T., Bergel, A., Anquetil, N.: Does JavaScript software embrace classes? In: 22nd IEEE International Conference on Software Analysis, Evolution, and Reengineering (SANER), pp. 73–82 (2015)

9. Silva, L.H., Hovadick, D., Valente, M.T., Bergel, A., Anquetil, N., Etien, A.: JSClassFinder: a tool to detect class-like structures in JavaScript. In: 6th Brazilian Conference on Software (CBSoft), Tools Demonstration Track, pp. 113–120 (2015)

10. Hafiz, M., Hasan, S., King, Z., Wirfs-Brock, A.: Growing a language: an empirical study on how (and why) developers use some recently-introduced and/or recently-evolving JavaScript features. J. Syst. Softw. (JSS) **121**, 191–208 (2016)

11. Gama, W., Alalfi, M., Cordy, J., Dean, T.: Normalizing object-oriented class styles in JavaScript. In: 14th IEEE International Symposium on Web Systems Evolution (WSE), pp. 79–83 (2012)

12. Nagappan, N., Ball, T.: Use of relative code churn measures to predict system defect density. In: 27th International Conference on Software Engineering (ICSE), pp. 284–292 (2005)

13. Fowler, M.: Refactoring: Improving the Design of Existing Code. Addison-Wesley, Boston (1999)

14. Apel, S., Kästner, C.: An overview of feature-oriented software development. J. Object Technol. **8**(5), 49–84 (2009)

15. Silva, L.H., Valente, M.T., Bergel, A.: Statically identifying class dependencies in legacy JavaScript systems: first results. In: 24th IEEE International Conference on Software Analysis, Evolution, and Reengineering (SANER), Early Research Achievements (ERA) Track, pp. 1–5 (2017)

16. Rostami, S., Eshkevari, L., Mazinanian, D., Tsantalis, N.: Detecting function constructors in JavaScript. In: 32nd IEEE International Conference on Software Maintenance and Evolution (ICSME), pp. 1–5 (2016)

17. Feldthaus, A., Millstein, T.D., Møller, A., Schäfer, M., Tip, F.: Refactoring towards the good parts of JavaScript. In: 26th Conference on Object-Oriented Programming (OOPSLA), pp. 189–190 (2011)

18. Siff, M., Reps, T.: Program generalization for software reuse: from C to C++. In: 4th Symposium on Foundations of Software Engineering (FSE), pp. 135–146 (1996)

19. Kyriakakis, P., Chatzigeorgiou, A.: Maintenance patterns of large-scale PHP web applications. In: 30th IEEE International Conference on Software Maintenance and Evolution (ICSME), pp. 381–390 (2014)

Tools Demonstrations

DyMMer-NFP: Modeling Non-functional Properties and Multiple Context Adaptation Scenarios in Software Product Lines

Anderson G. Uchôa[1]([✉]), Luan P. Lima[1], Carla I.M. Bezerra[1,3],
José Maria Monteiro[2], and Rossana M.C. Andrade[2,3]

[1] Federal University of Ceará, UFC Quixadá, Quixadá, Brazil
andersonguchoa@gmail.com, luan_pereira_lima@hotmail.com,
carlailane@ufc.br
[2] Computer Science Department, Federal University of Ceará,
UFC Fortaleza, Fortaleza, Brazil
{monteiro,rossana}@ufc.br
[3] Group of Computer Networks, Software Engineering and Systems (GREat),
Federal University of Ceará, Fortaleza, Brazil

Abstract. In Software Product Lines (SPLs), the modeling of non-functional properties (NFPs) and context adaptation scenarios are important activities, once they make possible the identification of inter-dependencies constraints between functional requirements (FR) and NFP, according to a specific adaptation context scenario. However, there are few tools to help domain engineers to represent NFPs and context adaptation scenarios. To deal with this problem, we propose DyMMer-NFP, an extension of the DyMMer tool to support the modeling of NFPs and multiple contextual adaptation scenarios in feature models. DyMMer-NFP uses a catalog with 39 NFPs. Each NFP in this catalog were mapped according to each quality characteristic and sub-characteristics presented in the ISO/IEC 25010 SQuaRE product quality model. To specify the interdependencies between NFPs and features, DyMMer-NFP has used the concept of contribution links. In order to make it easier to evaluate DyMMer-NFP two datasets, called AFFOgaTO and ESPREssO, were made available for free.

Keywords: Feature models · Non-functional properties · Dynamic Software Product Lines

1 Introduction

One of the main concepts in Software Product Lines (SPLs) is the variability, which can be defined as the possibility of setting or as the ability of a system or software artifact has to be changed, customized or configured for a particular context [3]. SPLs treat variability using a design artifact called feature model,

R.M.C. Andrade—Research Scholarship - DT Level 2, sponsored by CNPq.

G. Botterweck and C. Werner (Eds.): ICSR 2017, LNCS 10221, pp. 175–183, 2017.
DOI: 10.1007/978-3-319-56856-0_12

which captures the similarities and variabilities between the possible configurations of products in a particular domain [9]. This artifact represents the variations in software architecture. In SPLs, variants are typically set during the SPL development cycle at design time. However, recently, Dynamic Software Product Lines (DSPLs) were proposed as a way to promote runtime variability, where variants can be selected and change their behavior at runtime [3]. DSPL aims to produce software capable to adapt according to the needs of users and resources constraints at runtime. In a DSPL, variation points are firstly bound when the software is released, matching initial environment settings. However, at runtime, whether the context changes, it is possible to rebind the variation points, in order to adapt the system to the new, changed, environment settings [4]. Thus, in a DSPL feature model, the features can be added, removed and modified at runtime in a managed way [1].

Nevertheless, feature models do not capture Non-Functional Properties (NFP) explicitly neither influence these properties to achieve alternative configurations of a product variant. Representing NFP in SPL or DSPL might be a rather complex activity. Given a particular context, configuration rules, features constraints and preferences of stakeholders, must all be considered [10]. Although the NFP represent an important aspect related to the quality of a SPL, modeling NFP techniques are not completely suitable for SPL engineering, as indicated in an extensive literature survey [7].

A major challenge in DSPLs is to enable the support of scenarios with context adaptation and non-functional properties (NFP). The modeling of multiple context adaptation scenarios in DSPL feature models is an important mechanism for DSPL engineering, specifically in Domain Engineering where system features must be specified to accommodate context variations, and therefore, depending on the context, one set of features will be activated and the other will be deactivated [5].

In our previous work, we developed a tool called, DyMMer [2], to automatically support the evaluation of SPL and DSPL feature models based on a catalog of 40 quality measures. Currently, DyMMer is able to import a feature model in XML format, represent visually a feature model and edit it, adding context adaptations and context rules to the activation and deactivation of features. Besides, DyMMer is also capable of computing 40 quality measures, in which 8 are specific for DSPLs and 32 can be used in both SPLs and DSPLs [2].

In this work, we present an extension of the DyMMer tool, called DyMMer-NFP, to support the modeling of NFPs and multiple contextual adaptation scenarios in feature models. DyMMer-NFP uses a catalog with 39 NFPs (showed in Fig. 1), identified initially by [11]. Next, the 39 NFPs in this catalog were mapped according to each quality characteristic and sub-characteristics presented in the ISO/IEC 25010 SQuaRE product quality model [8]. Finally, to specify the interdependencies between NFPs and features we have used the concept of goal-oriented modeling, in particular the concept of contribution links [12].

The remainder of this paper is organized as follows. Section 2 the DyMMer tool is presented in detail, which includes the main features and architecture.

Section 3 describe the main features added to the DyMMer-NFP and presents a NFPs catalog to assist in the identification and NFPs modeling in DSPL feature models. Section 4 describes how to use the DyMMer-NFP to NFPs modeling through a set of tasks. Finally, Sect. 5 the conclusion and future work are described.

2 Background

DyMMer (*Dynamic Feature Model Tool Based on Measures*) is a tool originally developed to extract measures from different feature models, which can be described using the file format (XML) proposed by the S.P.L.O.T[1] feature models repository. So, DyMMer receives as input a XML file and creates an in memory representation for this feature model. The DyMMer was developed using JAVA and offers a series of functionalities, organized in three main layers [2]:

- **Feature Model Viewer** - allows the visualization of feature models according to the selected context;
- **Feature Model Editor** - allows the insertion, exclusion and edition of context adaptations. DyMMer considers that context and non-context features are represented in a single feature model; and
- **Data Exportation** - allows to export the values generated from the quality measures applied to the feature models with and without context for a spreadsheet in *Microsoft Office Excel* format.

Although DyMMer presents functionalities that allow domain engineers to extract quality measures and to edit feature models, it does not support the addition and removal of features and cardinality groups. Besides, DyMMer does not support the managing of NFPs, as well as multiple context adaptations scenarios in a same feature model. Thus, in order to surpass the lack of these functionalities, we extend the DyMMer giving rise to a new tool called DyMMer-NFP. The DyMMer-NFP code and its documentation are available *online*[2]. The new features incorporated by DyMMer-NFP are presented in the next section.

3 DyMMer-NFP Main Features

In this section we present the main features added in the DyMMer-NFP.

Creating a Feature Model. In addition to importing existing feature models which must be described in the S.P.L.O.T format, DyMMer-NFP makes it possible to create new feature models using the FODA method notation [6]. It is possible to create mandatory and optional features, XOR and OR cardinality groups, as well as inclusion and exclusion constraints (see Fig. 2. ③).

---

[1] S.P.L.O.T - http://www.splot-research.org/.
[2] https://github.com/anderson-uchoa/DyMMer.

Modeling Non-functional Properties. DyMMer-NFP makes it possible to represent NFPs in a feature model. For this, we have used a NFPs catalog (showed in Fig. 1), identified initially by [11]. Next, the 39 NFPs in this catalog were mapped according to each quality characteristic and sub-characteristics presented in the ISO/IEC 25010 SQuaRE product quality model [8] (see Fig. 2 ①). This catalog works as a guide for the identification of NFPs that emerge at runtime. Thus, the NFPs catalog was organized in several levels. The 1st level represents the root of our classification schema. The 2nd level is composed of each quality characteristic and the 3rd level represents the quality sub-characteristics related to each quality characteristic. Finally, the 4th level represents the NFPs identified in [11]. The quality characteristics mapped in this catalog are: *Functional suitability*, *Performance efficiency*, *Reliability*, *Security* e *Usability*. Currently, the DyMMer-NFP supports the modeling of 39 NFPs, which can also be used in both SPLs and DSPLs feature models.

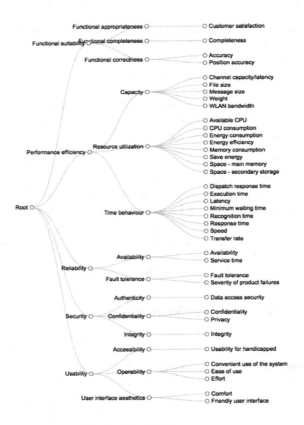

Fig. 1. The NFPs catalog.

Defining Context Adaptation Scenarios. DyMMer-NFP makes it possible to edit a specific feature model, adding or removing context adaptation scenarios. The addition of context adaptation scenarios is represented by a hierarchical list consisting of two specification levels (see Fig. 2. ②). Thus for each added context adaptation scenario a domain engineer must add context information with their respective variations, specify which features should be activated or deactivated, and define constraints. A DSPL feature model may have one or more context adaptation scenarios. DyMMer-NFP enables the domain engineer to handle DSPLs feature models. It is important to emphasize that the S.P.L.O.T does not support DSPLs modeling.

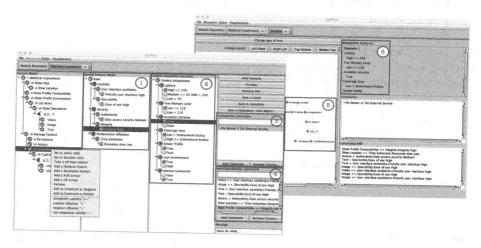

Fig. 2. An overview of the DyMMer-NFP tool: ① quality feature model editor, ② context adaptation scenarios editor, ③ cross-tree constraints editor, ④ interdependencies constraints editor, ⑤ visualizing feature model configuration, ⑥ selecting context adaptation scenarios.

Specifying Interdependencies Constraints Between Features and NFPs. DyMMer-NFP makes it possible to specify the interdependencies between NFPs and features (see Fig. 2. ④). To specify this constraints we have added a concept of goal-oriented modeling, in particular the concept of contribution links [12]. In this way, we assign interdependence constraints for each feature in a given context. These features may have four types of interdependence constraints over an NFP:

- "++" - the feature completely satisfies an NFP if it is activated;
- "- -" - the feature does not completely satisfy an NFP if it is activated;
- "+" - the feature has a positive influence on an NFP if it is activated; and
- "-" - the feature has a negative influence on an NFP if it is activated.

Visualizing Feature Model Configuration. DyMMer-NFP makes it possible to view the feature model configuration (see Fig. 2 ⑤–⑥). The visualization of the feature model configuration can be done in two ways: (i) after adding a context adaptation scenario in editing; and (ii) by means of the feature model viewer layer. The visualization of the feature model configurations after adding a context adaptation scenario, for example, is possible through the preview functionality, allowing the domain engineer to easily observe the feature model configuration during its editing. In this way, after each addition of a new context adaptation scenario the domain engineer can view one or more feature model configurations.

4   Using DyMMer-NFP to Modeling Non-functional Properties

The use of the DyMMer-NFP to modeling NFPs in feature models consists in running a set of tasks showed in Fig. 3 and in the tool demonstration video[3]. These task are discussed next.

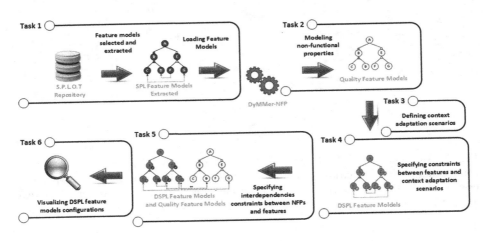

Fig. 3. Using DyMMer-NFP.

Task 1 - Importing Feature Models from S.P.L.O.T. The first task is to import a feature model from S.P.L.O.T repository or create a new feature model. In order to make it easier to evaluate DyMMer-NFP two datasets can be used, they are: (i) AFFOgaTO dataset is composed of a set of 218 feature models fetched from S.P.L.O.T repository; and (ii) ESPREssO dataset is composed of a set of the 30 DSPLs feature models extracted from literature and represented in the XML format, following the S.P.L.O.T specifications. The AFFOgaTO[4]

---

[3] Demonstration video - https://youtu.be/FCn0zEfAEBs.

[4] AFFOgaTO - https://goo.gl/gye5ma.

and ESPREssO[5] datasets are available for free download and can be used by the software engineering community.

Task 2 - Modeling Non-functional Properties. After to import or create a new feature model, we must represent the non-functional properties that are relevant for the feature model. These NFPs are specified according to the NFPs catalog and represented visually in DyMMer-NFP.

Task 3 - Defining Context Adaptation Scenarios. Next, a set of context adaptation scenarios can be defined for a given feature model. Context adaptation scenarios are added in a hierarchical list, where context information are added with their quantifiers and qualifiers. These quantifiers are defined by relational operators: greater than ($>$), less than ($<$), greater than or equal to ($>=$), less than or equal to ($<=$), equal ($=$) and different ($<>$). Followed by a value of type: *string*, integer, *float* or boolean. If this quantifier is defined by a numeric range, a logical operator is added that can be of the type: (OR) or (AND), followed by another value of type *string*, integer, *float* or boolean.

Task 4 - Specifying Constraints Between Features and Context Adaptation Scenarios. The next task is to analyze and specify the constraints between features and context adaptation scenarios. This task aims to verify which features should be activated and deactivated in a given context adaptation scenario. To perform this task we must specify which features are activated and deactivated for each context adaptation scenario.

Task 5 - Specifying Interdependencies Constraints Between NFPs and Features. After specifying the context adaptation scenarios, that is, which features are activated and deactivated in each context adaptation scenario, the interdependencies constraints between NFPs and the context features can be defined. Thus, for each context adaptation scenario, the user needs to specify the contribution links between each feature, activated or deactivated in this current scenario, and one or more NFPs.

Task 6 - Visualizing DSPL Feature Models Configurations. After modeling the context adaptation scenarios and the interdependencies constraints between NFPs and context features, we can visualize the configuration of a specific feature model.

5   Conclusion and Future Work

This paper presents DyMMer-NFP, an extension of the DyMMer tool to support the modeling of NFPs and multiple contextual adaptation scenarios in feature models. DyMMer-NFP uses a catalog with 39 NFPs (showed in Fig. 1), identified initially by [11]. Next, the 39 NFPs in this catalog were mapped according to each quality characteristic and sub-characteristics presented in the ISO/IEC

---

[5] ESPREssO - https://goo.gl/ONfTL3.

25010 SQuaRE product quality model [8]. Finally, to specify the interdependencies between NFPs and features we have used the concept of goal-oriented modeling, in particular the concept of contribution links [12]. The modeling of multiple context adaptation scenarios in DSPL feature models is at the same time an important mechanism and a challenging task. So, DyMMer-NFP can help domain engineers in creating better adaptive software, guiding the specification of the feature model, besides making it easier to model the NFPs established by the stakeholders and to represent the relationship (including constraints) between features and NFPs. Thus, DyMMer-NFP enables the analysis of the impacts that a feature have on one or more NFPs in different context adaptations, ensuring that products derived from the DSPL continue serving in a satisfactory way the NFPs previously established. In this way, the domain engineers are guided to build DSPLs that satisfies the specified NFPs: adding features that increases the possibility of achieving a particular NFP and removing (or minimizing) features that reduces this probability, ensuring an improvement in the quality of the DSPL. As future work, we intend to formally verify whether the NFPs in a specific DSPL feature model match the expected results of the process of runtime reconfiguration. In addition, we plan to add new NFPs in the catalog and to identify thresholds for each NFP.

References

1. Bencomo, N., Hallsteinsen, S., De Almeida, E.S.: A view of the dynamic software product line landscape. Computer 45(10), 36–41 (2012)
2. Bezerra, C.I., Barbosa, J., Freires, J.H., Andrade, R., Monteiro, J.M.: DyMMer: a measurement-based tool to support quality evaluation of DSPL feature models. In: Proceedings of the 20th International Systems and Software Product Line Conference, pp. 314–317. ACM (2016)
3. Bosch, J.: Software variability management. In: Proceedings of the 26th International Conference on Software Engineering, pp. 720–721. IEEE Computer Society (2004)
4. Capilla, R., Bosch, J., Kang, K.C.: Systems and Software Variability Management. Springer, Heidelberg (2013)
5. Capilla, R., Bosch, J., Trinidad, P., Ruiz-Cortés, A., Hinchey, M.: An overview of dynamic software product line architectures and techniques: observations from research and industry. J. Syst. Softw. 91, 3–23 (2014)
6. Czarnecki, K., Helsen, S., Eisenecker, U.: Formalizing cardinality-based feature models and their specialization. Softw. Process: Improv. Pract. 10(1), 7–29 (2005)
7. Hammani, F.Z.: Survey of non-functional requirements modeling and verification of software product lines. In: 2014 IEEE Eighth International Conference on Research Challenges in Information Science (RCIS), pp. 1–6. IEEE (2014)
8. ISO/IEC: 25010: Systems and software engineering - Systems and software Quality Requirements and Evaluation (SQuaRE) - System and software quality models. Technical report, ISO/IEC, Switzerland (2011)
9. Kang, K.C., Cohen, S.G., Hess, J.A., Novak, W.E., Peterson, A.S.: Feature-oriented domain analysis (FODA) feasibility study. Technical report, DTIC Document (1990)

10. Sanchez, L.E., Diaz-Pace, J.A., Zunino, A., Moisan, S., Rigault, J.P.: An approach based on feature models and quality criteria for adapting component-based systems. J. Softw. Eng. Res. Dev. **3**(1), 1–30 (2015)
11. Soares, L.R., Potena, P., Carmo Machado, I., Crnkovic, I., Almeida, E.S.: Analysis of non-functional properties in software product lines: a systematic review. In: 2014 40th EUROMICRO Conference on Software Engineering and Advanced Applications, pp. 328–335. IEEE (2014)
12. Van Lamsweerde, A.: Goal-oriented requirements engineering: a guided tour. In: 2001 Proceedings of the Fifth IEEE International Symposium on Requirements Engineering, pp. 249–262. IEEE (2001)

Identification and Prioritization of Reuse Opportunities with JReuse

Johnatan Oliveira[1(✉)], Eduardo Fernandes[1], Gustavo Vale[2], and Eduardo Figueiredo[1]

[1] Department of Computer Science, Federal University of Minas Gerais, Belo Horizonte, Brazil
{johnatan.si,eduardofernandes,figueiredo}@dcc.ufmg.br
[2] Department of Informatics and Mathematics, University of Passau, Passau, Germany
vale@fim.uni-passau.de

Abstract. Software reuse aims to decrease the development efforts by using existing software components in the development of new systems. Previous work propose tools to support the identification of reuse opportunities. Such tools apply different techniques, such as software design and source code analyses. However, none of them combines lexical analysis with prioritization and identification of reuse opportunities in several systems of a single domain. To fill this gap, this paper proposes JReuse, a tool that computes naming similarity for classes and methods of Java systems. Based on naming similarity, JReuse identifies reuse opportunities and prioritizes them by their frequency among systems. We evaluate JReuse with 35 e-commerce systems collected from GitHub by assessing the agreement among the JReuse recommendations and the opinion of a group of experts. We observe agreements of 89% and 72% for classes and methods, respectively. Therefore, our data suggest that JReuse is able to recommend reusable classes and methods in a given domain.

Keywords: Software reuse · Reuse opportunity · Supporting tool

1 Introduction

Software reuse is a development strategy in which existing software components support the development of new systems [4]. The reuse of existing components potentially increases the software quality and the developers' productivity, since reused components are recurrently evaluated and improved, instead of developed from scratch [6, 7]. Previous works propose tools with different techniques to support the identification of reuse opportunities [5, 9, 14]. For instance, the Guru tool [5] relies on source code analysis to identify reuse opportunities based on the similarity of attributes from different classes. Another tool, called Aesop [9], relies on the analysis of architectural diagrams. Finally, CodeBroker [14] performs run-time identification and prioritization of opportunities based on semantic code analysis and documentation. However, none of them combines lexical analysis with the prioritization of reuse opportunities. In addition, they do not aim to analyze several systems of a single domain.

This paper proposes and evaluates JReuse, a tool for identification and prioritization of reuse opportunities in Java systems. JReuse computes the naming similarity

© Springer International Publishing AG 2017
G. Botterweck and C. Werner (Eds.): ICSR 2017, LNCS 10221, pp. 184–191, 2017.
DOI: 10.1007/978-3-319-56856-0_13

(i.e., lexical analysis) of classes and methods among systems. Therefore, the tool aims to analyze systems from a domain with similar naming conventions. In addition, the tool prioritizes the identified reuse opportunities by their frequency among different systems. We evaluate JReuse with 35 e-commerce systems collected from GitHub[1]. In this evaluation, we compare the reuse opportunities identified by JReuse with the opinion of a group of e-commerce experts. We observe an average agreement of 89% between the tool and experts with respect to classes. Similarly, the average agreement was 72% between JReuse and the experts' opinion for methods.

Our main contribution with this paper is the JReuse tool. The potential users of the tool are software developers and engineers concerned about the identification of reuse opportunities at class and method levels in systems of a specific domain. The recommendations provided by JReuse have different practical applications. We provide some examples as follows. First, methods and partial classes can guide developers in the implementation of a new system. Second, the results provided by JReuse may support recovering a partial design for systems of a domain. Third, the recommendations provided by JReuse can support the evolution of existing systems.

The remainder of this paper is organized as follows. Section 2 discusses related work. Section 3 presents JReuse. Section 4 provides the tool's evaluation. Section 5 discusses threats to validity. Section 6 concludes the paper and suggests future work.

2   Related Work

Different techniques may support the identification of reuse opportunities. Maarek et al. [5] proposes the Guru tool that relies on the source code analysis. Guru groups code elements that implement similar functionalities based on the extraction of attributes of classes. However, Guru does not provide a general view of the reuse opportunities, via prioritization of opportunities, and requires that developers search for specific functionalities of interest instead. Monroe and Garlan [9] present Aesop that relies on architectural analysis. The authors assume that code analysis does not suffice to identify reuse opportunities, due to the limitation of representing concerns via code. Hence, Aesop analyzes the architectural diagram of a system to identify the main components and its interactions. Unlike Guru and Aesop, JReuse identifies and prioritizes reuse opportunities without requiring the developer to provide a search key.

Ye and Fischer [14] present the closest technique to ours, called CodeBroker, for identification of reuse opportunities at run-time using information retrieval. Their tool relies on semantic analysis and performs both source code and documentation analysis. CodeBroker provides a list of methods as reuse opportunities prioritized by their relevance. In turn, JReuse applies lexical analysis, i.e. a lighter technique for analysis of multiple systems at the same time. JReuse also aims to support reuse by identifying and prioritizing not only methods as reuse opportunities, but also classes.

---

[1] https://github.com/.

3   JReuse

This section presents the JReuse tool. Section 3.1 describes the tool's architecture and the algorithm adopted for similarity computation. Section 3.2 presents the main implementation technologies and the user interface of JReuse. An illustrative video of JReuse, as the source code of the tool, are both available in our research website [11].

3.1   Architecture

JReuse is an Eclipse plug-in that computes similarity among names of classes and methods to identify the most frequent terms in systems of a single domain. Figure 1 presents the architecture of JReuse. Four modules compose the tool, namely *Collector*, *Extractor*, *Similarity Calculator*, and *Ranking Calculator*.

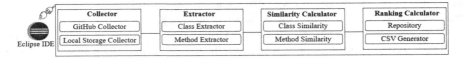

Fig. 1.   Architecture of JReuse

Collector collects a set of systems for identification of reuse opportunities. Two sub-modules compose this module: GitHub Collector and Local Storage Collector. GitHub Collector is responsible for collecting systems from GitHub given a search string provided by the user. Local Storage Collector collects systems from a local directory informed by the user. The user may choose between both means to collect systems. *Extractor* extracts the code elements necessary for computation of naming similarity. This module has two sub-modules. Class Extractor is responsible to retrieve both names and types of classes. Method Extractor does the same for methods.

Similarity Calculator calculates naming similarity among classes, through the Class Similarity sub-module, and Method Similarity does the same for methods. Both sub-modules use the Levenshtein's algorithm for naming similarity computation (details in the paragraph Similarity Algorithm). Finally, *Ranking Calculator* generates the sorted list of reuse opportunities. Such list prioritizes the opportunities based on a similarity score, i.e., higher scores come first. CSV Generator and Repository sub-modules export the JReuse results as CSV and persists the results on the repository.

Similarity Algorithm.   Previous work [1, 3, 15] propose algorithms for naming similarity computation. We chose the Levenshtein's algorithm [15] because of its simplicity. This algorithm relies on lexical analysis to computes a similarity score between two strings. Such score ranges from 0% to 100%. The higher the score, the more similar the strings are. We consider two names as similar if their score is at least 75%. We derived this value empirically, given naming conventions for classes and methods. Thus, we prevent elements with similar names that address different concerns. For instance, two classes named `Customer` and `CustomerDAO` have score equals 72%. The first one is an entity abstraction and the second one is a data base entity.

Limit for Recommendation. We defined two limits to the amount of classes and methods recommended as reuse opportunities. For classes, the limit is 15% of systems in the analyzed domain. For instance, considering the data set presented in Sect. 4.1, the limit of 15% means that a class should appear in at least 6 out of 35 systems. In our empirical analysis, several classes appear in a small amount of systems, eventually in just one system of our data set. Therefore, this limit aims to prevent the recommendation of non-frequent classes. For methods, the limit is 3, i.e. a method has to appear in at least 3 classes from different systems to be recommended. The limits of classes and methods can be adjusted depending on characteristics of the data set.

3.2 Implementation Technologies and User Interface

We implemented JReuse using the Java programming language with support of the Java Development Tools (JDT). JDT provides libraries for accessing and manipulating the Java source code and supports the source code parsing, as the retrieval of names of classes and methods of Java systems. We analyze the source code structure of target systems via Abstract Syntax Tree (AST). JReuse works only for Java systems, although the technique behind the tool applies to other object-oriented programming languages. The main reasons for selecting Java are: (i) it has a large support for code analysis, including libraries for AST generation, (ii) it is one of the most popular languages [2], and (iii) software reuse have been investigating in the context of Java software systems [8, 12].

Figure 2 illustrates the data grid view of JReuse with results for methods recommended as reuse opportunities. The grid for classes is similar. There are four columns in the view discusses as follows. "*#*" presents is an identifier per recommendation sorted by the prioritization score. *Class* provides the name of the source class for each method. *Method* shows the method name. *Prioritization* presents the frequency of each method among the systems of the analyzed data set (more details in Sect. 4). In addition, the button *Save as CSV* exports the results as a CSV file.

#	Class	Method	Prioritization
1	Product	productList	72%
2	Product	changeStock	68%
3	Product	delete	68%
4	Product	update	58%
5	Product	moveItens	58%
6	Product	processRegister	40%

Fig. 2. Data grid view with a list of methods identified by JReuse

4   Evaluation

This section evaluates JReuse. Section 4.1 presents the study settings. Sections 4.2 and 4.3 discuss the evaluation results at class and method levels, respectively.

4.1   Evaluation Settings

This evaluation aims to assess both the JReuse correctness and whether it is able to identify reuse opportunities in Java e-commerce systems. Regarding the tool correctness, we created many test cases and we manually searched for reusable classes and methods in the e-commerce systems. Then, we compared them with the results of JReuse. The results were equals. Thereby, we conclude that JReuse works correctly. In turn, regarding the ability of JReuse to identify reuse opportunities, we conducted a two-level evaluation. First, we investigate if the highly prioritized classes provided by JReuse are specific of a domain. Second, we investigate if the highly prioritized methods are meaningful to the class they were implemented. To support both evaluation steps, we rely on a group of experts composed of four software engineers with experience in software development and reuse, including e-commerce systems. We considered classes and methods as reuse opportunities just if all members of the group of experts agreed with the tool.

We designed three steps to the evaluation of JReuse. First, we run the tool with a data set composed by 35 e-commerce systems collected from GitHub. Second, we analyzed all classes recommended by JReuse. Third, from the top-ten highly prioritized classes, we verified the recommended methods. We chose the e-commerce domain for two main reasons. First, there is a large amount of systems of this domain available for download in GitHub. Second, since e-commerce is a well-defined domain in terms of requirements, e-commerce systems potentially have several reuse opportunities for identification. We collected the systems in November 2016. They have in total around 500 KLOC (mean of 46 KLOC per system), 3 K classes (mean of 368 classes), and 18 K methods (mean of 1 K methods).

4.2   Results at Class Level

Table 1 presents the reuse opportunities identified by JReuse at class level in our data set. The columns represent the class name, the class frequency, and if the classes are specific of the e-commerce domain according to the group of experts. We double the three columns due to space constraints, and the most frequent classes come first at the left side. As stated in Sect. 3.1, JReuse does not recommend classes that appear in less than 15% of the systems (limit). Thus, any class under this condition does not appear in Table 1. The column "Domain Specific" represents the opinion of the group of experts, in which "Y" means that all experts agree that the class is specific of the e-commerce domain, and "N" means that at least one expert does not agree.

Table 1. Results at class level

Class name	Class frequency	Domain specific	Class name	Class frequency	Domain specific
Product	80%	Y	Category	35%	Y
PaymentType	69%	Y	ProductService	29%	Y
Client	58%	Y	Order	26%	Y
ProductDao	52%	Y	LoginController	20%	N
ClientDao	52%	Y	UserDao	18%	Y
Item	49%	Y	ProductServiceImpl	18%	Y
ShoppingCart	49%	Y	ShoppingCartController	18%	Y
User	49%	N	OrderedProduct	15%	Y
Customer	40%	Y	ShoppingCartService	15%	Y

The classes presented in Table 1 appear in several systems. For instance, the class *Product* appears in 80% (28 out of 35) of the systems under analysis. Hence, this class probably will be necessary in the development of a new e-commerce system. Regarding the data reported at domain specific column, we observe that the group of experts agrees that most classes are specific of the e-commerce domain. The group of experts disagrees just in the case of *User* and *LoginController*. In summary, the agreement between the classes JReuse recommended and the group of experts is around 89%, a high value for agreement. We conclude that, in general, the reuse opportunities identified by JReuse at class level are actually reusable.

4.3 Results at Method Level

Table 2 summarizes the results for methods identified by JReuse as reuse opportunities. This analysis relies on the top-ten highly prioritized classes from Table 1. The rows list mean, maximum, and standard deviation for the last three columns. The second column presents of methods identified as reuse opportunities for the top-ten classes. The third column presents the percentage of methods in at least a half of similar classes in different systems. With this column, we aim to highlight the methods that occur more frequently in the analyzed classes. The fourth column presents the percentage of agreement from the group of experts with respect to the highly prioritized methods.

For the top-ten classes, we observe an average of 11 methods per class identified as reuse opportunities (maximum of 15). That is, each highly prioritized class has a high amount of similar methods that support the implementation of new e-commerce systems. In addition, we observe a mean of 60% (maximum of 100%) of methods identified as reuse opportunities and that occur in at least 50% of similar classes in the analyzed systems. Finally, regarding the viewpoint of the domain experts, we observe an average agreement of 72% of methods pointed as specific of their respective classes. The agreement reached up to 100% for methods of the class *User*. In summary, as stated in Sect. 4.2, we conclude that methods identified by JReuse are meaningful and, consequently, reusable in association with the identified classes.

Table 2. Results for methods from the top-ten classes

Measure	# Identified methods	% Methods with ≥ 50% frequency	Domain-specific methods
Mean	11	60%	72%
Max.	15	100%	100%
Std. Dev.	3	20%	20%

5 Threats to Validity

We discuss the main threats to the study validity, as the respective treatments, as follows. Our discussion relies on the guidelines proposed by Wohlin et al. [13].

Construct and Internal Validity. We conducted a careful filtering of systems collected from GitHub to evaluate JReuse. However, some threats may affect the correct filtering, as human factors that wrongly lead to the discard of a valid system for evaluation. We minimize this threat by adopting exclusion criteria described in our website [11]. Moreover, some threats may have affected our lexical classification of classes and methods. These threats include error in the nomenclature of classes and methods. To minimize this problem, and to identify bugs in the JReuse implementation, we randomly selected a sample of 10 e-commerce systems from our data set. We then identified the names of classes and methods manually from source code, in order to find synonyms. We compared our manually obtained results with the ones provided by JReuse and observed a low loss of 10% in synonym terms identified by the tool.

Conclusion and External Validity. We analyzed the data collected from JReuse manually, and two authors contributed to double-check such analysis. In addition, we derived empirically the limits for recommendation of classes and methods (see Sect. 3.1). Although both the analysis and the limit derivation may have been affected by human factors, we carefully conducted each activity to prevent biases and missing data, for instance. Finally, we evaluated JReuse with a set of 35 e-commerce systems collected from GitHub. Since our evaluation relies on a specific set of systems from a single domain, we may not generalize our study findings to any Java software systems. However, the systems of our data set are the most popular Java e-commerce systems on GitHub given by their number of stars. In addition to e-commerce, we evaluated JReuse in other three domains [10]: hospital, restaurant, and accounting.

6 Conclusion and Future Work

This paper presents JReuse, a tool for identification and prioritization of reuse opportunities in Java systems. Our tool relies on lexical source code analysis. JReuse computes naming similarly, using the Levenshtein's algorithm, for classes and methods extracted from a data set of systems from a specific domain. We evaluate the recommendations provided by JReuse at class and method levels. A group of experts assessed such recommendations with respect to their reusability in the context of e-commerce systems.

Agreements of 89% and 72% regarding classes and methods, respectively, suggest that JReuse is able to identify relevant reuse opportunities in both class and method levels for the e-commerce domain. These reuse opportunities can support, for instance, the reuse of parts of code, the recovery of a partial design for a system, or the evolution of existing systems.

As future work, we intend to implement the combination of similarity computation techniques, such as semantic analysis, to extend JReuse. We also aim to identify and prioritize reuse opportunities in systems implemented in languages other than Java.

Acknowledgments. This work was partially supported by CAPES, CNPq (grants 424340/2016-0 and 290136/2015-6), and FAPEMIG (grant PPM-00382-14).

References

1. Bilenko, M., Mooney, R.: Adaptive duplicate detection using learnable string similarity measures. In: 9th Conference on Knowledge Discovery and Data Mining (KDD), pp. 39–48 (2003)
2. Diakopoulos, N., Cass, S.: The Top Programming Languages 2015. http://spectrum.ieee.org/static/interactive-thetop-programming-languages-2015
3. Gitchell, D., Tran, N.: Sim: a utility for detecting similarity in computer programs. ACM SIGCSE Bull. **31**(1), 266–270 (1999)
4. Krueger, C.: Software reuse. ACM Comput. Surv. (CSUR) **24**(2), 131–183 (1992)
5. Maarek, Y., Berry, D., Kaiser, G.: An information retrieval approach for automatically constructing software libraries. IEEE Trans. Softw. Eng. (TSE) **17**(8), 800–813 (1991)
6. Mohagheghi, P., Conradi, R.: Quality, productivity and economic benefits of software reuse: a review of industrial studies. Empirical Softw. Eng. (ESE) **12**(5), 471–516 (2007)
7. Mohagheghi, P., Conradi, R., Killi, O., Schwarz, H.: An empirical study of software reuse vs. defect-density and stability. In: 26th ICSE, pp. 282–291 (2004)
8. Mojica, I., Adams, B., Nagappan, M., Dienst, S., Berger, T., Hassan, A.: A large-scale empirical study on software reuse in mobile apps. IEEE Softw. **31**(2), 78–86 (2014)
9. Monroe, R., Garlan, D.: Style-based reuse for software architectures. In: 4th ICSR, pp. 84–93 (1996)
10. Oliveira, J.: A method based on naming similarity to identify reuse opportunities. MSc dissertation, Federal University of Minas Gerais (UFMG), Belo Horizonte, Brazil (2016)
11. Oliveira, J., Fernandes, E., Vale, G., Figueiredo, E.: JReuse – Data of the Study. http://homepages.dcc.ufmg.br/~johnatan.si/jreuse
12. Roopa, M., Mani, V., Stefan, H.: An approach for enabling effective and systematic software reuse. In: 11th ICGSE, pp. 134–138 (2016)
13. Wohlin, C., Runeson, P., Höst, M., Ohlsson, M., Regnell, B., Wesslén, A.: Experimentation in Software Engineering. Springer Science & Business Media, Heidelberg (2012)
14. Ye, Y., Fischer, G.: Reuse-conducive development environments. Autom. Softw. Eng. (ASE) **12**(2), 199–235 (2005)
15. Yujian, L., Bo, L.: A normalized Levenshtein distance metric. IEEE Trans. Pattern Anal. Mach. Intell. (TPAMI) **29**(6), 1091–1095 (2007)

Doctoral Symposium

EcoData: Architecting Cross-Platform Software Ecosystem Applications

Marcelo França[1,2(✉)]

[1] COPPE/UFRJ – Federal University of Rio de Janeiro, Rio de Janeiro, Brazil
mafranca@cos.ufrj.br, mafranca@br.ibm.com
[2] IBM – International Business Machines Brazil, Rio de Janeiro, Brazil

Abstract. Software Ecosystems (SECOs) have been receiving an increasing amount of attention from both academia and industry. That could be explained by the open challenges pointed out by the Software Engineering community, as well as by the fact that many organizations adopt a more open and collaborative strategy to achieve innovation. While observing an evolution in the way platforms are used for developing applications, a specific type of SECO, which is centered on data, was identified: EcoData. It emerged in the "third model of computing platform", recognized by industry as the confluence of new technologies such as Cloud Computing, Big Data and Analytics, Mobility and Social Business – CAMS. By reviewing the literature, non-functional requirements for EcoData applications were identified, but without a reference architecture (RA). While a RA would be useful for new solutions, the research's goal is to provide a means for architecting and improving cross-platform SECO applications.

Keywords: Software ecosystem · Software architecture · CAMS

1 Introduction

From an organizational perspective, a Software Ecosystem (SECO) is defined as an environment where internal and external actors construct large software systems by reusing components, supported by a common platform [1]. As a relative new topic in Software Engineering (SE), its research has received more attention since 2007 [2].

At the same time, there is an everlasting demand for innovative solutions, since competitors are struggling to differentiate themselves by delivering more value to customers nowadays. Industry has to deal with the so called "digital transformation" [3], where changes associated with the application of digital technology are affecting human society. Thus, in order to reduce time-to-market whilst responding to such challenges, companies are moving from a traditional, independent strategy, to a more open, collaborative, and even agile approach, like crowdsourcing and SECO [1].

Despite the initial advances in SECO research, there are still several open challenges [4] and few contributions from industrial studies. Investigations performed for this PhD research helped us to identify two research issues: (1) the novelty of SECO research in SE implies in an incomplete SECO taxonomy [1], with the absence of a specific type of SECO that is centered on data, which is pivotal nowadays [5]; and (2) the lack of a SECO

© Springer International Publishing AG 2017
G. Botterweck and C. Werner (Eds.): ICSR 2017, LNCS 10221, pp. 195–200, 2017.
DOI: 10.1007/978-3-319-56856-0_14

reference architecture (RA) for applications targeting more than one platform, both on mobile (such as Windows, Android, and iOS) and in the cloud.

According to Taylor et al. [6], a RA is the set of principal design decisions that are applicable to multiple related systems with explicitly defined points of variation, usually within a domain – in our case, the SECO domain. RA could be leveraged as a roadmap for new SECO entrants, and a model for evaluating and improving existing SECO applications, due to the known correlation between software architecture and its quality and evolution, especially complex ones [7].

Three dimensions classically characterize a SECO: business, social and technical [8]. Focusing on the latter, this PhD's objective is to contribute to a body of knowledge with the definition of SECO architectures, by investigating non-functional requirements for today's applications targeting more than one platform (multihoming, for instance). The intent is to characterize a specific SECO type that is centered on data, spreading across multiple platforms and, then, to identify a set of non-functional requirements for applications targeting it (for example, portability and interoperability), and confirm it with specialists, i.e., subject matter experts (SME) from the industry. Finally, we will propose a RA addressing those requirements, documented as a set of architectural artifacts and a checklist plus a process, supporting the improvement of existing applications as outcome – since one could not be found in the literature.

Thus, the problem to be solved is how to architect and improve software applications targeting an EcoData, taking in consideration current technology trends, and according to the identified non-functional requirements. An important problem since there is not much information about data-centric cross-platform SECO applications.

The remainder of this paper is structured as follows: research questions are listed in Sect. 2, related work is discussed in Sect. 3, the proposed research methodology is defined in Sect. 4, and preliminary contributions are presented in Sect. 5. Finally, Sect. 6 concludes the paper with some remarks.

2   Research Questions

Based on the PhD objective, two hypotheses were established:

H_1: *A RA based on open standards and cross-platform mechanisms can address portability and interoperability requirements for applications targeting EcoData.*

H_2: *An EcoData RA that takes in consideration current industrial challenges (CAMS) is useful to architect new modern EcoData applications, as well as to evaluate and improve existing ones, by addressing a set of non-functional requirements.*

Considering the issues discussed in Sect. 1 and the aforementioned hypotheses, an initial research questions (RQs) set was established in order to help in narrowing the scope of this PhD research, and defining the RQs for answering H_1 and H_2:

RQ1: *What is already known about software architectures for SECO applications and platforms, especially when it comes to current technology trends and challenges?*

The goal was to study software architectures supporting existing SECO applications and platforms. To do so, besides conducting ad-hoc observations in industry, we conducted a systematic mapping study to find out what was already known regarding

SECO architectures and, at the same time, to identify common characteristics, besides problems yet to be addressed [9]. This RQ contributes to answer H_1.

RQ2: *What are the characteristics of data-centric SECO applications, which are cross platforms, i.e., not limited to a single technology or keystone organization?*

Throughout the investigation tasks performed in the first two years of the PhD research, RQ1 was answered and a specific type of SECO identified. It allowed us to establish RQ2 and propose seven EcoData characteristics [5], besides a complimentary SECO taxonomy. This RQ contributes to answer H_1.

RQ3: *What are the EcoData non-functional requirements, and how do they relate to current industry challenges?*

We are currently trying to answer this research question by conducting a survey with experts. This RQ intends to answer H_1 and contributes to answer H_2.

RQ4: *How should a RA be in order to address EcoData requirements, and how should we use it to evaluate and improve applications targeting that type of SECO?*

As Taylor explained [6], given two concrete architectural models of the system – "as is" and "to be" –, it is possible to create a diff. So, by using a RA, one could identify gaps related to implementation and define a roadmap for improving existing applications. We plan to conduct a case study with an industrial SECO platform. This RQ intends to answer H_1 and H_2.

3   Related Work

Bosch [1] has proposed a SECO taxonomy that identifies nine potential classes, according to a classification within two broad dimensions: category (end-user programming, application, and operating system) and platform (desktop, web, and mobile). He also argued that, before the desktop, mainframes and mini-computers existed and, in the era of ubiquitous computing, one can define other platforms besides mobile. As a result of our empirical observations, we adopted a "community focus", chronologically, as an additional dimension, proposing a complimentary taxonomy based on three SECO categories: Extra, Intra and Inter, respectively describing SECOs where developers focus on creating value-adding products on top of the platform, on growing the platform (with plug-ins, for instance), and finally on integrating platforms (interoperability). Bosch has also proposed a set of SECO architectural challenges [10], which includes integration via application program interfaces.

Similarly, Taylor [11] has discussed the importance of SECO software architectures, while also articulating a SPL-evolution view. According to him, a SECO's success may be assessed as regards to qualities such as reduced time-to-market, widespread use and adaptability, emphasizing SECO's platform. Conversely, our proposal focuses on applications targeting more than one SECO platforms.

Regarding a solution spreading across multiple platforms, Pérez et al. [12] proposed a RA for a domain-specific System-of-Systems (SoS). The authors developed their work from an industrial project and define a SoS as a composition of large heterogeneous and independent systems that leverage emergent behavior from their interaction. Albeit we ratify the importance of the integration among SECO components, the coupling seems to be lower than in a SoS, since it would be easier to replace them based on their APIs.

Finally, Christensen et al. [13] analyzed and designed a SECO architecture for a telemedicine platform. Their work could be considered broader, since it considers even the business SECO dimension, and at the same time more focused on design than architecture, since it describes low level implementation details. Our proposal is a high-level RA for EcoData. From an industrial perspective, our research is also interested in innovation enablers, in the so-called "third platform" [14–16], also known as CAMS - the confluence of Cloud Computing, Big Data and Analytics, Mobility and Social Business, plus Security and Internet of Things (IoT) technologies.

It can be concluded that related work does not completely exhaust the analysis of SECO architectures, at least related to EcoData. Also, they did not focus on CAMS challenges, although some of them describe desirable quality attributes. Most of the works focus on the platform itself and not on SECO applications, which is our case.

4   Research Methodology

The methodology used in this research is composed by the following activities:

STEP 1 (03/2014–08/2014) – Execute a broad and flexible literature review on SECO: a literature review was done in order to better understand SECO basis and its relations to SE. This activity is finished and helped in focusing the PhD scope;

STEP 2 (09/2014–02/2016) – Conduct an exploratory research on Software Architecture: a second literature review was done to better understand SECO from a Software Architecture perspective, while empirical observations in industry helped us to identify EcoData [5]. This activity is finished and helped answering RQ1 and RQ2;

STEP 3 (03/2016–08/2016) – Conduct a systematic mapping study to identify SECO's architectural challenges and desirable non-functional requirements: we wanted to find out what is already known about SECO architecture, and the challenges yet to be addressed. This is finished and helped answering RQ1, RQ2 and RQ3;

STEP 4 (09/2016–02/2017) – Evaluate the literature findings by surveying specialists: this activity is ongoing, and will help us to ratify the identified non-functional requirements, *i.e.*, to what extent industry's experts agree with them;

STEP 5 (09/2016–02/2017) – Write and present the Qualifying Exam: this activity is also ongoing, and will ratify this PhD proposal;

STEP 6 (03/2017–02/2018) – Propose a RA for EcoData: by addressing the identified non-functional requirements, the RA proposal will be described by a set of architectural diagrams, which were suggested by industry's SMEs during a survey (step #4). This activity, yet to be done, will help in answering RQ4;

STEP 7 (03/2018–06/2018) – Evaluate the proposed RA: considering the challenging nature of the process of evaluating a RA, we will adopt two methods: (i) instantiate EcoData RA in more than one platform as a service (PaaS) like IBM Bluemix [17], as POC (proof of concept), in order to conduct a case study based on a real scenario; and (ii) submit the RA's artifacts, plus the "roadmap" process and checklist, to a board of industry's SMEs (architects and developers from countries such as US and Brazil) for review. We will also compare it with other RAs, such as [12], with respect to commonalities. This activity, yet to be done, will help in answering RQ4;

STEP 8 (07/2018–02/2019) – Write and present the PhD Thesis: to be done, the following chapters are considered: (1) Introduction; (2) Overview of Software Ecosystems; (3) Architectural Evolution of Software Ecosystems; (4) EcoData: A Reference Architecture for SECO Applications; (5) EcoData: A Case Study; and (6) Conclusion.

5   Preliminary Contributions

As an initial contribution, we cite our complimentary taxonomy. One could claim that SECO arose with the first computational systems, even not being called that way back then, before the era of operating systems. We classify such type of SECO, which the community focused on providing value on top of the platform, as ExtraSECO. Later, we observed another type of SECOs emerged, one which its community focuses on the growth of the platform itself, named IntraSECO. Finally, we observed that instead of plug-ins architectures, SECOs based on Web APIs started to appear, spreading across multiple platforms. We call them InterSECO, i.e., a "SECO of SECOs".

Then, we have identified EcoData, which is a specific type of InterSECO. The distinction is possible due to the fact that it is centered on data, rather than on a set of platform features. Actually, this is the first of seven EcoData characteristics published in [5]: independence of the infrastructure platform. The other characteristics are: #2 hybrid application strategy; #3 enhanced data security requirements; #4 systems of engagements that are focused on data provided by instrumented people; #5 crowd-sourcing; #6 extra caution with the veracity of sensor data, and the necessity for model rules definition; and finally #7 An API-based Economy strategy.

EcoData may encompass software applications running on-premises, i.e. internally, but reusing components on top of one or more off-premise (cloud) platforms. One way of achieving platform independence is through the adoption of open standards, both on SECO platform and application side. Regarding data stores, it is possible to have them on the platform, in a separate infrastructure (due to large data volume), and also internally on organizations.

From a reuse perspective, Web APIs are the new components called Microservices: a granular SOA-style pattern. Integrating private and public APIs, and charging for them, is also a challenge that must be considered in future architectures.

Finally, our systematic literature mapping provided us with desirable SECO non-functional requirements, such as security, portability, interoperability and interface stability, besides a research agenda for software architecture for SECO.

6   Concluding Remarks

SECO research is still in its infancy, if compared to other topics in the SE area. Although plenty of research can be found for software architecture in general, there are still open questions when it comes to SECO architectures. Both industry and academy may benefit from a research that takes in consideration SECO challenges, especially regarding EcoData, since data's growing importance for organizations.

It was possible to detect a migration pattern regarding the behavior of community developers in relation to underlying SECO platform. Also, we were able to identify a very specific type of SECO, which is not restricted to a single platform, and where data are more important than functionality or technology.

Finally, by conducting a systematic mapping study, we gathered non-functional requirements for SECO platforms and applications. By analyzing those, we hope to be able to propose a RA for applications targeting an EcoData, achieving platform independence and interoperability, for example.

References

1. Bosch, J.: From software product lines to software ecosystem. In: Proceedings of the 13th International Software Product Line Conference, San Francisco, CA, USA, pp. 1–10 (2009)
2. Manikas, K., Hansen, K.M.: Software ecosystems: a syst. literature review. J. Syst. Softw. **86**, 1294–1306 (2013)
3. Stolterman, E., Fors, A.C.: Information technology and the good life. In: Kaplan, B., Truex, D.P., Wastell, D., Wood-Harper, A.T., DeGross, J.I. (eds.) Information Systems Research. IIFIP, vol. 143, pp. 687–692. Springer, Boston, MA (2004). doi:10.1007/1-4020-8095-6_45. ISBN 1-4020-8094-8
4. Serebrenik, A., Mens, T.: Challenges in software ecosystems research. In: Proceedings of the 2015 European Conference on Software Architecture Workshops, Cavtat, Croatia (2015)
5. França, M., Santos, R.P., Werner, C.M.L.: A roadmap for cloud SECO. EcoData and the new actors in IoT era. In: DCOSS, Fortaleza, Brazil, pp. 218–223 (2015)
6. Taylor, R.N., Medvidovic, N., Dashofy, E.M.: Software Architecture – Foundations, Theory, and Practice. Wiley, Hoboken (2010)
7. Shaw, M., Garlan, D.: Software Architecture: Perspectives on an Emerging Discipline. Prentice Hall, Upper Saddle River (1996)
8. Santos, R.P., Werner, C.M.L.: A proposal for software ecosystems engineering. In: IWSECO/ICSOB, pp. 40–51 (2011)
9. França, M., Santos, R.P., Werner, C.M.L.: Software architecture for SECO: a systematic literature mapping and research agenda. Technical report, COPPE/UFRJ (2016)
10. Bosch, J.: Architecture challenges for software ecosystems. In: Proceedings of the 4th European Conference on Software Architecture, ECSA 2010, NY, USA, pp. 93–95 (2010)
11. Taylor, R.N.: The role of architectural styles in successful software ecosystems. In: Proceeding of 17th SPLC 2013, New York, NY, USA, pp. 2–4 (2013)
12. Pérez, J., et al.: Towards a reference architecture for large-scale smart grids system of systems. In: Proceedings of 3rd International Workshop on Software Engineering for SoS, SESoS 2015, USA, pp. 5–11 (2015)
13. Christensen, H.B., et al.: Analysis and design of software ecosystem architectures: towards the 4S telemedicine ecosystem. J. Inf. Soft. Tech. **56**, 1476–1492 (2014)
14. Gartner: The Nexus of Forces: Social, Mobile, Cloud and Information (2012). https://www.gartner.com/doc/2049315. Accessed 12 Oct 2016
15. IDC: IDC Predictions 2013: Competing on the 3rd Platform, IDC Technical report (2013)
16. The Open Group: Convergent Technologies Survey (2013). https://www2.opengroup.org/ogsys/catalog/R130. Accessed 12 Oct 2016
17. IBM Bluemix. http://bluemix.net

Investigating the Recovery of Product Line Architectures: An Approach Proposal

Crescencio Lima[1,2](✉), Christina Chavez[1], and Eduardo Santana de Almeida[1]

[1] Federal University of Bahia, Salvador, Brazil
crescencio@gmail.com
[2] Federal Institute of Bahia, Salvador, Brazil

Abstract. Due to the complexity of managing architectural variability, maintaining the Product Line Architecture (PLA) up-to-date and synchronized with the project source code is a key challenge. Moreover, allow the variability traceability in architectural level of large-scale projects is a costly task. The systematic use of Software Architecture Recovery (SAR) techniques enables PLA recovery and keeps the PLA aligned with development. In this context, we present an initial proposal that consists of an approach to recover PLAs based on SAR techniques. We performed literature reviews and exploratory studies to investigate the relationship between SAR and PLA to identify gaps and define state-of-the-art. Learn how to combine SAR and PLA is an important strategy to address some issues of PLA design. We identified that few studies address architectural variability and provide empirical evaluation For this reason, more empirical research is still necessary.

1 Introduction

Software Architecture (SA) is "the architecture of a system that defines that system in terms of computational components and interactions among those components." [17]. According to Bass *et al.* [2], SA is the system structure, which consists of software elements, externally visible properties, and the relationships among elements. Making SA explicit and persistent is a key factor for using the potential it offers as an enabler for efficient and effective software development, specially in scenarios of increasing system size and complexity.

Nevertheless, applications evolve over time, so their architecture inevitably drifts. Recovering the architecture and checking whether it is still valid is, therefore, a relevant aid [14]. Software Architecture Recovery (SAR) is the process of obtaining the architecture of an implemented system from the existing system to promote enhanced understandability, and *reuse* of implemented systems [3].

Reuse is a key issue in the context of Software Product Line (SPL) projects. The SPL paradigm supports the development of software systems based on **reusable** parts [1]. SPL products share a set of common features (commonalities) and have variabilities that distinguish the applications [13]. Because the development of an SPL involves the implementation of different structures,

G. Botterweck and C. Werner (Eds.): ICSR 2017, LNCS 10221, pp. 201–207, 2017.
DOI: 10.1007/978-3-319-56856-0_15

processes, interfaces and activities, it is relevant for product line practitioners to pay sufficient attention to its architecture.

According to Nakagawa et al. [11], "the Product Line Architecture (PLA) refers to a structure that encompasses the behavior from which software products are developed." Moreover, Pohl et al. [13] defined PLA as the "core" architecture that represents the SPL high-level design, considering variation points and variants documented in the variability model.

The combination of SAR with PLA is critical to keeping assets (including architectural documentation and design artifacts) up-to-date [12], managing the variability at architectural level [15], and enabling architectural conformance among SPL products [7]. SAR can help in commonality and variability identification within the products [4]. However, Souza Filho et al. [18] points out the lack of guidelines for software architecture recovery in the SPL context. Shatnawi and colleagues [15] state that existing work is mostly focused on recovering variability at the requirement level. Few works aim at fully-automated PLA recovery addressing variability at the architectural level [6,7].

In this context, we present an initial proposal to PLA recovery that builds upon existing SAR techniques and tools developed for Single Systems (SS). We intend to understand PLA recovery, identify steps necessary to achieve it and provide guidelines to perform PLA recovery in a systematic way. Finally, we describe activities already performed during our research work and present related results.

2   Research Methodology

In our previous work [9], we performed a literature review on PLA and SAR relationship and its evolution over the years. We investigated how existing solution proposals supported PLA recovery and identified product line architecture recovery research trends. As a result from that study, we focused our investigation on bottom-up processes (i.e. tools and techniques) because we extracted information from SPL projects source code.

We also performed a literature review on metamodels to support Product Line Architecture design [8]. Moreover, we performed a set of exploratory studies based on experimentation in software engineering guidelines [19] to define our initial thesis proposal. Finally, we intend to perform empirical studies such as controlled experiments and mixed-methods to evaluate and calibrate the proposal.

3   Initial Proposal

In this research, we hypothesize that: "adapting existing single systems approaches, tools, and techniques from SAR will provide systematization in PLA recovery, and support PLA recovery replication and improvement". We propose an approach to verify this hypothesis by performing exploratory studies on recovering PLAs from open source SPL projects. We want to answer the following Research Questions (RQ):

- **RQ1:** Is it possible to use and adapt existing bottom-up recovery processes (i.e. tools and techniques) to recover PLAs?
- **RQ2:** What are the steps necessary to perform PLA recovery based on SPL projects source code?
- **RQ3:** How to identify and represent variability in PLA recovery?

To answer the above research questions, we are performing a series of studies, organized into 4 phases, to (1) identify frequent activities and steps used to recover PLA, (2) adapt or modify existing SAR tools and techniques for single systems, (3) organize information from the previous two phases in an novel approach – including the development of new tools to support the approach, and (4) define guidelines in a systematic way to support replication.

Currently, we are working on phases (3) and (4), which involves organizing the approach (and developing tool support) and defining guidelines that describe PLA recovery activities. We analyze how to perform variability identification relevant for PLA recovery. To the best of our knowledge, existing approaches lack detailed information regarding variability representation.

3.1 Preliminary Results

Based on evidence of our previous studies, we identified four main scenarios where the bottom-up recovery tools and techniques can be used in the recovery and/or adaptation of architectures of SPL projects:

- PLA Recovery directly from SPL source code;
- PLA Recovery based on the combination of SPL products architectures;
- PLA Recovery based on the combination of SS (legacy) architectures;
- PLA Recovery based on the combination of different versions of the same SPL project (e.g. Health Watcher and Mobile Media).

To understand the phenomenon, we performed two exploratory studies in the first and second scenarios – each one following the guidelines for controlled experiments [19]. We choose to work with this first two scenarios due to the lack of support for them. We identified these gaps based on available preliminary evidence.

In this way, the objective of the first exploratory study was to understand PLA recovery by identifying and adapting existing tools and techniques that support bottom-up recovery process. We recovered PLAs from fifteen SPL projects in different domains.

In the second exploratory study, we performed PLA recovery based on the steps identified in the first study. Moreover, to make PLA recovery systematic, we investigated the adaptation of Garcia *et al.* [5] recovery framework in the context of SPL projects. We worked with PLA recovery and two SPL teams. Finally, we presented the recovered information for the participants. After discussion, they suggested improvements and we identified lessons learned.

Finally, we considered the third and fourth scenarios out of the scope of our research. The third scenario presents the majority of studies and solution proposals. The fourth scenario focuses on SPL evolution – in other words, the use of different versions of the SPL is mandatory. In the latter, we performed studies recovering PLAs from different versions of the SPL.

3.2   Performing PLA Recovery

This initial proposal consists of an approach (and respective guidelines) for PLA recovery based on the use and adaptation of existing single systems SAR techniques and tools.

First, we gathered information about the SPL project. For instance, we download the SPL source code and feature model from the repository. The recovery technique and extraction tools may change according to the kind of variability implementation used. Moreover, in our approach, the SPL source code is mandatory because we recovered the PLA using bottom-up recovery tools and techniques.

Second, we selected the extraction tool based on the programming language used to implement the SPL project. Then, we extracted structural information from SPL (or/and products) source code. Third, based on the extracted information, we perform PLA recovery (including variability identification) using the technique suited for the scenario (e.g. merge of the recovered information). Fourth, we presented the PLA representation for analysis.

As mentioned before, one of our exploratory studies recovered the PLA based on the combination of architectures from the SPL products. After product instantiation, we extracted information **(phase 2)** from products source code using some existing extraction tool. We also developed a tool to support the merging process **(phase 3)** and provide the PLA representation **(phase 4)**.

4   Expected Contributions and Road Ahead

The expected contributions of our research are:

A novel approach to PLA recovery. The approach will provide a set of guidelines to support PLA recovery. Moreover, we will evaluate the approach based on empirical software engineering methods to support replication. We expect to drive efforts towards the definition of guidelines to support PLA recovery in details. In this way, we intend to use the approach to support different scenarios of PLA recovery.

Variability identification and traceability. During our exploratory studies, we have found that existing tools and techniques from SS do not support variability identification and traceability of the recovered information. We focused our efforts to identify variability (and enable traceability as a consequence) in the first and second scenarios. Moreover, we are developing tools to support this activity.

Metamodels to represent PLA recovery output. In our previous study [8], we defined a list of metamodels to support PLA design. Moreover, in our exploratory study with SPL developers, we investigated how these metamodels support them to understand the recovered PLA. We intend to organize these metamodels in a PLA Metamodels Catalog and represent recovered information based on the selected metamodel.

Raising architectural awareness of SPL engineers. This work intends to improve SPL engineers understanding about variability at the architectural level of SPL projects by providing up-to-date PLA documentation. We also expect that the proposed approach will help engineers to keep the PLA synchronized with SPL source code.

4.1 Evaluating the Approach and Results

We intend to perform a family of controlled experiments with subjects to evaluate the approach. Moreover, based on the execution of the experiments, we intend to calibrate and evolve the approach.

Two groups will participate in each study design. The group A will evaluate information recovered with our approach and group B will evaluate information recovered with existing SAR tool or technique. In this way, we will evaluate whether our adaptation to existing SAR techniques affected the PLA recovery activities.

We also intend to perform a survey to ask experts in SPL domain to validate the steps from the PLA recovery approach. Based on their knowledge, we believe that it will be possible to calibrate the approach according to the experts' suggestions.

5   Related Work

Shatnawi *et al.* [15] proposed an approach to PLA recovery based on the comparison of components recovered from different versions of the same SPL. The authors relied on Formal Concept Analysis (FCA) to analyze the variability and created a variability model. They extended the study in [16]. These studies focused only on the fourth PLA recovery scenario, and the approach did not support PLA recovery in the other three scenarios presented previously.

Linsbauer *et al.* [10] presented an approach for extracting information from sets of related product variants. The authors extracted structural information from the SPL products source code. They compared the information to recover the Feature Model (FM). We implemented a similar recovery process. However, instead of recovering the FM, we compared architectures recovered from SPL products to recover the SPL architecture.

Acknowledgment. This work was funded by FAPESB grants BOL2443/2016, and IFBA grants BP003-04/2014/PRPGI.

References

1. Apel, S., Batory, D., Kastner, C., Saake, G.: Feature-Oriented Software Product Lines. Springer, Heidelberg (2013)
2. Bass, L., Clements, P., Kazman, R.: Software Architecture in Practice. Addison-Wesley Longman Publishing, Amsterdam (2003)
3. van Deursen, A., Hofmeister, C., Koschke, R., Moonen, L., Riva, C.: Symphony: view-driven software architecture reconstruction. In: 4th WICSA, pp. 122–132 (2004)
4. Eixelsberger, W., Ogris, M., Gall, H., Bellay, B.: Software architecture recovery of a program family. In: 20th ICSE, pp. 508–511. ACM (1998)
5. Garcia, J., Krka, I., Medvidovic, N., Douglas, C.: A framework for obtaining the ground-truth in architectural recovery. In: WICSA/ECSA, pp. 292–296. IEEE (2012)
6. Kang, K.C., Kim, M., Lee, J., Kim, B.: Feature-oriented re-engineering of legacy systems into product line assets – a case study. In: Obbink, H., Pohl, K. (eds.) SPLC 2005. LNCS, vol. 3714, pp. 45–56. Springer, Heidelberg (2005). doi:10.1007/11554844_6
7. Koschke, R., Frenzel, P., Breu, A., Angstmann, K.: Extending the reflexion method for consolidating software variants into product lines. SQJ **17**(4), 331–366 (2009)
8. Lima, C., Chavez, C.: A systematic review on metamodels to support product line architecture design. In: 30th SBES, pp. 13–22. ACM (2016)
9. Lima-Neto, C.R., Cardoso, M.P.S., Chavez, C.V.G., de Almeida, E.S.: Initial evidence for understanding the relationship between product line architecture and software architecture recovery. In: IX SBCARS, pp. 40–49 (2015)
10. Linsbauer, L., Lopez-Herrejon, R.E., Egyed, A.: Variability extraction and modeling for product variants. Softw. Syst. Model. 1–21 (2016)
11. Nakagawa, E.Y., Oliveira Antonino, P., Becker, M.: Reference architecture and product line architecture: a subtle but critical difference. In: Crnkovic, I., Gruhn, V., Book, M. (eds.) ECSA 2011. LNCS, vol. 6903, pp. 207–211. Springer, Heidelberg (2011). doi:10.1007/978-3-642-23798-0_22
12. Pinzger, M., Gall, H., Girard, J.-F., Knodel, J., Riva, C., Pasman, W., Broerse, C., Wijnstra, J.G.: Architecture recovery for product families. In: Linden, F.J. (ed.) PFE 2003. LNCS, vol. 3014, pp. 332–351. Springer, Heidelberg (2004). doi:10.1007/978-3-540-24667-1_26
13. Pohl, K., Böckle, G., van der Linden, F.J.: Software Product Line Engineering: Foundations, Principles and Techniques. Springer, Heidelberg (2005)
14. Pollet, D., Ducasse, S., Poyet, L., Alloui, I., Cimpan, S., Verjus, H.: Towards a process-oriented software architecture reconstruction taxonomy. In: 11th European Conference on Software Maintenance and Reengineering, pp. 137–148 (2007)
15. Shatnawi, A., Seriai, A., Sahraoui, H.: Recovering architectural variability of a family of product variants. In: Schaefer, I., Stamelos, I. (eds.) ICSR 2015. LNCS, vol. 8919, pp. 17–33. Springer, Cham (2014). doi:10.1007/978-3-319-14130-5_2
16. Shatnawi, A., Seriai, A.D., Sahraoui, H.: Recovering software product line architecture of a family of object-oriented product variants. JSS (2016)
17. Shaw, M., Garlan, D.: Software Architecture: Perspectives on an Emerging Discipline. Prentice-Hall, Upper Saddle River (1996)

18. Souza Filho, E.D., Oliveira Cavalcanti, R., Neiva, D.F.S., Oliveira, T.H.B., Lisboa, L.B., Almeida, E.S., Lemos Meira, S.R.: Evaluating domain design approaches using systematic review. In: Morrison, R., Balasubramaniam, D., Falkner, K. (eds.) ECSA 2008. LNCS, vol. 5292, pp. 50–65. Springer, Heidelberg (2008). doi:10.1007/978-3-540-88030-1_6
19. Wohlin, C., Runeson, P., Höst, M., Ohlsson, M.C., Regnell, B., Wesslén, A.: Experimentation in Software Engineering. Springer, Heidelberg (2012)

Towards a Guideline-Based Approach to Govern Developers in Mobile Software Ecosystems

Awdren de Lima Fontão[1]([⊠]), Arilo Dias-Neto[2], and Rodrigo Santos[3]

[1] Institute of Computing, Federal University of Amazonas, Manaus, AM, Brazil
awdren@icomp.ufam.edu.br
[2] ICOMP/UFAM, Manaus, Brazil
[3] DIA/UNIRIO, Rio de Janeiro, Brazil

Abstract. Mobile application developers use repositories to store and reuse resources that support the development process. These repositories can be classified into internal – property of an organization that owns the mobile platform – or external – maintained by developers' communities in a open-source way. The app store is an example of an internal repository. As examples of external repositories, we can mention Github (code) and Stack Overflow (questions and answers). Such repositories can be used to support keystone's strategy to open its infrastructure in order to engage developers to meet the users' demands. This scenario refers to Mobile Software Ecosystem (MSECO) where keystones can use governance models to increase profits and reduce possible risks. However, it is necessary to understand how to monitor the engagement of developers using repositories as sources of information. In other words, it is important to define developers' governance guidelines to monitor the developer, contributions, technical questions, alignment with the keystone' goals, and developers' experience (DX). In this context, the goal of this PhD dissertation is to define a guideline-based approach to govern developers in an MSECO.

Keywords: Software ecosystem · Mobile application · Governance

1 Introduction

The organizations that sustain mobile platforms known as keystones, such as Apple, Google and Microsoft, have maintained mobile applications stores (app stores) and technical materials (developers portals) repositories as a way to govern the development of mobile applications (apps). The keystone with its internal structure cannot itself meet the users' demands and because of this there is a need to engage developers external to the keystone's infrastructure [1]. In Software Engineering, this scenario refers to the Mobile Software Ecosystem (MSECO), that is composed of elements competing and cooperating (e.g. developers and users) surrounding the app [2]. The developers collaborate with the keystone when producing apps or any other artifact (e.g. code snippets and technical documentation) to support building or evolving apps [5].

The original version of this chapter was revised: The name of the third author was corrected. The erratum to this chapter is available at 10.1007/978-3-319-56856-0_17

© Springer International Publishing AG 2017
G. Botterweck and C. Werner (Eds.): ICSR 2017, LNCS 10221, pp. 208–213, 2017.
DOI: 10.1007/978-3-319-56856-0_16

These developers' contributions are stored in internal repositories, for example, app store or developer portals. The app store works as a physical store where the keystone provides a set of apps in order to attract more users. The developer portal is a repository whose function is to provide and host technical materials to support the MSECO contributors in their activities. However, the developers also use external repositories that does not belong to keystone to exchange ideas, form communities and gain knowledge during the app development process. These external repositories help to maintain the interaction between developers influencing directly or indirectly the ecosystem [3], as examples we can cite Github and Stack Overflow. Github contains information about open source projects (e.g. code sources, commits). In turn, Stack Overflow has a set of developers involved in technical questions and answers in a social mechanism. '

In this context, Manikas [3] argues that it is challenging to reach conclusions in specific aspects of an ecosystem without examining (part of) the other aspects, for example, the elements' interaction during the software development. An external repository maintains the structure of archived communications between developers and it can be used to examine aspects of an MSECO. It can also support the keystone to have a good overview of the ecosystem providing effective measurements supporting the governance strategies [4] and helping to monitor the longevity and propensity to growth of the ecosystem (ecosystem health) [3]. This situation is known as synergy that is the relationship that exists between living organisms with each other (developers, keystone, and artifacts) and the ecosystem, ensuring the survival of them [6]. In this scenario, as a survival strategy, developers have expectations before and during their involvement in an MSECO, it refers to the Developer Experience (DX) [7].

If the keystone does not have efficient strategies for governing developers, the organization runs the risk of failing to meet the user's demands (e.g. number of apps, quality and variety). Successful ecosystem management and monitoring still remain as great challenges for software ecosystem practitioners [13]. This is partly because the ecosystems community lacks proper management theories, tool support, and real case studies [3]. The objective of this PhD dissertation is to define and evaluate a guideline-based approach to govern developers focused on monitoring developers from technical, social and business dimensions.

This paper is structured as follows. In the next section, related work is presented. Section 3 presents the proposed approach and discusses an evaluation proposal of the approach. Finally, the concluding remarks are discussed in Sect. 4.

2 Related Work

Ververs et al. [8] use data mining to map the influential factors that determine developer participation and evaluate the factors in a case study on the Debian ecosystem. The authors studied bug trackers, mailing lists and forums as a way to understand the community needs in the software ecosystem. Some conclusions are: influences have more effect on the degree of participation than causing more or less developers to become active; and developers respond differently to internal and external ecosystem influences. This reinforces our approach of analyzing internal and external repositories as a way to identify strategies of developers' governance.

Haenni *et al.* [9] present the results of a quantitative survey into the nature of information needs of 75 developers from open source ecosystems. The authors identified that in open source ecosystems mailing lists and internet search are the most popular tools that developers use to satisfy their ecosystem-related information needs (e.g. selection-, adoption-, and co-evolution-related needs). However, the authors conclude that the intersection of strong information needs, inappropriate practices and a new research field still remain as potential challenges for future impactful research.

Manikas *et al.* [10] argue that decisions related to the governance can influence the ecosystem's health and can result in fostering the success or greatly contributing to the failure of the ecosystem. From existing literature of software ecosystem governance and IT governance, the authors proposed the decomposition of software ecosystem governance into three activities: input or data collection (e.g. measures, information sources), decision making (e.g. data processing, scenario interpretation, alternative actions and their impact), and applied actions. The author identified five decision areas: principles, actor Interaction, software interaction, platform and ecosystem business and products.

Sadi *et al.* [11] proposed a generic approach built upon Android and iOS ecosystems to: identify types of developers, analyze the technical and non-technical requirements for collaborations and derive alternative solutions for designing an appropriate collaboration. The authors found out that Android developers choose the open-source platform to cultivate their intrinsic motivations, such as skills development and reputation enhancement. Regarding iOS developers, financial gain is one main requirement to sustain a collaborative relationship between developers and Apple. This study focuses on developers' objectives and decision criteria but does not provide specific guidance on how it can be performed.

This PhD dissertation focuses on the MSECO context. Manikas [3] argues that more in-depth studies are necessary. Focusing on a specific subset or type of ecosystem and studying the different aspects of this type in depth would arguably bring more realistic results rather than wide ecosystem studies focusing on a single aspect (e.g. architecture). In this scenario, this PhD dissertation focuses on mobile software ecosystems.

3 Proposal

3.1 Goal and Research Questions

The objective of this PhD dissertation is to define and evaluate a developers' governance approach by means of a set of support guidelines that impact the developer's experience within the MSECO. The following research questions (RQs) were defined: (RQ1) How to identify and assess (under social, technical and business perspectives) relevant sources of developer experience available in Mobile Software Ecosystems? (RQ2) How to deal in terms of developer experience with the use of internal and external repositories when governing developers in mobile software ecosystems? And (RQ3) What is the impact of using guidelines to support developers' governance in mobile software ecosystems considering business/social/technical dimensions?

Figure 1 helps to understand the idea involved in the proposed approach. We can capture the developer profile (e.g. expectations, country, MSECO name) and why he/she wants to participate in an MSECO, using this information we may identify the existing barriers in an MSECO that could make the developer onboarding difficult. The internal and external repositories can serve as source of information. This information serves as input to strategies, to control and support developers, based on input data from repositories, business, technical and social dimensions and also sources of developer experience (e.g. infrastructure development, feelings about the work, and the value of one's contribution). It will impact on developer health indicators (e.g. productivity, niche creation and robustness) that can be used to analyze the use of strategies helping the keystone to evaluate and evolve them.

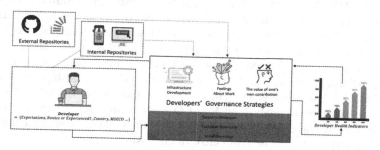

Fig. 1. An overview of the proposed approach.

3.2 Research Methodology and Emerging Results

STEP 1 (02/2016–05/2016) – Literature review about developer experience: building of the knowledge body about developer experience, research questions and opportunities, and defining the concept of DX in the mobile application development context. Applying the forward snowballing method on the string "developer experience", we retrieved 125 papers. In these papers, 58 (46%) have concepts related to DX. We have extracted proposed a definition of DX, 7 sets composed by research questions to understand what the researchers are working on and 37 existing opportunities to help to create a research agenda [12]. This step helped us to identify ways to monitor the developers from the use of repositories to the impact on health indicators.

STEP 2 (06/2016–08/2016) – Analysis of MSECO repositories: in an MSECO, there are some repositories where users search, download and evaluate apps, or where developers look for support material. These repositories can be used as part of an organization's strategy to monitor the ecosystem health. In order to explore the repositories, we performed four steps: (1) Design a governance process; (2) Interview experienced managers from MSECOs: Apple, Google, Nokia, Microsoft, and Samsung; (3) Perform an exploratory analysis of the repositories' structure, and; (4) Associate the repositories with ecosystem health indicators. Three main repositories (app store, developer central and apps' management portal) and also external repositories (e.g. code repositories as Github or Codeplex, Questions and Answers repositories as Stack Overflow) were analyzed. This study of MSECO repositories helped us to understand them as a source of information to governance strategies.

STEP 3 (08/2016–12/2016) – Literature Review about developers' governance in software ecosystem: a systematic mapping study was performed to investigate the following research question: *"Which strategies are applied to support Developers' Governance in Software Ecosystems?"*. We choose to explore Software Ecosystem as a way to identify directions that can be applied in the mobile domain. The following digital libraries were investigated: IEEExplore, ACM, Scopus, ScienceDirect, Springer Link, Engineering Village, and Web of Science. A total of 65 studies were analyzed. In summary, it is important to research on survival of developers. 43% (28) of the studies evaluate open-source ecosystems, 35% (23) proprietary and 22% (14) hydrid.

STEP 4 (01/2017–06/2017) – Business, technical and social studies: experimental studies aiming to explore strategies of governance and the impact on health indicators. In the technical dimension, data mining methods (extraction and clustering) were applied on Questions & Answers repositories such as Stack Overflow. In this study, we made comparisons among the three MSECOs: hot topics in recent and more commented/ viewed questions, developers' badges, sentiment analysis, relationship between questions and official developer events. It helped us to define a set of five propositions that can help the keystone to analyze an MSECO from a Q&A repository. In the social dimension, a study that explores the strategies from the point of view of the interaction between the developers will be conducted. In the business dimension, the objective is to raise hypotheses related to opportunities and economic barriers.

STEP 5 (07/2017) – Initial approach proposal: from the findings extracted in the previous steps, an initial version of the approach will be proposed. The approach will still take into consideration the following developer experience sources: development infrastructure, developer perceptions about work and value of contribution.

STEP 6 (08/2017–10/2017) – Surveys with experts: a validation of applicability and usefulness of the approach from the developers, researchers and community leaders viewpoint.

STEP 7 (11/2017–12/2017) – Write and present the qualifying exam.

STEP 8 (01/2018–09/2018) – Experimental studies with developers and community leaders: the set of studies (feasibility, observational, interviews) will have as objective to analyze the impact of the guideline-based approach from forms of governance with the developers: Top-down (organization guidelines as a way to support the developers, example, quality criteria of apps); Bottom-up (contributions from the developer that serve as input to the keystone's appropriateness of strategies, for example, an app that is purchased by the organization and becomes an official product), and; Inter-developers (the use of the MSECO infrastructure by developers but they create their own way of governing, e.g. startups).

STEP 9 (10/2018–12/2018) – Preparation to present the PhD dissertation. The writing of the dissertation happens during all the steps.

4 Concluding Remarks

The main contributions aiming to support the developers and keystones are: (1) body of knowledge about developer governance in the context of Mobile Software Ecosystems;

(2) Provide guidelines to support the developer governance using internal and external repositories as source of information, strategies that involves developer experience and the evaluation of health indicators; and (3) Assessment of the feasibility and application/ use of the approach using experimental studies.

Acknowledgements. The authors thank to CAPES for financial support for this research.

References

1. Fontao, A., Santos, R.P., Dias-neto, A.: Mobile software ecosystem (MSECO): a systematic mapping study. In: 39th Annual International Computers, Software & Applications Conference, pp. 653–658 (2015)
2. Lin, F., Ye, W.: Operating system battle in the ecosystem of smartphone industry. In: International Symposium on Information Engineering and Electronic Commerce, pp. 617–622 (2009)
3. Manikas, K.: Revisiting software ecosystems research: a longitudinal literature study. J. Syst. Softw. **117**, 84–103 (2016)
4. Eckhardt, E., Kaats, E., Jansen, S., Alves, C.: The merits of a meritocracy in open source software ecosystems. In: European Conference on Software Architecture (2014)
5. Fagerholm, F., Ikonen, M., Kettunen, P., Munch, J., Roto, V., Abrahamsson, P.: Performance alignment work: how software developers experience the continuous adaptation of team performance in lean and agile environments. Inf. Softw. Technol. **64**, 132–147 (2015)
6. Begon, M., Townsend, C., Harper, J.: Ecology: From Individuals to Ecosystems. Artmed (2007)
7. Fagerholm, F., Münch, J.: Developer experience: concept and definition. In: International Conference on Software and System Process, pp. 73–77 (2012)
8. Ververs, E., Van, R., Jansen, S.: Influences on developer participation in the debian software ecosystem. In: International Conference on Management of Emergent Digital EcoSystems, pp. 89–93 (2011)
9. Haenni, N., Lungu, M., Schwarz, N., Nierstrasz, O.: A quantitative analysis of developer information needs in software ecosystems. In: European Conference on Software Architecture Workshops, pp. 12–17 (2014)
10. Manikas, K., Wnuk, K., Shollo, A.: Defining decision making strategies in software ecosystem governance (2015)
11. Sadi, M.H., Dai, J., Yu, E.: Designing software ecosystems: how to develop sustainable collaborations? In: Persson, A., Stirna, J. (eds.) CAiSE 2015. LNBIP, vol. 215, pp. 161–173. Springer, Cham (2015). doi:10.1007/978-3-319-19243-7_17
12. Fontao, A., Santos, R., Dias-neto, A.: What we know about developer experience? In: 19th International Conference on Human-Computer Interaction (2017)
13. Rodrigo, S.: Managing and monitoring software ecosystem to support demand and solution analysis. Ph.D. dissertation. COPPE. Federal University of Rio de Janeiro (2016)

Erratum to: Towards a Guideline-Based Approach to Govern Developers in Mobile Software Ecosystems

Awdren de Lima Fontão[1](✉), Arilo Dias-Neto[2], and Rodrigo Santos[3]

[1] Institute of Computing, Federal University of Amazonas,
Manaus, AM, Brazil
awdren@icomp.ufam.edu.br
[2] ICOMP/UFAM, Manaus, Brazil
[3] DIA/UNIRIO, Rio de Janeiro, Brazil

Erratum to:

**Chapter "Towards a Guideline-Based Approach to Govern Developers in Mobile Software Ecosystems" in:
G. Botterweck and C. Werner (Eds.):
Mastering Scale and Complexity in Software Reuse, LNCS,
DOI: 10.1007/978-3-319-56856-0_16**

By mistake the name of the third author was stated as "Rodrigo Dias Santos". The correct name is "Rodrigo Santos".

The updated online version of this chapter can be found at
http://dx.doi.org/10.1007/978-3-319-56856-0_16

Tutorials

Building Safety-Critical Systems Through Architecture-Based Systematic Reuse

John D. McGregor[1] and Roselane S. Silva[2]

[1] Clemson University, Clemson, USA
johnmc@clemson.edu
[2] Federal University of Bahia, Salvador, Brazil
rosesilva@dcc.ufba.br

Abstract. Studies have shown that 70% of all defects are inserted during the very early phases of development, but most of those defects are not found until very late in development. The Architecture Analysis and Design Language (AADL) provides the basis for creating highly detailed models that support a "virtual integration" approach to architecture development. Through a set of domain specific languages, which support requirements definition, verification activities, and architectural modeling, the development team is able to incrementally design and analyze a system model. Those analyses are used to identify functional and non-functional requirements that are not satisfied at the time of the analysis by the architecture described in the model. This early "virtual integration" of the system using architectural-level components has been shown to facilitate early defect detection and a reduction of overall development effort by as much as 30%. This tutorial will survey this environment, present a specific example, and set the attendee up to explore the role of the tools in defining systems. This is a new tutorial although a similar tutorial at Saturn 2016 received very good reviews.

Bio

John D. McGregor is an associate professor of computer science at Clemson University, and a Software Architecture Researcher at the Software Engineering Institute. He regularly engages large software development organizations at all levels from strategic to tactical to the concrete. His research interests include highly-reliable software-intensive systems, software product lines, socio-technical ecosystems, model-driven development, and software/system architecture. He serves on the program committee of six to ten conferences per year. He researches, writes, and practices strategic software engineering. His consulting has included satellite operating systems, telephony infrastructure, cell phones, software certification, and software-defined radios.

Roselane S. Silva is a masters degree student of Computer Science at Federal University of Bahia (UFBA) and a member of RiSE Labs (Reuse in Software Engineering) at UFBA. She was selected for a study abroad program and studied

© Springer International Publishing AG 2017
G. Botterweck and C. Werner (Eds.): ICSR 2017, LNCS 10221, pp. 217–218, 2017.
DOI: 10.1007/978-3-319-56856-0

in the United States during the 2014–2015 academic year. For SPL research, Roselane is working with the Strategic Software Engineering Research Group at Clemson University on architectures for families of safety critical systems. Her architecture artifacts are being used by the Software Engineering Institute of Carnegie Mellon University as pedagogical examples.

Reusable Use Case and Test Case Specification Modeling

Tao Yue and Shaukat Ali

Simula Research Laboratory, Fornebu, Norway
{tao,shaukat}@simula.no

Abstract. Typically, use case specifications are structured, unrestricted textual documents conforming to a use case template. Since use case models are mostly text-based, ambiguity is unavoidable. This tutorial will present a use case modeling approach, called Restricted Use Case Modeling (RUCM), consisting of distinct restriction rules and an adapted use case template. Our objectives are: (1) limit the way users specify use case specifications with the goal of decreasing ambiguity, (2) provide built-in mechanisms to support reuse of use case specifications, and (3) enable automated analyses, e.g., generation of UML models and test cases.

Previously, we developed Zen-RUCM (a framework) composed of natural language-driven specification and modeling of requirements followed by generation of UML models and test cases. A chain of methodologies implemented in tools were developed and evaluated with real world case studies. These included: requirements modeling for real-time systems (RUCM4RT), test case specifications (RTCM) and automatic test case generation. This tutorial focuses on Zen-RUCM, RUCM, RUCM4RT, and RTCM methodologies, along with tool demonstration on real-world case studies. Particularly, we will focus on reuse of use case specifications, and test case specification.

Bio

Tao Yue is a chief research scientist of Simula Research Laboratory, Oslo, Norway and adjunct associate professor at University of Oslo. where she is leading the expertise area of Model Based Engineering (MBE). She is also affiliated to University of Oslo as an associate professor. She has received the PhD degree in the Department of Systems and Computer Engineering at Carleton University, Ottawa, Canada in 2010. Before that, she was an aviation engineer and system engineer for seven years. She has around 16 years of experience of conducting industry-oriented research with a focus on MBE in various application domains such as Avionics, Maritime and Energy, and Communications in several countries including Canada, Norway, and China. Her present research area is software engineering, with specific interested in requirements engineering, requirements-based testing, model-based product line engineering, model-based system engineering, model-based testing and empirical software engineering. Dr. Yue has been on the

G. Botterweck and C. Werner (Eds.): ICSR 2017, LNCS 10221, pp. 219–220, 2017.
DOI: 10.1007/978-3-319-56856-0

program and organization committees of many international, IEEE and ACM conferences such as MODELS, RE, and SPLC. She is PI and CO-PI of several national and international research projects. She is also actively participating in defining international standards such as Uncertainty Modeling.

Shaukat Ali is currently a senior research scientist in the Software Engineering department, Simula Research Laboratory, Norway. His research focuses on devising novel methods for Verification and Validation (V&V) of large scale highly connected software-based systems that are commonly referred to as Cyber-Physical Systems (CPSs). He has been involved in several basic research, research-based innovation, and innovation projects in the capacity of PI/Co-PI related to Model-based Testing (MBT), Search-Based Software Engineering, and Model-Based System Engineering. He has rich experience of working in several countries including UK, Canada, Norway, and Pakistan. Shaukat has been on the program committees of several international conferences (e.g., MODELS, ICST, GEECO, SSBSE) and also served as a reviewer for several software engineering journals (e.g., TSE, IST, SOSYM, JSS, TEVC). He is also actively participating in defining international standards on software modeling in Object Management Group (OMG), notably a new standard on Uncertainty Modeling.

Workshop

2nd Workshop on Social, Human, and Economic Aspects of Software (WASHES)

Special Edition for Software Reuse

Rodrigo Santos[1], Eldanae Teixeira[2], Emilia Mendes[3], and John McGregor[4]

[1] Department of Applied Informatics,
Federal University of the State of Rio de Janeiro (UNIRIO),
Rio de Janeiro, Brazil
rps@uniriotec.br
[2] Systems Engineering and Computer Science Department,
Federal University of Rio de Janeiro (COPPE/UFRJ), Rio de Janeiro, Brazil
danny@cos.ufrj.br
[3] Faculty of Computing Sciences,
Blekinge Institute of Technology, Karlskrona, Sweden
emilia.mendes@bth.se
[4] Department of Computer Science, Clemson University, Clemson, USA
johnmc@clemson.edu

Abstract. The Special Edition for Software Reuse of the Workshop on Social, Human, and Economic Aspects of Software (WASHES) aims at bringing together researchers and practitioners who are interested in social, human, and economic aspects of software. WASHES is a forum to discuss models, methods, techniques, and tools to achieve software quality, improve reuse and deal with the existing issues in this context. This special edition's main topic is *"Challenges of Reuse and the Social, Human, and Economic Aspects of Software"*. We believe it is important to investigate software reuse beyond the technical perspective and understand how the non-technical barriers of reuse affect practices, processes and tools in practice.

1 Motivation

Human and social aspects in software development have been discussed by researchers and practitioners since methods, techniques, and tools affect (and are affected by) stakeholders and their interactions. Similarly, software is a source of value for business in several organizations, either being software suppliers or acquirers, representing the key factor for their economic success. Decisions made in the software development processes and activities have economic implications on the profit and/or cost perspectives. Then, stakeholders, their interactions, and the software value notion are crucial to quality and directly affect the benefits promoted by software reuse. As such, it is important to discuss models, methods, techniques, and tools to achieve software quality, improve reuse and deal with the existing issues in this context.

© Springer International Publishing AG 2017
G. Botterweck and C. Werner (Eds.): ICSR 2017, LNCS 10221, pp. 223–224, 2017.
DOI: 10.1007/978-3-319-56856-0

2 Goals and Conclusion

The 2nd Workshop on Social, Human, and Economic Aspects of Software ("WASHES in Reuse") aims at putting together competencies and technologies focusing on the interaction between critical aspects that influence software engineering and software quality. This year's main topic seeks to bring together different perspectives in a specific forum in order to analyze software reuse in the light of social, human, and economic aspects.

In its first edition (2016) [1], the workshop was successfully co-located with the 15th Brazilian Symposium on Software Quality (SBQS 2016). WASHES 2016 had 50 attendees and received 30 submissions. After the final analysis, 6 full papers and 6 short papers were accepted. Additionally, 3 papers were presented as posters. A panel was promoted to discuss social, human and economic implications on software quality as well as to define the WASHES Research and Collaboration Roadmap.

WASHES Steering Committee is composed of 4 researchers from Federal University of Maranhão (UFMA, Brazil), Federal University of the State of Rio de Janeiro (UNIRIO, Brazil), Northern Arizona University (USA), and Pontifical Catholic University of Rio Grande do Sul (PUCRS, Brazil). This special edition is jointly organized by the 4 program chairs from Federal University of the State of Rio de Janeiro (UNIRIO, Brazil), Federal University of Rio de Janeiro (COPPE/UFRJ), Blekinge Institute of Technology (Sweden) & University of Oulu (Finland), and Clemson University (USA). WASHES Program Committee is composed of researchers with relevant expertise and production in the related research areas of the workshop. Program Committee Members conducted a rigorous double blind review process, in which each paper was evaluated and discussed in details by at least three members.

We welcome WASHES 2017 authors and other attendees, as well as ICSR 2017 participants. We would like to invite all participants to actively take part in discussions and integration moments provided by the workshop. Discussions on the investigation of reuse beyond the technical perspective will be performed in order to understand how the non-technical aspects influence (or are influenced by) software development management, processes and tools in practice.

Additionally, we would like to thank all researchers and practitioners who submitted their papers to WASHES 2017, the Steering and Program Committees' members, and the organizers and sponsors of ICSR 2017, for their support for the accomplishment of this workshop.

Reference

1. The First Workshop on Social, Human, and Economic Aspects of Software (WASHES 2016). http://reuse.cos.ufrj.br/washes2016/

Author Index

Ali, Shaukat 219
Alvim, Loreno Freitas Matos 31
Andrade, Rossana M.C. 65, 175
Assunção, Wesley K.G. 95

Bergel, Alexandre 155
Bezerra, Carla I.M. 65, 175
Blanc, Xavier 12

Charpentier, Alan 12
Chavez, Christina 201
Cleophas, Loek 77
Collet, Philippe 112

de Almeida, Eduardo Santana 31, 201
de Lima Fontão, Awdren 208
Dias-Neto, Arilo 208

Falleri, Jean-Rémy 12
Fernandes, Eduardo 48, 184
Figueiredo, Eduardo 48, 184
França, Marcelo 195

Garcia, Alessandro 48

Lee, Jaejoon 48
Lima, Crescencio 201
Lima, Luan P. 175
Lopez-Herrejon, Roberto E. 95

Machado, Ivan do Carmo 31, 65
McGee, Ethan T. 123
McGregor, John 223
McGregor, John D. 123, 217

Mendes, Emilia 223
Monteiro, José Maria 65, 175

Oliveira, Johnatan 184
Oumaziz, Mohamed A. 12

Santos, Rodrigo 208, 223
Schaefer, Ina 77
Schlie, Alexander 77
Silva, Leonardo Humberto 155
Silva, Roselane S. 123, 217
Sitaraman, Murali 139
Sousa, Leonardo 48

Tërnava, Xhevahire 112
Teixeira, Eldanae 223

Uchôa, Anderson G. 65, 175

Vale, Gustavo 48, 184
Valente, Marco Tulio 155
Vergilio, Silvia R. 95

Wang, Huaimin 3
Wang, Tao 3
Welch, Daniel 139
Wille, David 77

Yang, Cheng 3
Yin, Gang 3
Yu, Yue 3
Yue, Tao 219

Zhang, Xunhui 3

Printed in the United States
By Bookmasters